THE WEALTH OF POOR NATIONS
NEW EDITION

This updated edition of a book first published in 1984 and sponsored by the *London School of Economics and Political Science*, calls attention to the real experience of developing countries in the half century since, the end of the Second World War. It examines the factors behind the failure of much of the developing world to register rapid growth, belying the optimism of the early post-War years. It gives special emphasis to the structural factors and historical forces operating within the developed world which are seen to lie at the root of this failure. The new edition also explores developments in the second half of the 1980s and the opening years of the 1990s — a period when IMF/World Bank sponsorship and promotion of economic 'liberalization' brought a new set of challenges and problems before the world's poor. The failures of the developing countries themselves do not escape his attention.

Professor C. Suriyakumaran, economist, environmentalist, administrator and internationalist is currently Chairman, Centre for Regional Development Studies, Sri Lanka. He was earlier Deputy Executive Secretary of the United Nations Economic Commission for Asia; Director for Education, Training and Technical Assistance, UNEP; Regional Director for Asia and The Pacific and was directly associated in the creation, *inter alia,* of the Asian Development Bank, and many other institutions and programmes in development and environmen co-operation. He is visiting Professor at the London School of Economics and Political Science, and has lectured widely round the world.

Prof. Suriyakumaran is the author of publications on development, trade, finance, environment, governance and religion.

From –
The author

Sept '96

THE WEALTH OF POOR NATIONS

NEW EDITION

C. SURIYAKUMARAN

T.R. Publications

© 1984, 1996 C. SURIYAKUMARAN

First edition published in 1984 by
CROOM HELM LTD, KENT (UK)
in association with the
LONDON SCHOOL OF ECONOMICS AND
POLITICAL SCIENCE

NEW EDITION 1996
ISBN 81-85427-68-2

Published by
T.R. PUBLICATIONS PRIVATE LTD.
PMG Complex II Floor
57, South Usman Road
T. Nagar, Madras 600 017

Typeset at
LAKSHMI REALTIME GRAPHICS
Madras 600 024

Film Processed by
Dinippon Screen Imagesetter at
UNIVERSAL PRINT SYSTEMS LTD.,
Madras 600 008

Printed in India at
MULTICRAFT
Madras 600 004

Cover design by
MULTICRAFT
Madras 600 004

JK

A dedication to the
younger generation everywhere

And then Newton said to Halley, 'Why I have known it for years. If you will give me a few days, I will certainly find a proof for it'.

A child is a person who is going to carry on what you have started. He is going to sit where you are sitting, and when you are gone, attend to those things which you think are important. You may adopt all the policies you please; but how they are carried out depends on him. He will assume control of your cities, states, and nations. He is going to move in and take over your churches, schools, be judged, praised or condemned by him. The fate of humanity is in his hands. *Abraham Lincoln.*

vi

Contents

Foreword

This book is derived from an individual's intellectual and practical experience as a civil servant in the early years of independence of an Asian country, and his experience as an international official in some of the most vital and innovative outposts of the United Nations, watching at close hand both the changing problematique of development and the emerging problematique of environment.

These are rather formidable credentials for guiding a concerned reader through the avatars of conceptual framework within which national policies of development and international schemes of cooperation have evolved over a little more than three decades.

The result, however, would not have been so successful without a certain human quality and disposition of the mind that have infused his approach to contemporary problems and is rich in important lessons: an argument may be tightly knit without being contrived; its inner logic may emerge in the course of a relaxed 'promenade' through the history of ideas more effectively than from an elaborate preordained architecture; the gentle downgrading of ideas once sovereign, and pundits once allowed to pontificate, can be more persuasive than the iconoclastic message and arrogant ostracism with which new knowledge is sometimes announced. Modesty in the face of momentous problems goes hand in hand with a sense of history that is always redeeming in the uncertain areas of the social sciences, and particularly so in times of rapidly changing circumstances. For history bears witness that ideas may be ephemeral while playing a socially useful role. Both in the development of knowledge and the evolution of practical politics. The demonstration is strengthened when some of the most important sections are presented in their original version without the usual cosmetic effort to bring them up to date. It is thus possible to become more aware of what the author perceives so well, namely the interplay between what is constant and what is changing.

These remarks come to the mind because the present predicament requires from those who seek to analyse it, scholars as well as policy makers, just the type of approach that one finds in *The Wealth of Poor Nations*. The book covers a period of optimism and self-assurance, followed by one of great doubts and even gloom, which is still with us. The author manages the transition without the urge or the need for a recantation. His critical ability, rooted in a familiarity with the plight, overwhelming in South-East Asia, of unemployment and under employment was never quite convinced or misled by the simplicity of the prevailing neo-classical model of North-South growth transmission, only slightly modified by the recognition of structural gaps in savings and foreign exchange. Nor was he later ready to succumb to some of the more utopian entreaties of conviviality, frugality and repose, often too prone to underestimate growth in production and productivity as primordial ingredients in the development effort.

Not for the first time in post-War history do we believe to be at a 'crossroads'. Yet, although we loosely use the word 'crisis', it is still a matter of dispute whether the present circumstances are really exceptional, or whether the prolonged recessionary phase which we now experience is a normal, if somewhat overextended, avatar of the business cycle. We should at least admit to our perplexity. We cannot fail to observe that, more and more, the search for a credible explanation of the present tends to focus on long term trends. It addresses itself to the understanding of structural factors and historical forces, mostly operating in the capitalist world, which may give us more meaningful account of the recent evolution than the short term cycle theorems, and may also offer us useful clues to more successful development strategies. These factors include changes in the organic composition of capital, divergent trends in the growth rates of productivity and consumption, continuing exploitation of cheap labour by the industrial countries through the absorption of migrant workers or the relocation of industries in the Third World.

Even more relevant to the North-South perspective is the new challenge to a certain type of internationalism which had been usually acknowledged as being largely responsible for the spectacular expansion of the last thirty years. The growing internationalization of the world economy has been so pervasive that it must be seen as instrumental, not only in shaping policies of international cooperation, but in the indiscriminate adoption of outward looking patterns of national development in the Third World. That this model of interdependence is not attuned to the singularities of exchange between unequal partners, characteristic of North-South relations is now generally accepted, and perhaps even belaboured by academics. It does not really permeate the debutesan analyses of the United Nations or the North-South dialogue, although policy makers at home seem more eager to explore different options. This institutional lag in the modes of thinking may be explained by the frustrations of a never ending and fruitless negotiation over a certain set of measures, largely codified as far back as 1964. These should now be subject to qualifications and questioning in the light of new perceptions and knowledge, but they did atleast serve to establish a moral obligation of solidarity that may well appear even more essential when alternative strategies are seriously considered.

For it is not only progress in our knowledge, or even a change in ideological preferences, that make the call for a change in strategies so topical. The cumulative effect of demographic pressures and decades of disequalizing policies have in the last ten years resulted in increasing instability and unrest, often erupting in violence, and forced the consideration of social improvements as the first priority of development, indeed an imperious political necessity. As this is attempted, it becomes clear that planning for social improvement is far more difficult than planning for growth. It is particularly so in mixed economies with an important market sector, where voluntarist policies run the risk of being defeated by market forces, if these are not correctly identified and taken into account.

We are mentally ill-equipped to navigate in such a sea-change. It requires a revision of the traditional modes of economic analysis 'stricte sensu' and the incorporation of dimensions which have far too long been kept apart from it.

Environment is one of the new dimensions of the present complexity on which Suriyakumaran has much of interest to say. It intruded somewhat suddenly into our conceptual universe in the early seventies. In spite of impressive progress in pollution abatement, the monitoring of the climate and the other ecological phenomena, the field remains one of great uncertainities in respect of facts and of their treatment. Certainly, the present practice of dealing with environment as a negative externality which economists have learned to incorporate in their comprehensive models cannot be considered very satisfactory. A broader difficulty is that, early in its existence, the ecological school of thought expanded far beyond the mundane preoccupation with clean air and pure water or the rational management of resources. Ecology is a concept of such philosophical breadth that as soon as it gained the right of city in the political arena, it expanded into a comprehensive — though vague and not very coherent — system of values pertaining to the most important aspects of Society. It often projected itself forcefully in social movements and even political parties. It proposed new, non-utilitarian, 'ethical' precepts regarding the obligations of man to nature, beyond those embodied in the husbanding of land through labour, capital and technology for productive or welfare purposes. At times it came close to being coincidental with the Malthusian message of the Club of Rome and the zero-growth advocacy.

Scarcities must in fact play a part in the thinking on the future, perhaps not in terms of physical limits but in relation to the dynamics of exhaustible resources. For this factor must be incorporated in the planning process, an undertaking all the more difficult, because it had been a neglected branch of the economic science for several decades until the early seventies, when the power structure of the oil market changed in the midst of much misunderstanding resulting in unnecessary international tensions.

But to the practitioner or the student of development, it is the failure of relating the so-called *social factors* to growth and productivity which is the most embarrassing. Health, education, income distribution and employment must be seen as determinants as well as results of growth. Their relations to economic parameters need to be understood so that more reliable clues to the choice of investments and public expenditures might be discovered.

International relations are highly relevant to this problematique and should not be analyzed separately. Flows of goods and moneys across borders must be seen as either facilitating or constraining social choices and having under certain conditions — not infrequent in the Third World — perverse effect not only on income distribution and the plight of the disadvantaged, but also, through changes in the terms of trade, on growth itself. Such unexpected results, sometimes seen as paradoxes, are not easily accepted by the body politics, including the UN system. They are not unfamiliar to Suriyakumaran who chose a paradox as the title of his book. Paradoxes are indeed the very ferment that leads to what 'revisionists' sometimes call a 'change in paradigm' (a somewhat pedantic phrase) as they offer a proof that the dominant system of thought does not capture and incorporate important aspects of reality. They convey the message of a systematic and comprehensive re-examination, which has already begun and must unfold in the years ahead, providing new insights in the problematique of development and cooperation. The lines of the investigation emerge clearly from the *The Wealth of Poor Nations*.

It is the virtue of all good books that their findings are absorbed and remoulded by individual readers according to their idiosyncrasies, and then invested with their own extrapolations. A preface may be the ideal location for such chemistry.

The Wealth of Poor Nations

One approach to the 'revision' is to recognise that societies, however primitive, and at whatever stage of development, always pursue multiple and often conflicting objectives. This is not so trivial as it sounds; conventional wisdom has long held that social dividends in employment, distribution and other welfare components would derive from growth either through the operation of some automatic mechanisms or the instrumentality of a wise and benevolent State. Today we know that objectives and the means of achieving them must be *specified* in the planning process and analitically related in some coherent framework — not simply *declared* and juxtaposed. The discovery of the path leading to acceptable combinations of policies, to be pursued simultaneously or sequentially, require more sophisticated tools of analysis than seemed adequate for strategies focused on hardware investment, the stimulation of exports and the expectation of capital and technology transfers. National economies cannot be treated as homogeneous entities. Models must capture the phenomenon of poverty by introducing distinctions between groups, according to income consumption patterns and ownership of the means of production, including technology.

A policy aiming above all at the satisfaction of elementary needs will not be politically acceptable or even economically plausible, unless it makes room for rapid industrialization and recognizes the need to control inflation. Industrialization, in turn, may be oriented mostly towards the needs of the masses or the requirements of modernization, depending on existing resource endowments, the size and configuration of the economy, including its capacity to import, the nature and degree of its insertion in the world system, the political make-up and ideological bent.

In the present state of our knowledge, such a process of planning and policy making inevitably comes largely from intuition and empiricism, unless it is from the acceptance of a self-contained dogma inherited from the past. Intuition and empiricism, however (more than dogmas) can be informed and improved by *theoretical reflexion*, leading to the understanding of the mechanisms, economic, sociological, historical, which govern the functioning and evolution of society. That progress of theory is important to the improvement of practice has often been forgotten during the period of optimism which instilled in the decision makers an infatuation with pure pragmatism. Reflexion on theory was with few exceptions confined to the political 'dissidence' or applied to the elaboration, always more refined, of analyses with little relevance to the problem of development. Yet, in secularized societies, theory does contribute to the legitimacy of policies. It is not always explicitly invoked for such purpose, but it is tacitly operative as long as it remains unchallenged in the political class.

There can never be, and need not be, an international consensus on desirable national policies, but there can be one on the role of international action. In a world of diverse obediences and systems, and of strong nationalisms, this role must be seen as that of accommodating this diversity within the limits of acceptable standards of behaviour internationally defined. This is not achieved at present. There is no positive and adequate response from the international community, as expressed through its major institutions, to the efforts of those governments which embark on policies designed for more rapid social progress and less dependency. Such ambitions, involve a lengthy and difficult process, including a rearrangement in the composition of domestic demand and in external economic links that will almost inevitably aggravate the usual balance of payment and inflation problems.

The provision of liquidity must be seen in the light of these requirements. The international monetary system on which the author has so much useful to say, must not only aim at preserving its own overall stability or at facilitating adjustment toward the restoration of lost equilibria (which will again be precarious) but also at making possible a more drastic change in the macro-economic configuration of the economies; and more particularly in avoiding that increases in total demand shall be met only or principally at the expense of those who consume nothing but basic goods. Relaxing the constraints on the production or supply of these goods should therefore serve as a criterion for the provision of finance, by whatever name it is called, and such provision should be sustained for a longer period and probably at more favourable conditions than even the liberalized practices recently adopted by the International Monetary Fund can presently afford, given its Articles of Agreement and the structure of its governance. The dichotomy between long term development finance and short term supply of liquidity cannot be considered as immutable. It is not a natural or logical feature, intrinsic to international cooperation. It is subject to reform in the face of certain very present and precise economic realities, that exclusive attention to financial criteria will inevitably overlook. There is no reason why a change in the philosophy of 'conditionality' to permit strategies with social priorities to unfold without too many accidents should be viewed as being against the interests of those powers which persistently oppose the discussion of monetary matters within the United Nations, thereby blocking an international negotiation that the rest of the world regards as essential to its future.

As hypotheses are explored, it becomes apparent that the dichotomy between short-term demand management and long-term development efforts is the crucial dilemma confronting the 'revisionists', as the only measures available to meet an immediate crisis more often than not are liable to arrest or reverse for a period of unknown duration, the desired long-term policies. This is more visible today than ever, as the debt situation and continuing payment deficits are more alarming than they have been in the past. Therefore this is not the time to ignore or underestimate the pressing problems of the moment or to subordinate them too strictly and dogmatically to a new creed which has as yet hardly undergone the test of practical experience and confrontation to the real world. Yet, the search must continue and there should be much cooperative action, not only to encourage it but perhaps also to rescue those who try and fail.

It is a sign of the times and of changes in our understanding that no comprehensive approach to development could omit a reference to the 'cultural' dimension. Suriyakumaran does not shun this responsibility and in Chapter Fifteen, 'Cultures, Totems and Taboos'*, he displays the same seriousness and lack

* The above chapter reference is as in the first edition.

xviii

Foreword

of pretense that characterizes the rest of the book. He is of course well aware of the 'postures' so frequently exhibited in the work of social anthropologists, as well as of the 'fossilisation' in a set of values that have sometimes falsely been held to be sacred. His remarks on religion and nationalism, as often breeding and supporting the most undesirable taboos are refreshing and indeed courageous in view of so much indiscriminate reverence toward religious revival, as well as unquestioned worshipping of the Nation-State. Here again, his sense and knowledge of history serves him well. It preserves the sense of the relative, the ambiguities of the dilemmas, so necessary when one is bold enough to raise the problem of democratic institutions. No specific interpretations is forced upon the reader in the specific cases he chooses as examples, rather an invitation to observe caution in judging, and to pursue the inquiry.

As seen above, Suriyakumaran guards against 'postures'. I find no more appropriate word for the conclusion of my remarks. Those who strive to help others through their writings or their actions should accept that no change in policies can usefully be advocated from a high intellectual or moral posture. Rather, their work should proceed from a deep empathy with the universal struggle of human beings, through many hazardous paths, often in tragic circumstances, to organize their lives and societies, at times for sheer survival, but hopefully more and more for the fulfillment of their total potentialities.

In this also, *The Wealth of Poor Nations* is a precious lesson, as well as warning.

[1984]

PHILIPPE DE SEYNES
Director
Project on the future, UNITAR *

---

*Formerly, UnderSecretary General for Economic and Social Affairs of the UNITED NATIONS

Preface to the New Edition

When this book was first released in 1984, as a London-New York-Canberra publication, it became a product for a high priced market. It did indeed sell out in expected time, mainly, one thinks, as repository in major libraries, and similar acquisitions.

Quoted on occasions, it seems still to have been used in those high priced markets, such as in one instance brought to attention, of quotation by Knut Hammershoeld on a Canadian T.V. Panel Programme. The best known use of it in the Third World has been in its adoption by one university at least to one's knowledge, of the 'integrated environment-economic-cost benefit model' as an option for Ph.D. and Masters research students.

Yet, the reason for a revised edition of the book has been due to several reasons. The possible cheaper cost and wider accessibility was certainly one. That itself was based on periodic expressions of interest in such an issue.

The book had also firm substantive reasons for the present step. 'Plus de la change, plus de la meme'. While one may have expected, at the time of writing, that much therein would no more require reiteration, in many areas they have not only retained their value, but with perhaps even more urgent calls for attention. Academic journals and professional writings keep bearing repeated witness* to the present situations on all the major issues raised in the book.

The topic areas as in the original Contents are, therefore, virtually intact — 'The Long Wait', for still too many countries looking to growth; 'The Record' of assistance and co-operation in attaining that growth; the true content of 'Development Policy'; the still needed measures in the 'International System'; the state of 'International Trade and Monetary Co-operation'; the entire field of 'Environment and Development Relations and Management'; and not least, 'Culture Relegion and Politics'; and the Information Order.

In terms of formal structuring of the contents, certain chapters have been re-arranged in their sequences; later data or information have been added, as appropriate, in discussion of contemporary issues; a special chapter on development policy has been introduced, subsuming also certain earlier sections; so also on international co-operation; the chapters on environment development have been substituted in order to comprehend the latest situations; that on culture has been expanded for obvious developments since; and, select selections spelling out detailed designs or methodologies — valuable, even original as they probably are— have not been carried having in mind as well the need to contain the overall volume of the book. These include

1. An Indicative National Energy Design,
2. A Model for a Future City without cars,
3. A Model Commodity Flow exercise for Regional Economic Co-operation, and
4. An Integrated Environment-Economic c/b Framework.

The Foreword and Preface to the first edition have been kept virtually in their original form in view of their inherent relevance and usefulness.

The present New Edition has been done in close collaboration with its publishers, and concurrence of the publishers of the First Edition.

---

*Among notable recent cases are Robert Solow et al, (*The Journal of Economic Perspectives*, American Economic Associations, Volume 8, No.1, 1994); and

*Lawrence Summers and Vinod Thomas 'Recent Lessons of Development' (*The World Bank Research Observer*, July 1993).

Preface to the New Edition

The issues discussed, the analyses and discussions developed in its pages — for the most part coming down indeed from the First Edition — their high practical value, and conviction as to public interest in the policies and solutions advocated, suggest that perhaps, more needs to be done now than when the book was first written; in more areas than at that time; and at more sophisticated levels than before.

Most remarkable at times in the original edition at several points, is their prescience in seeing the trends of phenomena that were only emerging, even subdued then, which now continue to stalk our development scene, through to the nineties.

The urgencies in these matters are, therefore, even greater than before. It is in this background that the book is being offered for widest reading, hopeful acceptance of its many recommendations, and their eventual use. The Publishers themselves deserve special appreciation for the excellent support and co-operation given, and the product they have now put before the public.

*   *   *

Finally it is necessary, in a record of equal importance, to extend one's sincerest thanks and appreciation to those who helped in the preparation and production of this edition. As alwalys, their work has been tireless, willing and certainly more than may be evaluated in the market place. Thanks are due in particular to Mr. Maheswaran for overseeing and assisting, and to Ms. Jega Nalliah, Mr. A. Amsar and Mr. H.S. Ranasinghe.

Special personal thanks are due to Prof. V. Suryanarayanan, Director, Centre for South and South East. Asia Studies, Madras, for his personal interest and involvement in pursuing the initial actions that led to the publication of this edition under its present welcome auspices.

AUTHOR

Colombo.
1994.

Preface to the First Edition

This book is written out of the hopes, aspirations and failures of the decades that are now over. The hopes belonged to the forties, when the present passing generation belonged to the youth, and were carried with high expectation into succeeding years. During these years one thought of oneself as young and therefore, with time to meet obstacles and reverses to the goals that had all been set. But suddenly, now, one sees oneself as old; of a generation that must pass on to a younger generation, indeed which perhaps has already taken over, but to which the older generation has not transmitted the fruits of its own experience. This book therefore is addressed in humility, in the knowledge that what the passing generation of the Third World set out to do, despite semblances, it did not achieve. It is an attempt to recall those aspirations of the forties, after the 'war to end all wars' and to 'rid mankind from the scourge of poverty'; both as a reminder of the target of faith, and an attempt to re-live the basis on which the future was predicated.

If the Book has to be classified under a discipline, it is not on social or political philosophy, but an economic development and expectations and failings of the developing countries as much as of the cooperative world. It is a basic study, calling together the past and present, as testimony, for a renewed future action by the younger generation. It arises from the inequalities, inadequacies and some emptiness, of years of theories, prescriptions and imagined co-operative actions. It is, thus, addressed to the young everywhere, those in the rich as in the poor countries, the only basis for solutions to the problems, which are as much as the creation as the responsibility of both. Today more than ever before it is interdependence and all advancing together or all dragging themselves down together. Self-reliance, yes; it is the key to every nation's success, but also within this sensible world environment.

The hopes that were held out for the Third World prevailed for a long time; but perhaps by the seventies, the suspicions about the recipies for development and confirmations of their failures reached their peak. It was perhaps time then to have written on it. Indeed, at various times, innumerable publications have tried to focus disappointment. These were not only books but periodicals, journals, features, statements, speeches and debates. It is still going on. Now with years of such a situation, one perhaps may feel more confident and complete, to write about what in fact could have been written in the early seventies.

The purpose of this Book, whatever its limitations, is action. It is therefore not the least intended to be academic, particularly abstrusely so. So while it may be written as economic, whatever that word may mean, it is not intended to establish one economic development theory or another. It has much more serious purpose than that, of translating the realities of experience of these four decades, to the best possible extent for a deeper understanding of lasting trends and, fervently lasting solutions.

As will be seen in these chapters, ideas formulated out of concrete experience in trying to deal with issues have been fully used, irrespective of whether they were 'old' or 'new'. By the same token, no exhaustive cataloguing of various development 'theories' is claimed in these pages; nor even the academic indexing and footnote references to authority, expect as they occur incidentally. To scholars and observers of the international scene of these years, there are literally hundreds of references to the facets of development as we have them and they may be easily thumbed by most students, researchers and practitioners.

This is quite separate from the other question, not infrequently raised, as to how much of theories and prescriptions

Preface to the First Edition

of development have not been shibboleths after all. Indeed, we are brought close to the proposition, suggested seriously as truth, that in historical observation, economic theory has indeed never created development but only annotated it when it occurred. The only possible exceptions would be Marxist economics, not to the confused with being protagonists or antagonists of this economics, and possibly Keynesian General Theory. The Book is not written to prove 'isms' or to raise controversy in the abstract. It carried a strong conviction however that what is said must and will happen; at least, whether we like it or not, sooner or later.

The Book writes about development. In doing so, it includes, a conviction that development is everything. Without being a humanist treatise at all, it still touches on various facets: national and international, strategic and institutional, economic and environmental, political and social, material and spiritual. Inevitably, growth theory is not merely economic but politico-economic.

Some of the conclusions in the Book may appear nearly heretical. Long-held ideas on certain pillars, or pet concerns, of international cooperation and development-trade, payments, commodity price stabilisation, the political dimension, the social dimension, growth theory itself, human settlements, transport systems, others — would seem to come out in the discussions reflecting years of 'exposure', as in fact ideas or theories which are 'upside down' and which need to be put 'right side up'. These are presently imbedded in holy orthodoxy. If any ideas, theories or practices to solve problems had emerged, they are only as marginal theories or practices strictly within the framework of these orthodox moulds. In many of these cases, it will be seen that , perhaps bonafide, it is the short memories of the developed countries themselves, of their own development periods and the proselytizing advice and assistance now given by them which are at variance and the problem.

Although the Book is on development as a global issue, one must confess that its anchorage is mainly Asia, simply by reason of one's direct involvement in this area, if no other, although one has carried responsibilities in some ways in other parts of the world as well. The latter has, no doubt, helped.

The Wealth of Poor Nations

In many places direct evaluations are made of interests, which, knowingly or otherwise, impeded right developments . It is important to emphasize therefore that nothing in the Book is with animosity to any, in particular in the developed countries. Indeed, any other country in the 'developing' list, if it became developed tomorrow, may well behave exactly the same way, or worse ! The issue is therefore one of inherent characteristic and a genetic quality pertaining to developed country interest and attribute, expressing itself through its leadership. Individually, in the long years of international life, some of one's most cherished associations have been precisely among leaders and people from the developed countries themselves.

*   *   *

It has been mentioned that this Book is a dedication to the younger generation. Yet in a highly personalised sense on person, contrarily now very old, has to be mentioned, who was the Third Executive Secretary of the United Nations Economic Commission for Asia and the Far East (ECAFE), U Nyun of Burma. He spanned the sixties, starting a year before and ending two years later, in the leadership of the United Nations in Asia, a true founder of whatever was achieved in the name of international development and cooperation, in concrete achievements as also in laying the foundation for subsequent developments.

A true and humble Asian, also an internationalist, he carried a slogan of being 'poor but proud' and gave confidence to the countries at a time when none existed, in cooperation among themselves, through 'areas of agreement' amidst whatever their disagreements. In this sense, he was indeed stubborn and through this and through faith in the countries, he imparted concepts, ideals, and a philosophy for them which has abided. Without any reflection at all on his predecessors, one must say that he played a role of founding figure. Something more will be said about this in the Book; of institutions, for example, which those who to the hilt opposed him — and which came about only because he stood between them and these — then avidly took over and now control. Though now forgotten, most by those who may remember, this tribute is paid with gratitude by one who was privileged to work beside him. Many obstacles to the poor nations attaining wealth at the international level, indeed lie reflected in those efforts to succeed.

The Foreword, for which particular gratitude is due, is from another past soldier in the international scene, as magnificent as he is perhaps different from the other. Philippe de Seynes, Under-Secretary General in charge at the time, was in fact the Economic and Social boss of the United Nations system of the same sixties, a remarkably cool, mercurial and deeply knowledgeable servant. His commitment to world development was infectious, made enormously so by the extremely sparkling lucidity with which he would survey, sum up and prognosticate the world scene for his assembled audience of Heads and senior echelons of the United Nations and its Agencies. Along with his self-effacement and sense of humour, and impeccable capacity for that English 'garnished' in French culture, he was the centre around which others worked. He keenly observed and learned from all others, and when he differed, he only raised them as doubts, giving others food for thought rather than for opposition. He brought an abiding sensitivity and sure touch on the illusions and realities of development over the years.

Much was owed to him and now, personally, immensely for his kind Foreword to this Book, with which he was told he is not obliged to agree! Voltaire, that other Frenchman, had already declared, of a contemporary, that he may not agree with any thing he said, but would fight to the death for his right to say it.

The actual writing of the Book received much help along the way. I am grateful to Prof. Jan Tinbergen of the Netherlands for his ready, early, response to my draft for this Book, which provided me not only food, but great argument to go on. Among several others to all of whom my thanks are due, I must mention Prof. Hans Singer, presently of the Institute of Development Studies at Sussex and Prof. K. Velupillai, presently of the European University Institute of Florence, for the frank comments as much as their robust support; and B.R. Devarajan of the United Nations, for an intelligent man's guide to intelligence. I am also indebted for the friendly interest shown by several who may not have had time to help in details. Among them were Prof. J.K. Galbraith of Harvard, Mr. A.W. Claussen, President of the World Bank, Prof. Amartya K. Sen, Drummond Professor of Economics at Oxford and Prof. Martin Bronfenbrenner, Kenan Professor of Economics at Duke University. All the shortcomings still present are clearly mine.

I must express my utmost thanks to the London School of Economics for sponsoring the publication of the Book, thereby providing me as much satisfaction at having undertaken the study as the patronage for publication in an economy conscious book trade. The Book received its finishing touches during my period as Professor at LSE and owed considerably to my work there.

Finally, I extend my fullest gratitude and admiration to those who helped so overwhelmingly and unstingly to see the completion, production and publication of the manuscripts and the Book. They obviously suffered hours of long, enduring patience that must have been rewarding only to the author. For this remarkable contribution by all these kind people, sincerest acknowledgments indeed are due.

1984.   AUTHOR
London

A. History and Experience

Chapter One

The Long Wait

From the forties of this century, a broadly defined yet clear promise of rapid growth became available to developing economies. It was something that grew from the aura of post-War humanity and rising expectations everywhere. It was distinct from past economics of colonial patronage and assistance. Basically conceived on the theoretical foundations of growth economics of the thirties and early forties, it saw also strong pillars of international economic co-operation for development emerge. In addition to the prevailing political, economic and humanitarian climate, the developing countries, at that time called backward countries or under-developed countries, were also issued this confidence, in firm promise of concessions and assistance needed to realise that growth. The road to growth was thus taken by the devoloping nations with much expectation and confidence about the attainment of results. This attainment goal was broadly defined in terms of 'catching up' with the developed countries, not immediately but, yet, over a visible period. In order to assist in this effort, voluminous literature poured forth from economists and others through periodicals, pronouncements and learned studies, and from many parts of the developed and, to some extent, the developing world.

It was widely declared as known that the already developed countries had become so in a different climate, where the materials of industrialization were available to them on favourable terms, by force or other means, from within or without their national boundaries; and where their exports could also be marketed in circumstances that prevailed only then. Similarly, it was known that the social, political and even moral conditions which formed the foundations for the growth of those countries could not be replicated in the post-War World. Finally, it was recognised that the historical, wellmeant, social and, particularly, the health programmes developed in the poor countries during preceding decades, had created a surge in populations which was quite unknown and non-comparable with experience of the already developed countries. While population growth at best accompanied or otherwise followed the spurt of agrarian and industrial development in developed countries, in the developing countries the populations had in fact already arrived. 'The vertical invasion of the masses' that took place in Europe during the Industrial Revolution had therefore quite different characteristics from those of the post-War Third World.[1]

All these made the obtenance of two key components of sustained growth extremely difficult, if not well-nigh impossible. With the new countries treading the path of development, in the state of political sophistication and mass population, the accumulation of capital was no easy task even in absolute terms, much more so in terms relative to the pace of development required. Likewise, of course, given the code of international relations, affecting national sovereignty, the problems of obtaining the necessary materials as inputs or market for exports, were all the time under constraint; more so, to the poor countries.

The major import of the rising expectations imparted by the developed world to the developing world at this juncture, was the open recognition of the difficulties that the new developing countries must face concerning their capital requirements and their trade opportunities. The major promise, therefore, provided to these countries in the forties, in any case fully implied in the logic of the new world being created, was a corresponding required Aid and Trade, to enable the developing world to start up rapid growth, eventually closing the gap between them and the developed countries.

The Long Wait

Aside from the economic gap, the gap between promise and performance is also part of the story of this book, to be taken up later. Suffice to say here, that the promised rapid growth has not given indication of being realised. To many, it seemed that the promised land was even getting further away. This at least is the interpretation of situations where, at the end of a development phase, there were more unemployed in a country than less, or lower per capita income than more, and so on. There were very few exceptions, which themselves had exceptional circumstances - the 'four little dragons'[2] in Asia, each of them again different from one another - and were not applicable to the general case. This will again figure in our examination in later pages. As a general phenomenon for the developing world, it looked as if the catching up would almost never take place. Perhaps one statement good enough, as any other, was that from the then President of the World Bank, that 'the income of the United States rose more in a single year than it would in India over a century.[3] Thus the gap, rather than closing, kept widening. The gap was originally used to refer to average incomes of developed compared with developing countries. But it was not only the income gap; new gaps emerged to describe crises that needed naming. And so the trade gap, the foreign exchange gap, the technology gap and so on emerged and all became each more widening.

We shall go later into the well-meant theories, ideas, strategies and sophistications that kept being provided generously to the developing countries, both to explain their plight and to assist in overcoming it. Similarly also, we shall come later to the frustrations, even resentments, that overtook developing country leaders when the developing economies asked the world community to keep their contract for rapid growth. Some of the reasons for slowness were truly within the developing economies themselves. How much of this was autonomously created by national leadership and how much the result of outside patronage and advice - we shall try to see later. What is clear for the time being is that there has been no dearth of refinements of existing theory; but also no alternative breakthroughs have as yet been provided. Some pointers have

5

been increasingly clear, partly in literature and partly in practice, with the very few countries that have broken out of stagnation. One of them is also, the down grading that has occurred in economic sophistication as hitherto dispensed.

By the early seventies 'four presidents of great economic associations (had) called for more empirical, more applied, more relevant, more institutional and more inter-disciplinary economies. Reynolds, Phelps Brown, Worswick, Leontief, Frisch and Hahn call us back to pay attention to the important targets, not the attractive weapons.'[4] Meanwhile, another[5] was saying that 'saving time in the preparation and execution of investment projects and in getting them working at full capacity is likely to be of greater consequence for economic development than such economists' gimmicks as determining investment priorities according to accounting prices.'

Theory has been profound with the need for the simultaneous commitments for development of material production, of social welfare, of population planning, of environmental planning, health planning, rural development planning, income distribution and basic incomes planning, and many more. There has been very little unified planning except the label. In between the short promise in aid and trade and the inadequacies in national planning, there has been no fundamental position, with adequate answer, on the problem of the countries, namely rapid growth as a pre-condition and a basis for people's welfare and well-being. What makes for development, and whether there is a fresh principle sufficiently wide and determining, derived from theory or from experience, is a challenge still to be met. In what follows, an effort is made to do so, by describing the past short-comings in policy and institutions, national and international; but also by attempting to describe a path to growth as seems to have been known by some at least, in their practice and, sometimes, pronouncements.

Notes

1 The literature on these is extensive and not new. Some of the early references on them are cited, for instance, in the discussions in my

The Long Wait

Economics of Full Employment in Agricultural Countries with Special Reference to India and Ceylon (Colombo, 1957).
2 A complimentary term that refers to Taiwan, Korea, Hongkong and Singapore - China being the big dragon - all of whom together recorded remarkable economic breakthroughs.
3 Ecosoc/3347-3348, October 1972.
4 Paul Streeten, on the Three Worlds of Economics, by L.A. Reynolds, 1971 (Yale).
5 R.C. Repetto, Time in India's Development Programme, 1971 (OUP).

7

Chapter Two

The Means to Growth: Conditions and Invariables

We shall review in the next Chapter the actual record of the world-wide efforts made to promote the development of third world countries. This Chapter discusses something that is simple, even self-evident, but seems to lie buried under the mass of international policies, theories and refinements that have accumulated over the years: the invariable conditions for wealth creation in any economy. In this sense, it is a simple mechanics of growth which carries universal validity. The mechanics itself does not depend on, nor does it necessarily question, the innumerable theories of development in the literature of economics. It simply points to a constant process, under growth, which goes beyond the broad factors of production — of capital, labour and so on — and the aggregates — of savings, investment and the like. The Marxian dynamic, or the Tableau Economique,[1] perhaps provide examples of invariables on which development must depend, and on which governments may trace practical policies for growth. What is therefore, attempted at the outset is a simple description which is fundamental to the strategies of governments and central to the growth process but which is overlooked amidst the profusion of other sophistications.

The basis for growth, as for existence, is the presence of all our resources. They are 'land' (natural resources), 'labour' (human resources) combined to productive advantage by the application of capital (cumulative labour, management, or both) and organisation (perhaps labour or management or both).[2] But the mechanics of growth itself is determined by a process and not the existence of the factors; nor of the aggregates. The combination of the factors at a given time produces an output which divides itself partly into consumption and partly into investment. The production process creates a 'surplus,' however called, which has to be ploughed back into the process, for growth to be continued. This is the cause of wealth. There is no other cause. All the rest may accelerate or decelerate the process, sometimes halt it, enhance or adversely affect the composition of the wealth created, and so on. These are, of course, many and the pre-occupation of various national, as well as international, actions. But the mechanics of growth is single and invariable.

This is indeed, how the process of rapid wealth creation occurred in the nineteenth century. Consumer privation, exploitation, depressions, compensatory aggrandisements and even economic accidents determined the scale and composition of that wealth. But the mechanics was this. This was also the process of wealth creation later, in the societies having state ownership of the means of production. In this century, in contrast to the last, there has been less conspicuous consumption out of the 'surplus,' less privation and exploitation of the non-privileged class, a policy-based package of low priced basic consumption goods, mainly food, clothing and accommodation. Where countries succeeded, the accumulation process took place, necessarily and inexorably and the surpluses were repeatedly re-deployed into continued productive expansion.[3]

Thereafter it was the same mechanics which the Third World countries had to apply. It was an impersonal mechanics. But they were left without the means by which these mechanics were made to work, both in the countries that developed in the last century and in the countries that did so in this century. We shall need to look further, later, at the dilemmas of these countries that had willingly eschewed the nineteenth century mould, not pursued the twentieth century socialist policies, and been left without the Aid and Trade premises which were supposed to provide the brave new basis for the undisturbed operation, in effect, of this growth mechanics. Here, we are faced with the need to see how these may be overcome, because they are the only means to growth. Some basic characteristics seem to be part of such a growth mechanics and these may be considered here.

An essential pillar in growth mechanics has to be the consumption capacity of that part of production that is meant for consumption. In practice, these are not only the 'end goods' normally so understood, namely, the final consumption goods, like food and clothing. All ouput, intermediate and capital, are also each consumed at respective stages, and represent the consumption capacity of the disbursements from investment out of the national product. However, the end goods have a special connotation, not only as the end purpose, hedonistically, of a society's productive activity. Its level and its composition will also be crucial, firstly, to absorbing the portion of the production process set aside for consumption goods. Secondly, it will reflect on the ability to market what are called 'investment goods'. In other words, both capital and intermediate goods can continue to sell only if the consumer 'end products' they are producing, or will produce, are such in quantity and composition as will be consumed. The quantity and composition of the end goods are therefore crucial. Given proper decisions as to what these shall be at a given phase in an economy, each of the innumerable segments and items of both investment and consumption outputs will complement each other, and through this interlocking support, become each other's own markets.[4] The above pattern of producing goods becomes the basis for economic movement and sustenance. If the consumers in a society are seen, as wage-earners or workers, then the most visible basic industries in developing economies are the wage-goods industries.

It must be pointed out however in the context of the foregoing ,that the basic industries are not merely consumptions goods in the popular sense. They are also configuration of closely related intermediate and capital goods that are involved in the rational sustenance of the pattern of the planned wage goods themselves. Nations that were dependent on advanced

10

countries in the past, politically or economically, typically never had this basic essential of self-reliance, or self-development. Later, in the post-War phase, the promise of Aid and Trade eschewed the adoption of this strategy as a basis once again. Yet there was no commensurate outlet in exports to absorb the increasing production that was not in any case diversified enough for the low income domestic market to take, but had to be sold, if the pace of reinvestment[5] and the growth rate were to be maintained. Having adopted a development style that was internationalist, it also became practically impossible later for a dependent country to find the margins to reduce imports, since these were mostly development imports.[6] Nor could they find leverage in expanding exports, since these were practically primary, or similar, goods. In any case, when it came to bargaining, the buyers knew who was dependent on whom. The concept of progressive non-dependence, in significant form, on imports for developmental inputs was a crucial component of the growth mechanics that was not adopted.

This non-dependence was also crucial in another, somewhat interesting, way. Developed countries that originally relied on colonial patterns in order to develop, did not collapse after that pattern was lost, but continued to prosper, in fact, contrary to many opinions in the early post-War years. While advantageous inputs and sale of outputs were crucial in their early stage of development, they ceased to be relatively important with the technological advance and giant superiority that they had attained subsequently. These provided the new competitiveness and even price advantage for their goods subsequently. In a different situation, even Marshall Aid to West Europe would have had to take a longer, varied, course before 'reconstruction' took place.

Parallel with this, the transition 'from the first shovel to the first hydraulic forklift' proved similarly crucial. For too many developing countries, the transition achieved was chimerical, since what came about was the end of the indigenous 'shovel'or handicraft industry and the beginning of a vigorous import industry for the hydraulic 'machinery'. This could be multiplied with a thousand more examples in various production lines in the history of these economies. In effect, there was no transition in which a machine or component became also a prototype to fabricate and to multiply appropriately as domestic equivalents. This distinction — between countries which failed to do so and those that did, runs like a golden, or not so golden, thread dividing today's new prosperous countries and those still 'developing'.[7] Japan, and in certain ways, the 'four little dragons' of Asia illustrate the former; too many countries exist around the world illustrating the later; while a few, like India or Brazil illustrate a mid-way mark.

Thus, internal fabricating capacity, without at all presuming that everything is to be fabricated internally, is integral to planning for wage goods industries, being the bedrock of growth mechanics. Indeed, no country has become developed, without a highly advanced agricultural system, a meaningful industrial pattern, a wide range of wage goods outputs and, coupled with it, the internal fabricating capacity as appropriate to each economy. If one may exclude ready exceptions, like small city states, the pattern seems invariable. Where one or two such countries have been lucky, so as to receive a much larger volume of per capita aid and foreign market opportunities than others, the pace of growth has been faster. But the basic pattern for this growth was the same.

Yet some of the developing countries that have so far failed must also take some of the blame. They have complained long and loud about the international system. All too true, but they have not complained enough about themselves. In that sense, so far at least as the growth mechanics described here goes, the still developing countries have lessons to learn, irrespective of ideology and whether they are so-called market or socialist economies. Given the invariables that we have talked about, other issues, ideas and theories, advanced from time to time, on how to develop, can find their due place. That goes for ideas of balanced versus imbalanced growth, export related versus domestic based growth, agriculture versus industry, environment versus development, social versus economic growth, consumption versus investment, monetarist versus non-monetarist economy and others. More important than even 'catching up', was establishing the basis for 'self-sustained' growth; catching up would then take its own course.

12

The Means to Growth: Conditions and Invariables

In summing up the growth mechanics described, that is the only process by which growth must take place in any economy, at all times, under any political or social system. In some, especially in the past, the means to development were morally reprehensible or physically possible only at that time. Also in certain areas, it may have been achieved largely autonomously; in others, in cooperation with partner countries. But the process was the same. Money supply did not by itself create this growth; nor wages and employment by themselves. The structure had to exist first, or be created, that could use these as instruments in a growth process. Money management, income policies and others could not create 'growth'; bad management and policies could certainly arrest growth!

It was once observed that 'the failure of economic historians to provide the economists with a historical dimension to their perspective had reduced the effectiveness of economists in dealing with contemporary problems. In other words, 'failure of economists to appreciate the transitory character of the assumed constraints and to understand the source and direction of these changing constraints is a fundamental handicap to further development of economic theory'.[8]

As for more sophisticated attempts, Leontief's Presidential Address to the American Economic Association in 1970 would encourage one to leave this well alone! 'Mathematical model-building industry' as a branch of economics is questioned for its ability to support itself on an empirical foundation, with assumptions not assessed or verified against observed facts. 'If you do not like my set of assumptions, give me another and I will gladly make you another model'. When it comes to normative models, which are frequent in literature, there is even less obligation to test assumptions. He considers the situation scandalous and does not think it is redeemed by the large volume of econometric work. 'In no other field of empirical enquiry has so massive and sophisticated machinery been used with such indifferent results', due to pre-occupation with hypothetical rather than observable reality. One review of this[9] echoes Leontief's call for reassessment of the balance between pure theory and inductive theory.

13

The Wealth of Poor Nations

What follows is based on the premise that history has had, in effect, only three growth models. As mentioned before, one was the 19th century free market model; the other, the 20th century socialist economies model; and the third is the predicted post-War model for the Third World. The Third World has to examine these models as they contain the conditions and invariables of growth and establish a viable mechanism for development.

In subsequent chapters, we shall try to address some of the major issues in national action and international co-operation, that are absolutely essential if we are to emerge from the present stagnation. But before we do so, as earlier stated, we should examine something of the record of development and of international co-operation and assistance from the developed world.

Notes

1   Marxian economics posited persistent surplus which was expropriated by the exploiting class and used to enlarge the capitalist economy, underconsumption implied in such a system being met in later stages by imperialism. While it was genuine and unique in that it sought to discover a system, perhaps its weakness was that it did not foresee fully the type of State-level demand maintenance policies that would then make decisions on investment and consumption in a social context. The Tableau was by a French school of thought known as the Physiocrafts in which agriculture became the basic sector and its output the basic economic output, or Wealth. See also my *Economics of Full Employment in Agricultural Countries with Special Reference to India and Ceylon*, p.83 for some references.

2   The 1980 World Bank survey, World Development Report, quotes with approval Adam Smith, that the prosperity of a nation is determined mainly 'by the skill, dexterity, and judgement with which its labour is generally applied'.

3   A long-standing source of reference on these is, for example, Dobb's *Studies in the Development of Capitalism*. See also my *Economics of Full Employment in Agricultural Countries with Special Reference to India and Ceylon*, especially chapters six and seven.

4   There is long established pioneering basis, in select writings, on this, especially Rosentein Roden (also quoting Allen) *The Economic Journal*, June-September 1943; Mandelbaum, *Industrialization of Backward Areas*. See also my *Ceylon, Beveridge and Bretton Woods*; Colombo 1946; and

14

The Means to Growth: Conditions and Invariables

Economics of Full Employment in Agricultural Countries with Special reference to India and Ceylon, p. 92.

5 Some of the 'surplus' generated for re-investment was, in the real world, not only investment goods but also consumption goods, which however are exported against capital goods imports. Such leeway however presumes adequate trade opportunities.

6 Or 'maintenance' imports, as they came to be called in India in the fifties, in which several intermediate goods and food items figured; the argument being that other aid and domestic capital were going into production.

7 This core distinction — determining terms of trade, income, sustainable growth and scale of that growth — is illustratively described in the eighth and last chapters, as among the major foundations in a manifesto of future actions, under the theme of transition from 'dependent to non-dependent' development.

8 Journal of Economic Literature, September 1978, p.963, Douglas C.North.

9 *The Economic Journal*, December 1979, p. 993.

Chapter Three

The Record

When the compact for the development of the Third World was begun in the forties, it was within a specific political and economic framework, namely that of political democracies with multiple obligations — on working conditions, welfare benefits, and other social benefits, and infrastructural provisions. They were also in the climate of thinking that premised cycles of prosperity and depression in the course of development, the mode that basically obtained in the countries that developed in the last century. The question of clearing the market of the total goods and services produced was one in which the international monetary and trade system was to be a key agent, replacing the colonial export-import pattern of the past.

The developing economies were thus already attuned at the beginning of this long journey in search of growth, not only to dependence outside, and to cycles of peaks and troughs in the progress, but also to periods of low level equilibrium, as much as the equilibrium at high level, at which post-War thinking was aimed.

In the end, what the co-operating developed countries brought as recipes to the developing countries were models and theories derived from themselves. To begin with, the forties were the period of applied Keynesian thinking. Demand management and deficit budgeting were held up as the mechanisms for development. Lending themselves easier to government manipulations, they also seemed acceptable to the countries receiving the concomitant supporting aid resources. That these aid sources and trade openings were woefully inadequate, given the premises of the particular philosophy, is a tortuous story which we shall later touch on. Nothing in fact was wrong with the Keynesian model. But its attempt to extend beyond its environment without first establishing the economic structure to make it relevant was obviously wrong.

The sanctifying of budget deficits for development proved attractive to indigent governments struggling to find consumption incomes and investment resources at the same time. However, while going along, at least some leaderships in countries had the prescience to see the primacy of establishing the structural frameworks first. Whatever other shortcomings then or still existing, the establishment in India even before Independence, of two foundations became the most lasting creations of these decades. One was the unequivocal assertion of the need to increase dramatically the volume of total agricultural production. The Indian National Congress under the leadership of Jawaharlal Nehru simply declared, 'the whole success and failure of all our planning hangs by the single thread of our agricultural production and, specially, food production'.[1] More than anything else, this has been responsible for the rise, in round figures, of Indian food grains production, from around 50 million tons at the end of the forties to near 150 million tons at the end of the seventies. The second stand taken by Nehru and the Congress was the decision to develop, unswervingly, a strong network of basic heavy industries for India. That meant dams and generating plants as much as factories and industrial plants, infrastructures as much as rolling stock, and, not least, machines that made machines as much as machines that produced the consumer goods. As events developed, when the reckoning came later with the expectations in aid and trade turning sour, it was the structural foundation and its capacity to enable the growth mechanisms to operate that has emerged as the country's most important asset.

Perhaps a more remarkable development, also illustrating the case of growth without classical type external dependence, was of course China, from the late forties. A sturdy combination of the state in large-scale production, with the communes at the lowest ground level, produced a remarkable transformation in the outputs of agriculture, industrial materials, small-scale industry, components manufacture and integrated planning in the most realistic form possible, of health, education, population, environment and economics. Whatever may be said about shortcomings and weaknesses, still, the position remains that it is these foundations that assured the success of the steps instituted from the late seventies towards an ultimate high-mass consumption stage by the end of the century. As for the earlier phase, it is also evident that such aid and trade as obtained were almost fully exploited to establish self-reliant productive capacity in concrete lines of production and certainly not to import machinery that merely produced consumer goods. At the higher levels, a similar pattern to that in India may be said to have emerged, with industries producing a range of planned consumer goods, as well as producing planned machine goods.[2]

The classic case of Japan belongs to a much earlier period beginning with 1875. Both the mechanics and the structure tell the story of agrarian transformation, surge in outputs of various consumer goods,[3] with gradual growth and later dominance of capital goods. The earnings of foreign exchange as in the other two countries, in Japan's case originally from export of silks, were geared singularly to create the self-reliant structure and sustaining the re-investment of surpluses. As one writer observed in early stages, 'most of the capital goods required in the wider industrialisation of Japan were produced domestically.'[4] Comparing India, another writer stated.[5] 'India's position with regard to foreign capital (was) very different from that of Japan — Japan borrowed abroad to finance her industrial development but retained control of capital in her own hands and eventually evolved from a debtor to a creditor nation. But India suffered from the limitation that her use of imported capital carried with it outside control over the choice of investments, and hence over the general trend of economic development.'

Taiwan and South Korea again demonstrated the basic necessity of the agrarian transformation. Their construction of

18

industry enjoyed massive support in aid terms, which for once lived up to the premise of the early forties supposedly to apply to all the developing countries. It showed how on such a premise, fully applied, rapid growth could and would take place and also how the need for aid gradually tapered off as theoretically intended. The case of the other two little dragons, namely, Hongkong and Singapore, is special, they being essentially city states. Their story is one of how self-reliance came to be established by highly practical policies first through use of commerce, then of light manufactures and then of sophisticated skilled manufactures. The ingredients for self-reliance, whether by physical production, or by attracting money markets or other ways, as the means for the mechanics of growth, had nonetheless to be established and this is what was done. In Singapore, for example, productive lines of world scale have thus resulted in the process. It has among the world's largest ports, refining capacity, and international financial markets. These, as well as the wide range of other economic activities, relate very much to the local environment of the countries concerned. Some strong, sudden change of winds may shift this environment, with effects on the economic structure, since these are not large countries. But what has been done and achieved is what should have been done, notwithstanding this. There is no corresponding economic theory on it.

Many other developing countries, charted their developmental course on the philosophy of political democracy, Welfare State and international co-operation that was to be their guide in and after the forties. Thus they readily used also many theories that came from the source of the expected aid and trade.

In the early years, development based on 'import-substitution' was such a theory. It was impeccable and, further, attractive to the developing countries. In practice, however, this became mostly and at best import of machines which produced consumption goods and had to be each replaced by imports. We discussed this earlier in terms of the lasting implications to a developing economy in its capacity to reduce imports, establish tolerable terms of trade, reduce continual

19

dependence on aid flows, or the ability to build up its own internal structure.

With the end of the import-substitution phase as a solvent, the international co-operative community went into a new idea, of 'export-led growth' and of lead sectors. As will be seen in the previous case, as well as in this, and others none of these by themselves are false. But what has been curious, and wholly false, is the way in which international and national dialogues have got on to one or other of panaceas singly as the solvent. Lead sector and export-led growth were in the same category, except that each failed for its own reasons. In this case, there were two reasons. One, that internal agrarian and economic revolution was never established. Secondly, the so-called export lead mostly came from the same colonial type primary or quasi-primary production lines, with their own capacity to earn foreign exchange or to produce adequate local incomes quite inadequate to the demands of development.

Then there were the theories of 'balanced growth' of a type, which said that what was wrong with the development efforts was the lack of a balance between agriculture and industry and that something should have been done with agriculture much earlier. The failure to do so explained the foreign exchange and debt servicing limits and even the capacity to produce inputs to industry within the countries. Again there was nothing new or objectionable, but countries during a certain phase were all practically giving up everything else and single-mindedly pursuing this development as the panacea. While interest in agriculture revived, it was presumed industry was less important, whereas what was less important was the dependent type of industrialisation pointed out earlier.

Then there were also supporting facets of ideas to prop up one or other of such theories. One of these facets was a series of imported policies for rural development. At one time, it was all 'community development'. When disillusionment came upon this some years later, serious examination had to be undertaken internally to realise what should have been realised at the beginning, in order to start an alternative strategy. Community development — as community services and public

20

works programmes, even with some economic and related assistance as obtained - was a thing apart from integrated resource-based planning and development by the community itself at the autonomous level. In such context, infrastructure and other support had a place and had to be given a place, but in accord with needs directly of the production resources and of production. Block development schemes in India were different from the commune in China, the Kibbutz in Israel, or the Shemaul in Korea, or the earlier rural programmes in Taiwan and Japan. But each shared this integrated resource based planning and production approach.

Another concept that offered to come to the rescue during these times was that of 'employment intensive development', as having been the missing link and the explanation for the massive insoluble unemployment, low income, foreign exchange constraints, budget deficits, costly subsidies and many other ailments. We shall see in one of the cases, in a separate chapter, where such an approach should lead. Here we may note that, along with a somewhat diffuse slogan about appropriate technology, it carried wide charisma which it became difficult to overthrow. The countries that 'suffered' seeming benefits failed later to obtain self-sustaining growth.

More recently, we have had the philosophy that what was wrong was the failure of the so-called trickle-down approach to development, whereby the massive large-scale production programmes were to have beneficial chain-effects in employment and productive activity down the line, to the populations at lower income levels. It was very quickly agreed that the trickle-down theory was wrong, forgetting that in fact it existed as a fact of life in the experience of the last century, even this century. What the present day developing countries did not have were the conditions in which the trickle-down 'theory' worked, including the political, social and moral conditions thereto. The same effect however may be said fairly to have been simulated, partly at least in the socialist economies, subject to the initial provision of basic consumption goods by these economies to the population. Most other growth was highly capital — intensive and large-scale in most cases and the benefits

21

gradually worked themselves down. It is not that the trickle-down theory is needed at all today. But from this, an alternative was next developed to help the poor countries. This is what was called 'the basic-needs approach'.

Under this concept, it was declared that the problem with non-development was the fact that the lower income deciles did not have basic incomes to meet basic needs. The meeting of these needs would be development by itself; would also be efficient and economic use of local factors of production; and would, through demand effects, generate other growth. This again was not something to quarrel with by and large, and by itself. But as a single panacea it was rather a trap, like the many traps that the poor countries have had, than an adequately compulsive theory of growth. As in the employment intensive theory, so in this too, there remained a serious question of the optimal combination of factors in every production process to ensure maximum surplus creation, as well as to ensure overall full use of national resources. It has been aptly said that 'the determination of the optimum size of total savings and that of the optimum capital intensity of investment are interdependent problems.[6] To discard this rule, in favour of labour-intensiveness and basic needs *per se* as salvation, would be to ignore the constraints which prevented under-developed countries from accumulating capital and thereby developing.[7] 'If the primary object of government was to raise the rate of growth of output, then it should maximise the rate of investment at each moment'. Subsequent writers have recognised that the level of modern sector employment and rate of investment are inter-dependent.[8] In discussions on attaining full employment during early years too, it was noted that 'the labour intensive ideas could be pursued only in conformity with the principles of optimal grouping of factors in the unit.'[9] 'It is the capital labour ratio of the development process as a whole which has to take account of the relative capacity of the various factors and not the choice of productive techniques in each production unit.[10] These are fundamental points of view which, in a practical way, the Chinese have questioned in international forums, suggesting that this may border on being simply another trap to be cautious about; diverting countries away from the essential strategies for lasting growth. Sound development planning will inherently have basic needs, both as benefit and as instrument for high rates of re-investment of surpluses and rapid growth.

Then of course there was the other set of ideas provided to the developing countries around new headings of development. For example, it was important to have 'social planning' and provide for social changes as pre-conditions to development, perhaps including cultural and spiritual conditions as well. There was hardly anybody to consider the fact that social change precedes development, but also accompanies it and flows from it. Similarly, there was the concept of 'population planning' as one more pre-condition for development to take place. There was again hardly any to consider the fact in history that development was the most assured solvent to the population problem. This is again another special issue which we shall look at in one of the later chapters. Or again there was 'environment' as something to be preserved and considered 'before development'. There were few to consider the fact that environment management, as sustained resource use management, was a support with current resource crisis, an essential support to development. This too we shall see in a later chapter.

And so on. They all add up to a somewhat simple fact that there were as many theories or philosophies as there were 'disciplines'. There was no integrated theory of growth which after all must be more in conformity with the realities of life. It is somewhat surprising that all these separate theories have carried weight and conviction with the developing countries. One reason at least that they did so, surely, is that they were tied to the grants and loans and the markets that were supposed to be made available by the developed countries.

As one of the final steps to advice on development, there was 'dethroning of GNP', without knowing of or finding an alternative. GNP itself was always a means to welfare in the end, even to the Mercantalists! The change that had to be made was in the automatic inference of social welfare from economic production. But GNP was needed for welfare, and this fine thread was not really researched.

23

The Wealth of Poor Nations

Neither the conventional financial ingredients of sustained growth - given savings and investment ratios, plus demand maintenance by incomes policy; or 'monetarism'; nor the establishment of Rostowian indices, of percentages to national output and savings and so on, can or will, assure take-off for these countries. These are indices, not causative instruments. The structural changes posited will inevitably reflect later in emergence of Rostow and Colin Clark type phenomena - critical mass investment ratio to GNP and thinning of agricultural work-force and population in favour of industry and tertiary sectors.

Amidst the slow growth, it must not be thought that developing countries had not increased their GNP. They have doubled and trebled in some cases. They have passed from the stage of the 'shovel' and gone to the stage 'hydraulic forklift', but the forklift by and large continues to be imported or assembled at best, not fabricated internally. International forums have already laid targets for them in which they participated. For example, the UNIDO Lima Conference set a target for the year 2000 which seems impractical now. Similarly, in other forums, from time to time, great promises have been held in trade concessions, stated to be granted, to be followed only by fresh phases of disillusionment and further conferences. The process is still going on and will continue, so long as the present development style remains, with its package of international technical assistance, foreign loans euphemistically called aid, market concessions marginally given, and structural dependence on the developed countries.

A classic statement of the position to which the process has been reduced, voiced sometimes in the most respectable places, is the serious proposition that the continued growth of the developed countries is most important, because the growth of the developing countries depends on that. The markets of the former were needed to provide the off-take for the exports of developing countries not to mention their loans to the developing countries. A strange syllogism, since, by definition, developing countries must forever be developing; and the developed countries forever developed, so that they may provide the motive for the former's growth.

24

The Record

The Third World is tied to 'a system' and cannot immediately change over to another system which it can build. Such a system is essentially the core of the growth mechanics and the self reliance structure, posited at the outset, at the first chapter, as should have been the basis for the developing countries.

The syndrome of international consultations, confrontations, discussions and conferences is going on. But now increasingly, the developed countries are asserting that it was time to cry halt to continued aid and continued trade concessions. The developing countries must learn to look after themselves. A sad rounding of the circle indeed.

The post-War growth system for the democratic countries, as also the United Nations system, was created by the potential aid givers, and the rules by which the growth game was to be played flowed basically from them. Then came the flow of prescriptions, advice, patronage, and finally, resentment, accusing the developing countries of demanding too much, when all the time the game was being played according to the rules. In actual performance down the years, countries varyingly had to go hat in hand seeking the promised international assistance, often in order to stand still or to prevent themselves from slipping back. It was a co-operation that also carried heavy burdens and barriers to the receivers. Often developed countries would lecture, call to account,[11] or berate them for situations to which in fact the donors were, by the socio-political and co-operation terms, implicitly party. As we shall see, there was also quite obvious use of 'double standards' by the developed group, on trade, based simply on strength a situation well illustrated when one of the countries, New Zealand, on being hit with the EEC walls , accused them of 'economic vandalism'. Also as we shall see later during global trade negotiations , the same syndrome prevailed, of the rich giving to and taking from each other, with the others standing by.

By 1969, in a representative view of developing countries, Singapore found itself compelled to state that the big powers are setting up a separate international network of their own where decisions of greater consequence than resolutions passed by the United Nations are being made and implemented. The less developed countries should wake up to this new and significant development in international affairs. The reality is, it is in this separate international network, this new free masonry of big powers and advanced nations, that the significant decisions on world issues, whether they be political, economic or military are being taken. The rate of progress in advanced countries is reaching geometrical proportions. The validity of this contention... would be put to the test not many generations hence... (but) ... when those now in their teens in less developed countries reach maturity by the end of this century. Whether this emerging generation is put in new bondage will depend to a great extent on what those now in charge do or fail to do. This is the measure of urgency of the real and significant problem before the less developed countries.'[12]

There is now need for the closest reassessment by developing countries of how they should determine their growth. This Book has expressed a clear point of view. In the following special chapters, we shall try to take up some of the main issues in this point of view, issues that are both national and international, and attempt to discuss them in practical terms.

Notes

1   Quoted in Gunnar Myrdal *Asian Drama*.
2   On China's Policy at that time, including its aid policy, see for example, *Far East Trade and Development*, July and October 1972 (London); also China's statement at Ecosoc (Fifty-third section).
3   Rice and fish were a smaller ratio of imports in later years than in the early years of development.
4   Buchanan, *E.J.* December 1946.
5   Hubbard, *Eastern Industrialisation and its Effects on the West*. Of interest also is, H.W. Singer, *The Distribution of Gains Between Investing and Borrowing Countries*.
6   A.K. Sen, *The Choice of Techniques* (Third Edition, Oxford), 1967.
7   W. Galenson and H.Leibenstein: Investment criteria, Productivity and Economic Development, *Quarterly Journal of Economics*, August 1955.
8   See Newberry, *E.J.* June 1972, p.567 et seq - Public Policy in the Dual Economy.
9   My *Economics of full employment in Developing Countries with Special Reference to India and Ceylon* (1957), p.171.

10   Adler, *AER* May 1952, p.589. Fiscal and Monetary implications of
     development Programmes. See also *Yale Brozen*, May 1951, Investment,
     Innovation and Initiation, pp.241-2.
11   Something that has actually occurred at some conferences. Years later by
     the early eighties when the issues split over and hurt rich countries too,
     Australia, using Third World phraseology, complained that the EEC
     sugar policies had cost Australia over A$1,300 million for the decade
     preceding; and A$8,150 for producers outside the communtiy. 'It was
     high time' it said 'the EEC did something about the serious damage it was
     doing to efficient sugar producing and exporting nations'. (Reuter,
     Feb.1982).
12   Foreign Minister of Singapore, S. Rajaratnam, at the United Nations
     General Assembly, 1969.

B. Issues and Options - National

Chapter Four

Return to Growth — New National Decisions

The development that has taken place and can continue to take place in developing countries may seemingly give satisfaction and maintain still some hope of "catching up" at some future time. Spurts in glamorous production lines, in commerce, shipping, certain industries, sometimes in the plantations can take place, often through the leadership of multinationals.[1] The economics of these developments have shown, and unfortunately are most likely to continue to show, that increases in national outputs in this form are one thing and closing the so-called gaps with the developed countries are quite another. As we said, even closing of the gaps is not as important a target as the establishment of self-sustained growth capacity. This, structurally, continues to elude. Developing countries' governments keep going to international parleys and forums, coming back with nothing; or, perhaps worse, with something that is only marginal but mistaken for a solution. This is what has occurred over trade rounds, compensatory agreements, commodity stabilisation, and others.[2] Thus, new national decisions have to be taken that can help earliest to establish the conditions for growth, to build appropriate internal structures, to re-adjust the import pattern, and to sharpen further the use of export potentials.

This is not easy, but possible. Before we can get to impersonal and economic considerations, the social political context is a necessary premise. In the political-democratic context of such societies, some characteristics must be natural. The leadership would tend to be elitist and may not always distinguish between relative national priorities. This is of course not an aspersion but simply an interpretation of what occurs most of the time. An extreme example of this could be the view of private vehicles as if they were an essential backbone to transport and to commuting, a consideration made more dramatic of late by the oil and energy crisis. But as mentioned, this example can be replicated in many sectors and areas of the society with tremendous implications for resource allocations between investment and consumption and, within consumption, between self-sustaining growth-oriented consumption and that in which the multiplier leakage abroad is dominant. It goes without saying that an additional imposition is on the already scarce foreign exchange resources.

In this situation, there have been hasty pontifications purporting to diagnose and to give advice to these countries. They have been called 'soft societies' and therefore unable to take hold of themselves for development. Corruption has been described as a determining component, like other elements of a theory, affecting development. An observation overlooked was that all countries had a genius for corruption at all times, except that, while the developed countries can afford it, the poor countries cannot.[3] But this is not the main argument concerning 'softness'. The oligarchic/elitist commercial and political structure of the democratic societies carries per force elements of 'inducement', commission and pay-off which are common in entrepreneurship and touch other leadership as well easily, when a country is poor. If so, one has to consider at the same time the nature of social organisation.[4] Meanwhile, in the given social, political, democratic context — the silent premises of the post-War expectations — these were to have been met by massive, honest international co-operation, with Aid and Trade support that should have been at least equal to those extended to the very few countries which, for one or other reason, received such support. Thus, simply pointing the finger at so-called 'inherent' retrogressive factors in developing societies, even when they are present, was not conceptually mature or comprehensive. These societies had 'foreclosed' on alternative political systems for development, which could well have different effects on social standards, however mixed.

Yet, to say this simply does not answer our problem of what new national decisions to make. This Book is not one on revolution but on rapid development. There are of course ample instances of countries in this ill-defined democratic group which have reactionary leadership and have simply been stationary. This would obviously point to the need for an honest system of participatory government as the basis for development. What seems even more interesting to our question is perhaps a phenomenon which seems consistently observed in the democratic countries which showed conspicuous development.

For one thing, historically no country was in fact a political democracy at the time of its achieving industrialization and take-off. Those countries which have in this Century, as developing countries, built up strong economic structures, or raised per capita incomes notably, or ramified into sophisticated production lines, all fall in the category of having benevolent, firm, almost one-man leadership. One does not wish to go into the details of these. The purpose is not to make political value judgements. But it is clear that in all these cases, large countries or small, or very small, political democratic private ownership based societies had to have firm, singular leadership which benefited them through establishment of the economic structures that were appropriate to each of their self-reliant growths.

Thus, it seems a social compact within a given country is a pre-condition. It is a compact, which if achieved, cannot continue if the leadership continues to fail. Development then becomes a strong political-economic decision-making process, in which once such a compact can be forged, the organisational and production decisions in the economy must be set out and exploited rapidly and fully. Otherwise, there is an erosion not only in development but in governmental process. Countries that became independent after the War amply carried examples of both consolidation and erosion. On this basis, we may briefly review some of the major organisational actions that

33

should be put into effect, before we could talk of economic nuances and levers of development.

The essential national decisions package would consist of: (i) country-wide rural areas autonomous development organisations; (ii) agri-crops, agro-industries, and agro-related infrastructures; (iii) across-the-board fabrication capacities in machinery, equipment, components, and at rural and industrial levels; (iv) wage goods industries, primary, secondary and tertiary; and (v) exploitation of all unique potential developmental enclaves or nodal points (harbours, free trade zones, etc.). This is not new but, in fact, what successful countries have done. On (i) are Japan, China, China-Taiwan, South Korea, and Israel. Note that, while political systems were varying, there is a clear distinction between the paths taken by these countries and those that did not, for example, India (partly), Sri Lanka, even Malaysia and so on. The record on (ii) is based on respectable classical economics, except for the absence earlier of fullest possible agro-industry processing; where countries were doing it, as in India or Malaysia, it has paid, although how those incomes were used may be another matter again. As for (iii) it has been a poor record, and how crucial is shown by the examples, comparing for instance Japan and, partly, China and India, with other countries. As for (iv) the similarities with (i) that is those that carried agricultural modernisation, are repeated, with additional cases like India perhaps, being above the line rather than below. On (v) the classic records of those like Hongkong and Singapore, or earlier, by different circumstances, of those like the United Kingdom and Netherlands, are example.

In most so-called democratic developing economies, the agrarian revolution remains only an objective and the rural base as uncared for, at least relatively speaking, as always. A complete change in thinking for the basic rural organisation level — call it commune, village area, or whatever — must be put into effect. The efficiency of land re-organisation, irrespective of ownership philosophy, requires a drastic abolition of two existing approaches. One is the so-called public services, infrastructure and loan finance, concepts of what is rural

34

organisation for production. This has to go. The second is the widespread persistence of segmented sectoral programmes for an essentially unified rural area. They come down as economic programmes, health programmes, population programmes, social programmes, education programmes, public works programme, environment programmes, agricultural programmes and many others, leaving the village area more confused and disorganised. Worse still, these leave the village area with misguided impressions that these capital disbursements rather than the increases in their own production are the source of their income. This is another source of corruption, since the village area was never given productive opportunities, nor the involvement by its own people in the planning and implementation. A unified rural area development organisation, with resources-based planning as distinct from programming for governmental budgets, has to be instituted with maximum strength. The important point is that this can be done with much less difficulties than political-democratic governments seem to imagine for so long. So long as this is absent, one of the central basis for self-reliant development will be absent.

One, perhaps minor, but interesting instance of an attempt to introduce this in a colonial type rural administration system, may be worth recalling. About the late forties, in a district in Sri Lanka, then called Ceylon, an attempt at unified production planning by village areas was initiated. The ground seemed right for an experiment of this type, about whose success however nobody was quite sure. It was initiated by a small group, led by the writer, of what were called district heads of departments, governmental officials concerned with local organisations, co-operatives, agriculture, health, public works, small or cottage industries, and one or two other related lines. The district in question was a high intensive multi-cash crop rural agriculture zone, dependent mainly on underground water sources and manual labour even for irrigation at that time. It was, however, a high-yielding area in the country, on the various cash crops it produced. The customary approach by the rural population and its leadership to development dialogue with government authorities was, as expected, simply in terms

35

of bringing a shopping list of works to be done and money needed. It was an obvious divorce from the mainstream of economic production, that induced an easy climate for the sharper elements in the society to use such a process as fecund source for corruption and personal gain. Such public works as were constructed, while of benefit, were not directly integrated into production targets and for the most part, did not result in production increases. When some select local communities were introduced to the idea of addressing themselves to resource based production planning, and its implications were discussed at informal rural meetings, the impact was immediate. It was an impact on both sides. The local communities reacted with forthright enthusiasm and eagerness to participate in such a process, which they immediately saw as the real thing. The bureaucracy were equally astonished by the proficiency and capacity shown by the participating elements in creative practical terms. It was clear that the common basis was the area's soil, water, production capacity and other techno-economic categories, all ingredients for a start on unified production planning. In a short series of informal, almost classroom, exercises, a simple outline of categories for preparation of production plans and for their aggregation as well as conversion into financing terms was prepared. This was sent out to a few local areas for the data to be entered, providing at the end of the process, simple but effective information and data of production in that area, possible additional production; strictly related infrastructural input and marketing needs; repairs and maintenance facilities in the local area; education, including technical training and health and other services programmes. One category in view of the special situation, was on energy for irrigation, in order to convert from manual and diesel oil power to electricity. The biggest stumbling block was the economics of the proposition, in view of the natural low density of consumption per unit of area, even including domestic and street lighting. Fortunately, similar to the rural reticulation schemes that had obtained in certain other countries, some provision for central government support existed. Armed with these intentions and possibilities, a series of rural areas, again through induction at informal sessions got to know the elements of electricity installation and, very quickly, had numbers of households effectively preparing the required data information. As it turned out, or the first time in that area, rural electrification came into being. Except for the electrification process which progressed from that point, the others somewhat languished because of the gap between the local initiatives and the colonial type law-and-order perspectives that seemed to linger still at the higher levels. But the experiment, conducted in an ordinary market economy developing country, was highly indicative.

Far better known and far more successful has been of course the case of the rural communes in China. Despite the remarkable achievements in the thirty years after the revolution, there were naturally, in a vast country, some better and some worse examples of rural reorganisation. Yet, it was they that led rural China away from the abject Landlordism of the past, sufficiently to enable the later phenomenal developments from the eighties onwards.

The foregoing is not exclusive of other development potentials. It by no means excludes, for instance, major production categories of national scale, which are outside the scope of competence of local areas but imply large potential outputs. Such an area for national decision in a new orientation in many developing countries is a much better appraisal of new agro and plantation industries, their pursuit to final agro-industries stage, and the assignment of priority to infrastructure for these. This is quite distinct from relying on the primary sector as a basis for growth. In quite a few countries, large potentials remain unexploited, for want of local foresight and leadership.

Supportive of these an original point that was discussed earlier would apply across all sectors. This is that from the lowest to the highest level, the feasibilities of internal fabrication capacity of machinery, components, equipment, etc., should be constantly pursued and constantly implemented. As mentioned again before, it is not that a country can at all fabricate all its requirements, just as obviously it cannot produce all its consumer requirements. The fabrication capacity, as demonstrated earlier has a central place in the self-reliance mechanics. In addition to what it yields in specific areas, it has another quality, namely of creating a skilled society and the concept of skill orientation which has always assured societies of a capacity to exploit technological opportunities as a normal process.

This is a subject with considerable early literature particularly in the form of the foundational quality of applied skills and the multiplier quality of even limited development of domestic machine and tools manufacturing. We do not intend to go into details of cases and experience though some reference is again made at Chapter Five. The evidence of the countries that developed in this century, not to mention earlier, are record enough. The implementation of the earlier mentioned actions, themselves, constitute much of the needed advance in entrenching the wage goods structure in the economy. The completion of this phase really implies industrialisation as it need be, and establishment of the basis for self-sustained growth.

In the matter of imports, quite obviously they would be directed to support the framework of a self-reliant growth structure. It is necessary that aid, as euphemism for loans, can be received only in proportion to exports that will be purchased against them. It is meaningless to consider otherwise and the crisis of present years simply bear this out. As development proceeds however, and national capacity expands, these economies would undoubtedly participate increasingly in patterns and levels of exports and imports of varying consumer goods as well as of development inputs.

As major actions, again discussed earlier, the range of basic wage-goods industries must be instituted as central, in the package of the new national decisions. We have introduced this point already and, therefore, shall not go into its details again. However, within such a structure, and on this basis, it should be open policy to utilise all opportunities, based on each country's national endowments, in high investments leading to capital creation, exports and rising incomes. Of course, national endowments may not only be natural - such as harbours and their hinter-land — but created. This is in effect what many countries achieved, such as Japan, Hongkong, Korea, Taiwan,

Singapore; or others such as the United Kingdom or Netherlands in an earlier period. For today's developing countries, various natural endowments should be fully studied early on and exploited to maximum national benefit.

We mentioned earlier that a persistent idea that had kept catching the attention of leaderships was the so-called employment-intensive theory. Naturally, that has no place in this structure. Obviously, it is not that employment has no place but that the means to ensure this employment on a high and sustained basis and on accepted income levels, could not be that way. In the subsequent chapter as a special issue, we recall the example of a particular international study in one of the countries, as an illustration of limitation in this approach and of the alternative direction that has to be taken.

A set of national decisions for development as above, would also clearly bear on several ideas of fiscal, financial and other policies normally used as apparent aids to economic development. Some of these are protection or liberalisation, high or low domestic cost structures, devaluation or appreciation, stationary or flexible wages, and global commodity agreements or producers agreements. These have long histories, some from colonial times, some under international agencies, some by developing country groups. In each case, some of the conventionally entrenched views could be highly questionable. It is not the intention, nor is it necessary, to discuss each of these in detail here. However, it could be useful to mention some of their limitations and needs.

For example, on protection, while there is now acceptance for development, many prescriptive steps of international aid sources seek reversals under liberlisation 'pakages' involving devaluation and free markets. Devaluation itself has become too freely dispensed as a prescription. Similarly, on internal cost structures, such packages frown also on subsidies to domestic production;[5] as distinct from subsidy to consumer imports. Then there is wages which, both when lower or higher, have seemed artificially determined, without priority either to development or to labour itself. Perhaps this is the most difficult issue on which to arrive at, decisions, due to various political and human considerations. Yet, many labour situations today are also due to other preconceptions about labour-intensive development or the sanctity of high costs or devaluation and so on. Finally, we have buffer stocking and price stabilisation schemes, having jumped into new prominence at the end of the seventies due to international parleys under UNCTAD. Even if all major world commodities were covered, which is far from the case. the benefits would be deceptive. Quantitatively appearing substantial, the benefits will be absolutely marginal in terms of developmental needs - as in the trade negotiations benefits we shall see later. The poor countries also would have accumulated even more deficits and problems by the time it would take for such commodity agreements to be at all worked out even minimally. Also, they are not on par at all with the type of commodity agreements, as for oil producers, silently partnered by developed oil producers too. Such marginal trade concessions, also divert developing countries away from urgent, more fundamental, re-organisational actions they should take for more assured future growth.[6]

In a discussion some years ago, the question was posed whether it is not the expanding conditions that create the entrepreneurs and not vice versa (in the same way as capital creation is held to be a result of a stage of development and not its cause); and that therefore whether it was not futile to wait for entrepreneurs to create the conditions.[7] As stated earlier, the conditions suited to each country vary widely. But whether due to Nature's bounty, or to historical advantage, or to the creation of Imperial Power, it would appear that development in various countries proceeded not by swarms of entrepreneurs developing the economy, but by entrepreneurs emerging as, successively, the growing conditions appeared fertile (in terms of materials, cost, saleability,etc.) for germination.

The above study noted the ready and flourishing existence of assiduous entrepreneurs in plenty in India, East Africa, S and S.E.Asia and similar places, but confined to commercial trading and allied activities where the conditions for successful development of the field were present. There seems no doubt that if a parallel were drawn with the conditions of developing

40

economies, it could not stop with mere creation of infrastructures, a few State industries, state policies for private capital and general incentives or exhortations. An approach such as we have outlined is more likely to lead to a structure that automatically creates obvious needs and opportunities that are possible for entrepreneurs to meet. Even as from a particular seed will grow only a particular type of tree, a particular economic structure, or a 'partial' and incomplete one, will provide the momentum for its own self-fulfilment and no more. The example of entrepreneurial activity in the 'commerce of colonial economies' was referred to; the stationary under-developed economies as a whole themselves provide other examples. The importance then of moulding the correct structural basis should be as urgent as it is evident.

Notes

1 The transnational companies control about three-fourth of the capitalist world trade, and about one-fifth to one-quarter of it is simply inter company supply. (They) make extensive use of transfer prices; and in many fields the world market prices are monopoly prices (not only OPEC) (Tibor Palankai, Karl Marx University of Economics, Budapest, in *AER*, June 1981). See also Ian Steedman, *Trade Among Growing Economies, (Cambridge Univ. Press, 1979)*.

2 On the limited capacity of primary exports to solve development problems, see, e.g., my *Economics of Full Employment with Special Reference to India and Ceylon*, pp 137-150, presenting a production possibility analysis for one country. But also see below on 'commodity communities' as potentials, in preference to buffer stocks arrangements.

3 A point made in fact at a United Nations technical conference in 1966 on administration for development.

4 The most serious corruption, as Arthur Lewis has suggested, is not the pecuniary bribe spirited into a pocket, but major, fateful, wrong decisions on development taken or not taken - acts of omission and commission - by a poorly motivated leadership and bureaucracy.

5 Protection has always been part of developed country armoury despite public statements. Even as a developed country, the U.S. had its Buy American Act in 1933 requiring local purchase by agencies up to at least 25 per cent over imported cost (*Eastern Economist*, January 6, 1950, p.15). Much later, it was Japanese imports. Thus, for all countries, a sound national economic base is considered supreme for sustained growth.

6 Views and literature are naturally wide and varied on all these. Also see,

for some early discussions and references on each, my *Economics of Full Employment with Special Reference to India and Ceylon:* on protection pp. 200-1; high costs, pp. 204-6 and 212-5; devaluation, pp. 244-5; wages, pp.217-8; buffer stocks, pp.186 and 278.

7 c.f. A.O. Hirschman, *American Economic Review*, May 1957; also B.F. Hoselitz in same number — Non Economic Factors in Economic Development; and my Ceylon Association for the Advancement of Science Paper, early 1960, 'Some Less Accepted Factors in Economic Growth' (which Gunnar Myrdal thought arresting enough to   want to discuss on his visit to Sri Lanka at the time).

Chapter Five

A Case of Employment —
Intensive National Development

In 1971, under an international programme of employment promotion, team studies were commissioned for selected developing countries in order to outline action programmes. One such was a programme of Action for Ceylon (Sri Lanka).[1]

In Chapter Three, we recalled certain theories and prescriptions suggested to developing countries, so they may develop. Among these, the employment intensive approach, along with the concept of appropriate technology, attracted considerable attention at various levels of society. They also seemed to prevail, or at least to linger, since they seemed to conform as well to what the countries could in any case do in their poor, even harassed, circumstances.

This Chapter seeks, through the specific case study on Sri Lanka, to examine the ideas put out as applied to the case and draw certain lessons, obvioususing intended as applicable also to other countries in the same situation.

What follows is based on a paper prepared on request at that time (1972). It is being kept largely in that form in order to retain it in the climate of that period, at which perhaps the employment, appropriate technology preaching was at its peak.

The essential purpose (of the Report), according to its Letter of Transmittal, 'is to serve as the basis for further national discussion.... it does not attempt to give final answers to the unemployment problem in Ceylon'. It is in this spirit that this contribution to the discussion[2] is being made.

The Wealth of Poor Nations

The Report is the result of a specific request from Ceylon for an examination of developmental policies and progeammes with a view to meeting the unemployment situation. It is natural and proper that the tenor of the investigation and analysis should reflect this emphasis. It would seem, at the same time, looking back now at the end product, that this pre-occupation has also acted somewhat as a constraint, particularly in meeting the continuing goals of employment itself. The reluctance to follow through with more productive oriented policy or programme vis-a-vis an immediate employment situation does not go unnoticed. This occurs in the overall, and also in specifics.[3]

It is not that the Report itself has not referred to the production imperative as a prime objective. The terms of reference as set out for the study[4] themselves seek advice on a long-term strategy to achieve a high-level of productive employment. Elsewhere, many references unavoidably compel a corresponding reflection of such priority; for example, the reference to the increasingly inappropriate structure, and the imperative need now for economic transformation.[5] Correspondingly, there is more than one reference to the nature of the opening or openings in such transformation. The failure to develop new exports, conspicuous in comparison with the achievement of many other Asian countries, and the historical failure to develop a comparable foreign exchange source to support the social welfare structure, and so on, find their place in these pages.[6]

However, at the point of confrontation as it were with the nature of the challenge, the Report stops short by assumption of no further, structural opportunity or capacity. It, therefore, proceeds thereafter to national policies that will help arrange the fiscal and foreign exchange balances on more or less two assumptions of employment absorption by a target year.[7]

It does so, notwithstanding the conclusion that from the second half of the 1970s the enormous task involved will come to depend more and more on exports.[8] In what follows it is sought to set out in a little more detail the nature of this policy presentation, its implications for growth along with productive

44

employment in the long term; as well as to suggest certain much desired policy shifts. It is intended to show that the policy package as now provided represents too much of a prescription for stagnation. The trend of the desired policy shifts will refer to a type of production potential areas which together may constitute a set of leading sectors as it were, rendering the level of balance between given employment need, purchasing power and foreign exchange resource more meaningful.

Before proceeding to this, it is only fair and necessary to agree wholeheartedly with the fresh approach on many matters of high relevance to any policy. Among which are also many that have been enunciated, though not subsequently pursed or utilised in the analysis. To mention at random, among the former are the thoughts, for example, on shadow pricing (para.289), exchange rate adjustment (para. 689 fn), administrative policy areas (paras.496 et seq, 533 et seq, 584/9,590), statistical signalling (para.514), education (chapter 9), aid (paras 761 and 874, notwithstanding para.750 read with para.539),trade (para.766), and technical assistance programming (para.733). Among other excellent points made, though not utilised later for policy formulation are: the discussions on science and technology (paras.269, 356 and 630, etc.), local organisations (paras.491-2, 500 and 529 et. seq) and, of course, the major concerns referred to earlier on import substitution and exports industry potential. There are one or two specific points of discussion such as on cost benefit evaluation of multi-purpose schemes which leave room for doubt; but these do not detract from the numerous valuable positive discussions.

The summary position of the programme of action in the Report may be set down in the following way :

Movements in international prices were very much exogeneously determined. But their effects could have been contained if the opportunities in the post-War period up to the end of the 1960s, had been used to develop other exports and import substitutes. This failure was more marked in the 1960s. The political economic system remained unresponsive in the 1950s ; it became more glaring thereafter.[9] If unemployment

45

was to be reduced substantially by 1976, employment would have to increase by over 4 per cent per annum, leaving virtually nothing for increases in average consumption; if those at the bottom of the income scale were to be slightly benefited, average consumption for others would even have to fall. Even at a slower rate of reduction in unemployment, that is having a target year of 1985 instead of 1976, total consumption can increase at best only by 1.5 per cent per annum.[10]

Even if unemployment were not a serious problem, the mere reduction of the payments deficit would require removal of several hundred million rupees from consumer expenditure.[11] The reduction in the future deficit accounting for nearly one third of the investment financing so far, implies the lifting of domestic share of income saved, to make up for the former and also to account in all for the required more than 20 per cent gross investment by 1985. This, together with the need for consumption restraint in order to provide for increased employment, constitutes the measure by which the growth rate and the consumption increase [12] must both remain at a low level.

The basis for this prescription is that foreign exchange accretion by import substitution and export earning cannot be more than the equivalent of Rs.5,000 million by 1985(at 1968 prices) or nearly Rs.3,000 million above the 1968 level.[13] This increase is just enough to give the employment absorption rate, and the dim prospect of a stagnant consumption level right into 1985. The dilemma is all the more severe since Ceylon will need to change course in the second half of the 1970s, up to which time it can still meet the balance of payments situation by reducing imports of rice and other food stuff; thereafter the import requirement will depend increasingly on expanded and new exports.[14]

A situation such as this calls at least for a courageous hard look at necessity of such a prospect, and therefore validity of an analysis on which that prospect is based. The silent premise in the Report is that non-traditional exports, presently about 10 per cent of the total cannot, by 1985, provide the required significant increase in exports[15] to lend a different premise for policy and for target setting of growth and consumption. This

46

aspect seems clearly to be a major blind spot in the report. It is not sure in this connection to what extent the report based itself on data available and therefore left it to the later national discussions envisaged by it to enlarge the scope of national opportunity within the broad framework of analysis developed by it.[16] One may therfore begin by taking a look at the export potential as set out in the report. It is expected that of the current major exports, tea, also carrying some processing forms to a further stage, could yield about Rs. 1,500 million by 1985.[17] Similarly, rubber is estimated to yield over Rs.1,000 million;[18] and coconuts over Rs.1,000 million.[19] As for what may be loosely called non-traditional export — a mixture of elements such as tourism, gems, forest products, fruits, cut flowers, fish, spices, and manufactures — a total not exceeding Rs.2,000 million is anticipated.[20] Thus, among the foregoing taken together, a balance on foreign account is estimated at the figure of about Rs. 5,000 million odd referred to earlier.[21]

In these estimates, the figure for manufacturing exports is set, at the outside, near Rs.200 to 300 million for 1985.[22]

The excess purchasing power for consumption by 1976 (that is the amount of private disposable income for consumption less the amount of consumer goods and services available) is set at Rs.1,000 million and the excess purchasing power in 1972 is set at Rs.550 to 700 million.[23] Given the income and price policies prescribed in the report it is not certain as to what the figure of excess purchasing power may be by 1980 or 1985. It is perhaps anticipated that the monetary policies will curb this excess beyond 1976 in any case. On the other hand, an alternative overall development policy option of higher production and export performance would entail more purchasing power in the economy. A starting point for some measure of this could be the current external resource gap, estimated for 1968 at Rs. 657 million. One purely hypothetical way of approaching the problem of stagnation or austerity would be to consider a given foreign exchange gap — whether Rs. 600 million or thousand million or more — as the measure of the challenge involved in raising national consumption simultaneously with employment. Naturally, this challenge is additional to the export capability of current export categories already anticipated; and for this purpose, the estimates of increase for 1985 should be considered normal.

Whatever the figure of the additional challenge therfore, the likelihood of more than the estimated export / import-saving performance will sharply influence both development policy and income and price policy. It could mean the difference, while pursuing the employment objectives, between low productivity, low 'surplus', low consumption, and 'stagnant growth' on the one hand, and rising consumption expectations plus growth on the other. A main gap in the report , which has competently set out a frame of analysis for consumption and the foreign exchange gap, is of a different type. It is in its marked neglect of the potential for export in what may perhaps be called the 'forgotten sector'.

Certain parts of this sector have been touched upon, including manufactured goods, some new crops and the like, as well as science and technology development for fabrication. But the scale of opportunity in these has been so overlooked that the failure is both qualitative and quantitative. It is, if one may dramatise somewhat, as if a view had been taken of the economy last century before the plantation phase without providing for it in its prognostications. It is this type of opportunity which is available, not confined to a crop alone, which must be examined.

Such a type of need is brought in focus in the report, for example, in the point mentioned earlier that after 1975 the enormous task of keeping the country supplied with imports will come to depend more and more on exports, as opposed to only import substitution of rice and other food stuffs. The task of problem solving becomes therfore not merely one within almost existing rigid frameworks, but one of examining the production framework in a dynamic sense. New export crops, under-utilised capacity assesment and utilisation, and more effective policy for science and technology development, would all be involved. There would be lines within these which could assume some of the nature of new leading sectors as well. All these potentials could, taken together, certainly constitute a type of leading sector thrust.

48

A Case of Employment — Intensive National Development

Any precise assessment would naturally need a more systematic probe and a team effort; but the picture seems sufficiently clear to be able to indicate a scale of opportunity. Approaching the problem in this vein, therfore, one may aptly start with two illustrations. In the case of a country in the region, Thailand, a new 'crops programme' was initiated at the beginning of the 1950s which, by the end of that decade, accounted in terms of foreign exchange earning/saving, from a zero position to something of the order of 16 to 18% of total exports. These crops were normal tropical crops such as maize, bean, kenaf, tapioca and sugar cane; and of course, would not have been available in any input-output table or projection frame if such had been attempted before the 1950s. In India, in the area of Kerala State, the gross foreign exchange earning from cashew which stood at about Rs.180 million around 1960, was about Rs.300 million by 1965-66, and apparently is of the order of Rs.600 million by 1971. These are crops which do not by and large compete for land use with rice and equivalent produce. Their gestation period could be about five to seven years; their technology is ideally appropriate to the work force and skills endowment in developing country situations; and they provide employment and income. They also provide an ideal basis for industrial application in the form of agro-industry. By virtue of the nature of the factor mix or resource endowment, the agricultural aspect and the agro-industry aspect carry the minimum foreign exchange input implications.

One is only too well aware of the need for precise establishment of rationale, in terms especially of markets, before launching programmes (and for this, a large re-orientation of the foreign mission network of the country would be required as an administrative reform measure). But, it should be possible to say in a preliminary way that the potential for export realisation from such a programme by 1977 or a little thereafter could well be of the order of an additional Rs.500 million. The main mental dimension required in this achievement would be a departure from traditional land development and extension approches on such crops: annual increases in such new cultivation of the order of a few hundreds, thousands or a few thousands of acres are 'radically' conservative. The programme has to be conceived in selected cases in terms of tens of thousands of acres, with medium and long-term perspectives, the latter finally determining the national optimum over a secular term. There are certain implications also of administrative organisation and systems (which need not at all be a simulation of the early phase of opening up in the existing plantation sector) in keeping with the country's socio-economic policy framework. We shall come to this later.

Before leaving this, one could of course add to the list. Fruit farming and similar development (some mentioned in the report too), shrimp exploitation (Thailand is on the way to realising a target shortly, by about 1975, of nearly Baht 600 million) and so on. But these are not being quantified here at this stage.

As noted earlier, the scope for manufacturing exports has been set in the Report at a maximum of Rs. 300 million by 1985. Right now, there is no more doubt, as may have existed earlier, on the availability of under-utilised capacity in industry as a whole; but the problem of estimate of under utilisation still remains. All indications, that one may tentatively use as basis for judgement, suggest a figure nearer Rs.500 million as attainable, and well before 1985, perhaps over the next five years. Here again, there is the background of contrast between existing and required administrative mechanism and approaches, which may currently be more regulatory in nature and also more applicable to the 'deviationist' than to the possible mass of potential performers; this is very much a matter of administrative organisation and streamlining wherein the much larger total foreign exchange accretion rather than specific marginal deviations would be the prime object of attention.

Science and technology infra-structure development and development of capacity for fabrication of machinery and components are not as remote, much less as unnecessary, as implied in the *final* result in the report. The latter does indeed carry excellent thinking in a few places.[24] But the potential in development terms does not come out finally. In the early years of post-War industrialization among the developing countries, there was a natural rush towards import substitution for purposes

50

of saving foreign exchange. Notwithstanding a few who focused attention on some of its constraints precisely in foreign exchange terms, the process gathered momentum. It was not sufficiently realised that in an early phase of industrialization today the first impact of industrial investment, given the factor mix, was not foreign exchange saving but additional foreign exchange commitment. This flowed, both from the fact in many cases that machinery, intermediates and other components, and even basic raw material inputs and so on, were imported; and the fact that in any case there is a great cumulation, or 'crowding in', of foreign exchange commitments for investment goods without the corresponding capacity of the existing economy, or a strategy for this purpose, to meet the liabilities in foreign exchange terms.

In some ways, the phases of transformation from simple agrarian through diversified agriculture, to agro-industry and later other industry, which could be seen in successful experience elsewhere, such as Japan from 1875 and after, Taiwan later, and so on, were not part of a policy package in many other developing countries. In one sense, this is understandable, given the post-War silent premise for international growth and co-operation based on the concepts of international aid and access in international trade[25] about which countries now engage in continuing international conferences (or confrontations, depending on one's choice of view). However, the consequences did not fail to arrive. Perhaps the particular foreign exchange problem was best given a name in the course of the second Five-Year plan in India (helped also by mounting debt servicing). It became necessary to invent the phrase 'maintenance aid' in order to earn entitlement to special soft term foreign financing to support imports of consumer items, including intermediate goods for industry.

Science and technology development and industrial fabrication are thus not marginally desirable ends. An investment strategy that optimises the utilisation of limited internal factor or resource potentials will still unceasingly generate heavy foreign exchange leakage. In the absence of an optimisation policy of all feasible production inputs, such policy must sooner

51

or later become not only a long-term objective, but the one which will prevent the phenomenon of ever running and staying in the same place.[26] This is the relevance of science and technology and fabrication. It is well understood that fabrication as a concept is not for generalised application, for example, in the sense of including, in the early stages especially, fabrication of full scale machine plants.[27] In a given developing economy, and one with limitations in size of market and other elements, such a strategy would begin with maximum exploitation of areas of component manufacture, small machine fabrication and the like. The scope for this is not difficult to observe.

In the plantation sector there has been a historical development of tea machinery; the rice sector has shown some indications in the milling, hulling and related processes; with the effect of the so-called Green Revolution the demand for small agricultural machinery of various types is evident; so also in domestic agriculture as a whole, including the scope for pumps; small industry and agro-industry carry numerous areas of potentials; similarly fishing, including outboard motors; and perhaps several areas in infra-structure, including power generation, transport, housing fabrication, etc. In the so-called large-scale industries themselves in Ceylon, there is much scope for fabrication of selected components. The Report adverts in passing to the existence of local skills and ingenuity in machine repair and maintenance. One is in fact further aware of specific striking instances of technological initiative and success in private sector industries where, as in one typical case, a particular machine unit was duplicated entirely domestically with the result that the factory had on its floor about a dozen units in all of which only one was imported. The Report's negative evaluation of endowment for export promotion in another connection[28] is surprisingly drastic. The economy does not, in immediate potential terms, lack technological capability or managerial skills. What it lacks just now is a sense of priority for science and technology development.

Science and technology in its application may be described in terms of two broad needs. One is the development of domestic capability to apply systematically, continuously and at

52

a practical level, scientific and technological knowledge, to transform large, already existing undeveloped resources into production capabilities. The whole area of existing tropical crops and other produce, and potential crops, clearly constitute the basis for applying scientific research towards utilization of by-products and processing[29] in the acres that together constitute millions of coconut, rubber and other plantations. Such crops are simply continuing, non-exhaustible, self-reproducing, natural resource for economic transformation in innumerable uses, both as internal consumption and in foreign exchange conservation. The second area of science application is in what was discussed earlier, namely the fabrication of machinery and components, the priorities for which will flow from the pattern and scales of major sectoral growth areas.[30]

This type of approach provides a type of interlocking internal demand pattern in which stepped up investment and consequent demand increase will be conserved within the economy and reduce significantly the contradiction of increased investment involving equivalent increased import burdens. Once more in this field, there is a whole area of administrative and organisational pattern to which high priority attention will be needed.[31] It may involve specialized research units for separate crops, a new orientation in relationship between industry and scientific research organisations and so on.

It may not be possible readily to compute the foreign exchange benefit in such a programme, but in a position where 75 per cent of total physical inputs into industry are imported,[32] not to mention those in infra-structure and other sectors, it must clearly be considered a significant quantitative change, as also one of relevance to an immediate programme. The scale of opportunity for fabrication of machinery may be broadly computed from the present import structure, as also from the needs reflected in a larger view of a new crops-and-agro-industry programme. Assessment of scope for productive conversion of tropical natural resources would need the first results from a concentrated crash programme in science application on these. As to the scope itself there should be no doubt. As emphasized earlier, it is based on the concept of the availability of continuous, inexhaustible, or self-reproducing resource (what is the present plantation sector, other 'new crops', fruit and cut flowers which in certain already developed countries account for millions of dollars of exports — and so on) awaiting only application of applied research and organisation to alter these latent resources from inert waste to economic produce.

Whether conceived as a special aspect of science and technology contribution, or, as the report does,[33] as industry for export expansion, the idea of a duty free zone constitutes an important and useful element. For our immediate purpose of establishing additional export potential in the short term this proposal may not be valid. What would be important is immediate action to establish such a zone without prolonged delays in refined studies of feasibility. If so pursued, it could even assist in the short-term with flow of foreign capital, and later on also assist in that aspect of science and technology application relating to fabrication of machinery.

One recent healthy trend not apparently dealt with in the Report deserves special mention. It is well-known that, among the invisible, ocean freight rates do constitute a heavy drain on the economy's foreign exchange resources. Both in its pace of development and the administrative impetus for it, striking results seem to have begun to appear which merit commendation. It would seem that about 45 per cent of the exports on the Western route is now to be carried under domestic shipping arrangements; it would also appear that by about 1975 a similar proportion of the total exports would be so carried. Naturally, this is not currently being undertaken entirely under the national flag; chartering arrangements are very much part of the operation. Undoubtedly, however, the gains in foreign exchange must show and there is everything to be said for pressing forward on these very sound lines.[34]

The foregoing are by no means a comprehensive indication of potentials. It is also understood that the additional foreign exchange potentials in these are to be interpreted in a 'netted' sense in two ways: (i) for foreign inputs in the value added by the new activities; and (ii) for the estimate of foreign exchange

54

earnings already surmised in the Report.[35] The foregoing indications are sufficient, however, to suggest an additional export capability over the next five to seven years (depending on the gestation period in the case of crops) of at least a further Rs.1,000 millions. As seen before, the Report directed itself towards its given employment target, on the basis of no consumption rise for those already employed if the target year is 1976; with a minor consumption rise if the target year were 1985.[36] The additional production potential set out in this Note may, therefore, be taken to imply a higher productivity out of the work force, since by definition the work force is already to be virtually fully employed.[37] Additional national production, therefore, means a redeployment of the same work force in more efficient terms; meaning also, therefore, a greater mix of efficient methods of production involving mechanized uses in varying degrees.[38]

On such a basis as this, certain significant policy conclusions also result. A drastic move against efficient production methods using appropriate mechanization does not follow. A new scope is provided for stronger science and technology development and for fabrication. A higher growth rate and consumption rise become foreseeable; as also the potential for providing a sound techno-economic base for sustained future growth and employment, which become rightly the targets rather than only foreign exchange saving and employment. In internal resource terms, income and price policies become more manageable; the means of handling the surplus consumer purchasing power could be different. In the new crops programme which is bound to have some consumer demand effect, monetary policy could even rely, given the production gestation period, on export increases and allow some extent of 'forced savings' to operate (in any case, the strategy for domestic investment resource increase in the Report would also operate to some extent in this way). There could also be other policy results. For example, on the view of FEECS[39] in relation to required production inputs (it should be remembered that their imports are determined by volume under over-all planning, while the non-application of FEECs would also assist in maintaining lower product prices); or on the view concerning major colonization.[40]

All this is not detracting from the Report which as mentioned at the outset reflects considerable perspicacity and realism in the areas it discusses. The export targets for tea, rubber and coconut,[41] are accompanied by practical pointers to organisational and production improvement needs. In the same way, the additional potential set out in this Note calls for careful sustained organisational effort. The Report's discussion on implementation mentioned before are among the best seen recently. In endorsement of these and perhaps by way of some supplement this comment concludes with certain needed observations on the organisational and administrative aspects of carrying the production targets forward to realization.

Administrative organisation has traditionally been conceived, of course, in terms of smoother operations and work methods in given systems or units. This continues to be valid. Any observer of some of the public utility or service organisations would readily see the scope and need for simple, easily realizable streamlining of work methods which are bound to enhance the public image apart from enhancing revenues. For the economy as a whole, what is involved is also much more. A major need is (i) frank examination of the relevance and irrelevance of given organisational, structures or patterns presently obtaining to deliver programmes and production; and (ii) to formulate organisational structures at macro and micro levels which are in keeping with the socio-economic philosophy of the country itself. When we realize that much of the administrative structure is inherited from outside, even if somewhat adapted thereafter, and that the more recent organisational developments themselves carry the impression of this general inheritance we could see the need for such examination. Administrative organisation here — this again is an inherited concept — does not refer to public departmental structure alone. In the context of a developing economy, administrative structure and organisation comprehends all participants in the productive process.[42] An inherited structure does not necessarily mean the total discarding of all its origins. For example, the plantation sector, having been developed under a private enterprise joint stock concept, while not necessarily reflecting present socio-economic philosophy, still carries lessons in organisation. It does not follow that a new crop programme should not, therefore, be large scale; what is needed is to formulate the relevant organisational pattern — whether it be the large co-operative, or small holding with central inputs and marketing services, or the collective concept — that will not lose the economic benefit of given scale of operations if that were technically the more desirable. The same would apply in innumerable other areas, whether at the centre or in sectors or at local levels. A type of 'administrative ecology' approach is fundamental for national economic efficiency, in which the particular relevance of implementation, or administrative machinery and organisation is unremittingly related to the socio-economic 'environment'.

The administrative organisation may be viewed in three categories — the apex, the vertical (or sectoral) and the horizontal (or local). The first touches on the highest level organisational frame-work for planning and implementation and, of course, not only includes the planning function proper or implementation of financial and fiscal policy, but the two other elements as well. One is the highest level policy group element which provides the directives not only for growth targets but also for administrative organisation; the other is that of associating non-governmental areas at this level as well.

At the sectoral or vertical level, the tendency for reliance on departmental responsibility alone for production results would be inadequate; so also any reliance only on 'advisory' groups or committees, even associating non-governmental elements. The Report refers in discussing the Government's earlier short-term programme to the idea of Boards[43] for given production items (for example, coconut is mentioned). This concept would need to be carried right through the major production areas, combining both the scope and responsibility for achieving results. Besides, the apex level boards should be equally able to pass down scope and responsibility to the 'implementers' below.[44] In some cases it may not be advantageous to compartmentalize each particular produce; for example, the plantation sector, especially in the short term, should carry specific targets for fruit and dairy development notwithstanding a separate programme for these items.

57

At the local or horizontal level, the discussions in the Report, which are very much in the right direction, imply the need for much devolution of responsibility and initiative for development programming and implementation rather than the allocation of given limited sums of money to these local organisations. The needed approach would seem to be one of their being allowed to look at their own area[45] - the land, possibilities of existing production increases, possibilities of new production on the land, agro (and other) industry — all of which would then give meaning, and nationwise quantitative significance, to the economic programme.[46]

Full attainment of promise in such a framework requires a particular element which can be described in terms of links or linkages. There are two such types which are fairly well-known and for which the jargon is often used in discussing inter-sectoral consistency within a development plan. One is the planning 'model' idea relating mutually the implications of various targets and thereby the premises for the targets as well.[47] The other is the forward and backward linkage concept in plan and programme preparation, which is related to the first but which also specifically identifies in given production categories, the potentials for development of inputs, with implications for domestic investment or foreign exchange budgeting; and the potentials for end products as inputs to other activities (and by-products and similar utilisation).

A further linkage, not often applied in implementation, is the extension of the linkage concept to comprehend a multiple array of currently needed physical, financial, marketing,(domestic and foreign) and organisational essentials.[48] It is an anti-compartmentalization approach in product planning or programming at the apex, sectoral and local levels. A given new production possibility must entail its own inputs such as material and services immediately related to it and so on; also infra-structure, road access and the like. There is also, importantly, an advance market information or intelligence system that is essential. In foreign marketing, a two-way process of supply capabilities and market possibilities must obtain. This is valid both for the Report's target of Rs.5,000

58

million export and the minimum feasible addition suggested in this Note of Rs.1,000 million.

The structure, orientation and method of work of the country's foreign outposts, which its Missions abroad represent, would become as much a part of the development plan as the physical targets and programmes themselves similarly in the two-way process between the apex and the local level.

Towards the end, the Report[49] has a passage with which it seeks to make compulsive the need for timely decisions, suggesting that there is no alternative to rational development, failing which the consequences would be only destructive, anarchic and explosive. This is not only a basis for firm imaginative domestic policy decisions; but at the least as much for policies of the country's international partners. Nor is it confined to purely economic and financial decisions. For example, technological and administrative development are also urgent priorities. The development of science and technology infra-structure as discussed earlier is also a key foundation in cushioning the helpless impact of current export price fluctuation, and in redressing the current aid, trade and technology transfer policies of the external world,[50] among whom there is much espousing of ideas on 'Welfare Statism', population policies and so on, without corresponding espousals of the needed aid, trade and technology transfer policies.

One is aware that in a brief review of this nature, certain provisos and details may not be fully spelt out. For example, there could be a hasty impression that a given orientation implies restrictive autarchy, when that is certainly not the case. So also on the details of additional product capability; and so on. It has been attempted to keep this brief in order to concentrate attention on the important lines of presentation. It has been written in order to convey the country's capability for growth at a higher level than presumed, thus ensuring also the only basis for continued self-sustained growth in later periods. Else, one may need another Employment Mission in another five years or so, to avoid which one needs to grasp the 'nettle'[51] and establish a basis for continuing growth. In this sense, one cannot have an 'excessive' attention to the growth of income;[52] only a wrong strategy, or policy, in attaining that end.

The Wealth of Poor Nations

Notes

1 The Employment Mission Report on Ceylon (1971).
2 The Transmittal Letter emphasises that it is not a Report to which at this stage the sponsoring Agency is committed; at this stage, the later seeks open discussion.
3 For example, paras 254, 249, 247 and 245; the footnote to para 247 would almost suggest the continuance of the economy as under developed.
4 Para 22.
5 Para 194.
6 For example, paras 54, 63, 73, 149 and 787.
7 For example, paras 801 and 865.
8 Para 568.
9 Para 73.
10 Paras 195, 204 and 865.
11 Paras 673 et seq.
12 Paras 202 to 204.
13 Para 198
14 Para 568
15 Para 801
16 Para 20
17 Para 216
18 Para 220
19 Para 221
20 Paras 208 to 212.
21 Para 222
22 Para 208
23 Paras 683, 684. The equivalent of something between five to six per cent higher than the current consumption level per year.
24 For example, paras. 269, 356-9, 361 and 630 already referred to.
25 Which Taiwan enjoyed.
26 Without such strategy, even a simple growth of agriculture and industry in present conditions will soon face arresting foreign exchange constraints. It is not a policy of autarchy, but the only basis for enabling imports; required thus by exports and not by unpayable debts. (Though in different context, para 245 and its footnote are also of interest.)
27 Regional co-operation can, of course, yield large fabrication possibilities, through opportunities of enlargement of agreed production categories, perhaps even certain machinery manufacture for its own sake (in time). Para 363, etc., of the Report provide some indications. Much work has now developed for countries to use in ESCAFE (ESCAP) forums; and include commodities, agro-industry, industry, shipping and so on. All of these constitute potentials long overdue for political decision-making and implementation.
28 Para 377.
29 e.g., para 363.

30 To quote a review on historical experience in the 'mechanism whereby traditional agriculture is transformed into a branch of modern industry', it is not enough, however, to import technology from a different economy; each country must be enabled to develop a technology appropriate to its own conditions. One extremely interesting section describes how, at the turn of the century, the Japanese began trying to modernise their agriculture by introducing English agricultural machines which proved hopelessly unsuited to Japanese conditions. They again started using German scientific methods to evolve a technology suitable for Japan, and in this achieved notable success. Graham Hallet on Hayami and Rutton, 'Agricultural Development: An International Perspective', (*Economic Journal*, June 1972, pp. 792,793).

31 Providing also a 'Positive' framework in which to view the so-called brain drain.

32 Para 349.

33 Para 378.

34 Of course, for purpose of foreign exchange saving, there must be a distinction between profit in an enterprise (or firm) sense derived from total turn-over and profit attributable on own shipping account; in other words, between, say the commercial results of rupee plus foreign currency net receipts, and receipts in the latter denominations.

35 Especially paras 208-212.

36 Paras. 727 and 865.

37 The Report assumes not more than 5 per cent unemployment in its targets (para 727).

38 See in this connection, the reference to A.K. Sen and others at Chapter III, fn 6-10.

39 Para 249 (FEECs was an exchange arrangement in which an amount in excess of an official exchange rate was provided against sale of hard currency).

40 Paras 260 and 305; also paras 302 and 806. The Report makes the usual error in assessing cost-benefit, in the scope of inputs and outputs considered, time span, etc. (Also, it is clear that in assessing the production potential by intensive cultivation methods there is a tacit embracing of the earlier colonization benefit in terms of additional area).

41 Para 213 et seq.

42 This is implied in paras 496 and 497.

43 Paras 574, 576 and 584.

44 On one aspect, vide para 328 (fn 1 - p. 98 of Report). This and similar cases have been the subject of note and evaluation in the Ceylon Association for the Advancement of Science (Section F) in past years.

45 Para 500 emphasises rightly the integrated development planning concept.

46 Long years earlier, under Prime Minister Mr. Bandaranaike, when Minister for Local Government, the first concepts in local area economic planning and development budgeting were initiated; a model development budget was even formulated and tested unofficially with remarkable lessons. In a sense, there was a gap thereafter till the recent (1963) idea of the

District Development Council, which in some respects, seems still to lag behind the original concepts.

47 This is referred to in para 507.
48 One aspect is reflected in paras 362 and 590.
49 Para 748.
50 Paras 761 and 766.
51 Paras 715 and 80.
52 Technical papers, Chapter 4, para 2. See also *Economic Journal*, June 1972, p.567, referred to earlier.

Chapter Six

Post-Keynesian Model of Employment and Equilibrium

I n the thinking of the nineteenth century, economic systems were considered to be always moving towards full employment and equilibrium. It was a tradition based on Adam Smith, through Ricardo to Marshall, in which private benefit would equate with public good. In the Ricardian system growth was almost implicit, whether due to the technical functions within the economy or to the presumed ability of prices and profits to clear the market of goods produced. Say's Law, that supply creates demand, development naturally in this thinking. Controversy continues in interpreting Ricardo's view of the equilibrium process, but this does not concern us here and we are happy to leave it to others for theoretical exploration. With the assumption of inherent equilibrium and growth, the residual major concern was naturally with the efficiency of the individual firm. Thus, the dominance of micro-economics and concentration on advances in the theory of marginal equilibrium, that characterised economic literature, especially up to the thirties; even now, occasionally, as when economics is to be applied to a new field, say environment. There was of course no steady equilibrium or steady growth during this period in actual fact. Cycles of prosperity and depression were notable, but they were accommodated as variation from the norm, to be explained by supportive theory. The main concepts behind such supportive theory were that the cycles were caused by under-investment due to under-saving and that the problem therefore was in essence, over-consumption. Thus, savings had to be enlarged at the expense of consumption, so that capital creation and deepening of capital, in the best traditions of what was known as the Austrian School, could continue to take place. These naturally required high flexibility in wages or employment or both, which also then enabled exchange rates to be kept steady for maintenance of foreign trade. The broad dichotomy of world economic structure in trade, with inflow of primary products and outflow of finished goods, helped to maintain consumption demand. So, free trade was seen as another, natural, axiom of growth and equilibrium.[1]

By the thirties, the whole world situation had taken a different turn. Previous theories and prescriptions proved insufficient to explain either the collapse of countries generally or to show how any or all of them could return to full employment and equilibrium. The Keynesiam Model particularly pointed to the fact that the problem of growth was not in under-saving, but in under-consumption. Demand had to be revived as the means by which, through rising expectations, investments may revive and with them, also, profits, employment and wages. In a depression, a start with conscious governmental demand stimulus was initially necessary in one form or another. The system would then pick up from there.

This meant implicitly an opposite of much of the policies and prescriptions that were held to be immutable in the previous thinking. Wages, instead of being flexible, were to be steady. Full employment, instead of being presumed, had to be yet attained and maintained. Exchange rates, instead of being fixed may be flexible, to be responsive to the needed demand maintenance. The full employment of resources, not only labour, instead of being automatic, would have to be sought. In fact, without such action, an economy could even continue at a sub-optimal equilibrium level, that is below full employment level and below full utilisation of its resources; just as for different reasons, some of the Third World countries presently do.

These ideas, as also their application and effects worldwide after the war, are well-known. Inadequate awareness is, therefore, not the purpose in recalling them, but rather to view them in relation to the developing countries real needs. The Keynesian Model was specific not only to the developed economies that it was concerned with. It was specific also to apparent persistent depression in those economies. Hence the over-riding, pervasive, emphasis on demand maintenance and, quite obviously, not on demand reduction. Of special relevance when considered by the developing countries, then, is the structure itself. This is because the success held out for demand maintenance presumed very clearly the existence in an economy of unused capacity is the typical situation of developed country. This was the conceptual linkage — physically the absence of linkage — between Its applicability to developed economies and its inapplicability to the developing countries.

As for the one-way traffic of demand maintenance, the Keynesian Model is equally conceivable, at the peak of full employment and inflationary pressure, as lending itself to the application of demand reduction. It would seem that the controversies on Keynesianism and non-Keynesianism, or monetarism and non-monetarism, allow interesting room for sophistication, but mainly by presumed preconditions about each other. We are again not concerned with this here. The Keynesian Model could be quite applicable to developing countries, but if they have the same economic structure as the developed countries, with potential unused capacity at the time of depression. The problem of the developing countries is that, to start with, they do not have the capacity and the issue is to create this capacity. This was the basic structure we discussed earlier, on which the mechanics of growth could operate. At present, as once remarked, it was like discussing fuel mixtures when first there was no combustion engine! In another connection symptomatic of the type of problems of the transplant that developing countries often have, a developing country delegate once declared at a conference in the early seventies, 'What is the use of talking about black smoke or white smoke, when we do not have any smoke at all ?'

It is indeed surprising how we would allow events to overtake our thinking. Too often, we would go to all intents on post hoc interpretation of circumstances of an earlier phase, seeking to approximate it to the present. Too often thereby, we probably suit the needs to the thought; and not the thought to the needs. The constant necessity to think afresh, often from basic principles, gets lost in the technical niceties of an 'orthodox' pattern of thought. And thus it is only exceptionally that theory becomes significantly more than mere systematization of the mode of approach (the prescriptions and the proscriptions) of the time. The utility of theory (in fact otherwise it could be even misleading) is in the interpretation of practice to enable change of policy well in time before events overtake us completely and render policy incomplete once more.[2]

The fact is, whether we like it or not, many policy prescriptions from these past theories still lie among developing countries as hang-overs and sole refuge. In the late seventies, the problems of their use were further compounded by world-wide stagflation, with policies based on controlling money supply and on devaluation figuring prominently as solutions for growth. Often, they were conditions for assistance by international institutions like the IMF and WorldBank. What Prof. Arthur Lewis concluded on these as instruments of growth sums up, as well as one might, the limits of their use.[3] Current world inflation is a result of shortage of various raw materials, including oil, on the one hand; and price rises through wage and salary increases under pressure of organised groups, on the other. Controlling inflation, through controlling money supply, touches neither of these primary sources, unless unemployment is pushed to politically untenable levels. The rate of growth is slowed down. As for devaluation, it is palliative rather than curative, in situations where it triggers further increases in domestic costs that reinstate the differential that it was meant to eliminate. Thus the price level can no longer be controlled by twirling general control levers, namely the rate of interest, supply of money or rate of exchange. If the economy has attained sustained growth then we are into a new world. Instead of trade determining the rate of growth, growth will determine the volume of trade. Growth itself will be determined by internal forces. The conclusions in the foregoing were clear, that the basic economic structure had first to be created, before one could talk of surplus capacity to re-activate.

The literature on post-Keynesianism is among the most wide-ranging and profuse, as well as being rich. Without offence to such a background, but partly taking refuge in the wide range of interpretations of this theory, one may try to set out in a very simplified form, the apparent behaviour of major variables in their progress from one peak period in and economy, through a downturn, to its next peak. It is of interest not because of applicability to growth in the developing economies, but, as mentioned, since much of Keynesian economic prescriptions loomed large in financial and economic policies of developing countries. The attempted scheme is not a professional model presentation but one which would share the essential concept of a model, namely that it provides a framework in which one may introduce an input at one point which, one could then assume, will move with predictability through its successive stages to a destination. A converse quality in such a framework is that change of any one component must produce corresponding change in the other components towards a new and rearranged equilibrium. The framework, as it would appear, is outlined at the next page.

At stage (7), the growth process is back to a new peak stage, hopefully at a higher equilibirium level. Thus gross and per capita income in the economy would be higher on attainment of phase (7). Given market economy conditions and Stage-engineered demand support, the whole represents capitalist growth process, through disequilibrating/equilibrating interactions of wages, demand, technology, profit, employment and investment.

A point of some practical interest is that, at certain phases in such a process, two different variables may move in opposite directions. For example, as a result of a previous rising profit trend, despite the beginning of a wage fall, technology inputs could rise in the next succeeding phase while demand could fall. But, in addition, in a given phase, the same variable, for example profits, could both rise and fall. As earlier indicated in a situation where technology has risen but demand begins to

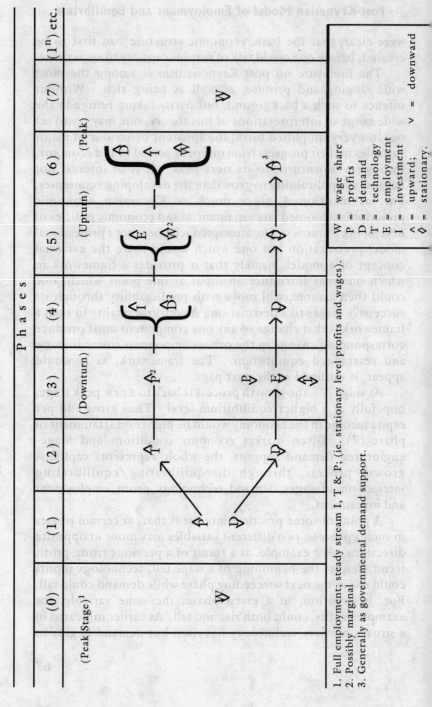

A Disequilibrium/Equilibrium Dynamic Growth Model

Phases

(0)	(1)	(2)	(3)	(4)	(5)	(6)	(7)	(1^n) etc.
(Peak Stage)[1]			(Downturn)		(Upturn)	(Peak)		

W = wage share
P = profits
D = demand
T = technology
E = employment
I = investment
< = upward; v = downward
◊ = stationary.

1. Full employment; steady stream I, T & P; (ie. stationary level profits and wages).
2. Possibly marginal
3. Generally as governmental demand support.

fall, the former will register a profit rise in the succeeding phase, while the latter will register a profit fall. Thus there is never a crystal clear trend, with unitary, fiscal, financial, or other policy to be applied as a rule of thumb at a given moment. It seems that much more selectivity and sophistication is required than we have perhaps exercised in the past, in using our instruments of economic management for steering growth as it goes along. Demand, liquidity, interest, investment schedules, may all have to be touched, and in varying directions, as levers that move and economy.[4]

Such a disequilibrium could, within limits, still be the order of the day for developing countries as well, while building up their structures and structural capacity. It would seem therefore that some scrutiny of this process and, in particular, of wise incomes policy, while not being a substitute for structural development, should be an important adjunct of good economic management.[5]

Notes

1 In the beginning, the metropolitan countries simply brought their mercantilist, free trade traditions, clothed in Adam Smith — Ricardian academia, serving to rationalise their particular successes. Investments produced goods, supply created demand (in any case foreign markets were there, so it did not entirely matter that the domestic wage fund did not absorb all), Cycles were sought to be explained as aberrations and seemed so, at least in the expansive world economy at that time. What was, therefore, left was the efficiency of each firm. Thus, the 'framework' of economics was contained very much satisfactorily within equilibrium of the firm theory and trade cycle theory.

2 From my 'Some Less Accepted Factors in Economic Growth' (CAAS, Paper 1960).

3 From Nobel Prize Lecture, The Slowing Down of the Engine of Growth (Stockholm, 1979. The wording above is not direct quotation).

4 This thought is in fact in the original Keynes, though lost amidst the enthusiasm in applying the under-consumption function and public works to fight the great depression of the thirties. For example see my *Economies of Full Employment with Special Reference to India and Ceylon*, pp 35, 41,94. As Keynes said of himself on one occasion, 'I found myself the only non-Keynesian present' (*E.J.* June 1972).

5   While being entirely responsible for specific views expressed, I wish to acknowledge with thanks the stimulating discussions, in this area of economic theory and practice, with Dr. Kumaraswamy Velupillai of Lund and Cambridge and presently European University Institute, Florence.

Chapter Seven

Wages in a Developing Economy

For no economies nor at any stage in their development, is the question of wages easy of determination or handling. We have already acknowledged this in an earlier context. The hard core of the mechanics of growth which we defined in Chapter Two obviously implies the availability of reinvestment surpluses and arithmetically, therefore, some relation and balance between costs — in which wage is dominant — and receipts. This has been interpreted in history sometimes in terms of a wage fund theory, leading to an Iron Law of Wages, which in practice called for keeping the total wage share more or less invariable and even depressed. Such a static arithmetical relation between wages and investment surplus is both factually and analytically faulty. In particular, a dynamic view of wage shares, involving rational adequate wages, working hours, and working conditions, as well as providing the essential means and tools for production could yield a much larger re-investment surplus out of out put. There are also exogenous conditions, particularly in situations of inflation, which are not wage induced or , as we saw briefly in Chapter Ten, are as much the result of concentrated economic power on the side of capital as of trade union pressure. As from the mid-seventies, when inflation has been brought to the doorstep of labour, the solution for them may have to be found on the supply side first.

As far as developing countries are concerned, we have mentioned the idea of wage goods industries as a concrete constituent in a growth mechanics. Of course, work ethics is a basic consideration, not only for labour but for other partners in production. Its attainment has to be the result of a multiple process — from having a right production structure, favourable international co-operation arrangements, and a sensible approach to the natural resources base, to development of integrated planning, maintaining a favourable cultural, social and political ethos, and a sound communications and media climate. There could be others. These are much more than can fall, or be handled under, a chapter on wages; many are indeed the subject of other chapters here.

The purpose of this Chapter may be more modest, perhaps also more pointed, taking a slightly more mechanistic approach. What is done here, therefore, is to take up what was undertaken some years ago at a national symposium on wages in a developing economy, in which leading proponents of various political views from various segments of the society, along with academics, took part. What are set out are personal conclusions, but very much based on this 'mix' of the discussions and exchanges that took place in practical terms.

As a prelude, it may be interesting to note that in developing countries, as sometimes elsewhere, there is always the constant conflict between socialist politics and capitalist economics; in other words, the need for capital in large quantum in the hands of those who could use it, whether individual or the state. Very often in capitalistic democracy, it is the socialist politics that has surprisingly prevailed over capitalist economics. Equally surprisingly, it is the capitalist economics that has prevailed in people's democracies over socialist politics. In certain crucial essentials there is, contrary to popular ideas, no difference between socialist and capitalist economies, at least there cannot be if economic growth really takes place. Wages arrangements and husbanding of capital are two inescapable cases. It is no less than the concept of balance between the capital goods investment (or supply) and consumption goods investment (or demand) relation, generally accepted as needed in economic growth; in another form, it may appear as a balance between agriculture and industry (as in the early soviet experience), or

Wages in a Developing Economy

between natural or warranted growth in dynamic economics (under western formulation). The subject of planning may one day come to be written as the story of how familiar economic realities do make the practices equally in what are acknowledged to be vitally divergent systems.[1] In pursuing the accumulation of capital, capitalist democracy suffered under that very label for it was expected to enrich a small autocracy; something under which people's democracies did not labour, as the enrichment was ideologically of the state, even though wages may have been lower or stagnant. Entrepreneurial investment becomes more difficult thereby, as also restraint on wages.

On the question of wages, the field is very vast. The subject has had a long history, as old as social organisation — a history, both of stark realities and of unreal illusions; of fight against regulations, and of chimerical confusions of prosperity with the means to prosperity. The Iron Law of Wages, the Wages Fund, Surplus Value, and many more — all made Wages one of the more compelling, even romantic, fields of interest down the years. Was that a Wages Fund? What was Surplus Value? What was the value judgement relevant to these, their amounts and the purposes for which they were used? Were they talked of in a static or a developing economy context? Today the subject is even more real, absorbing and worthy of highest attention. The Wage was present always, and remains associated with development — in investment, in work, in production, and in productivity. Each of them had special interests, fears, but also a pragmatism.

One could have asked whether a critical discussion on wages should not instead have been a critical discussion on profit. Indeed so, for profits, especially for development, where in a special sense the obverse of wages. Yet, the wage was not a residual. It had also a special aspect in relation to other factors of production — and flowed from the distinction between material and human 'factors'. An over — supply of factors could reduce their returns to abnormally low levels — Keynesian economics would talk of zero rate of interest on capital. In the case of wages, even to talk of zero return as something that could happen would have been profane. Whatever the technical nature of a supply situation, wages could not go below a certain norm, however undefined, and whatever the particular historical or socio-economic forces. The 'wage problem' involves directly the very people for whom the developing economy was being planned. Precisely for this reason, one's thinking could also be subjective, depending on where one's livelihood was based — on rent, interest, profit or wages! Hence its special categorization, its peculiar interest and its undenied importance in the development process.

An important aim is, while bringing out the points of departure, also to identify some common threads. It might appear that very little of common element could be identified. At least superficially, there are views in regard to the basic facts on wages which are diametrically opposed; and if there is similarity of views, it may be on matters which are not vital or fundamental. Granting some of this, it is still possible to point to some ingredients in wages and wage policy in relation to increasing the national product which from the point of view of developing a common understanding, are noteworthy.

It has been mentioned that wage is an element in the gross national product. Alongside, is also another concept of the wage, as part of national income or national expenditure. Without seeking to be technical, one may distinguish by this two particular aspects in regard to wage responsibilities, or duties that attach to the wage earning sector. What happens when the national product is increased is that the value added component is increased; that is, in place of what goes in, in the form of materials and the lot, one gets out, at the other end, a product whose value is higher than the sum total of the components that went in earlier. The wage is a share of this value added component. When the national product increases in this sense, there is the problem of sharing out. From the point of view of what is produced , labour naturally has a view not only in regard to its share in the general sense, but also and more importantly, in regard to the relative share vis-a-vis the shares of the other agencies in the production process. It is at this point that one might see the position of wages in relation to profits. In the sense, and from the point of view, of development or of increasing the national product, profit — using the word loosely at this point — is the obverse of wages. What is not consumed is utilised for purposes of investment. Profit, if we might borrow the phrase in capitalist terminology, includes the remuneration to the entrepreneur and a reward for the risk element in investment for production. Yet the point is that there is now a surplus and a decision has to be made as to how much of the surplus we are going to syphon off for future investment.

In a planning sense, this is synonymous with the volume of consumer goods that country is going to produce as a whole ; because, in the overall context, if we produce a given volume of consumer goods in the economy, then the balance is for investment goods. One may perhaps try and draw out certain elements of agreement from this. For instance there were, long ago two policy statements, one from Soviet and one from the British background, on the question of how decisions on wages are made, or must be made.

In the Soviet experience, decisions on wages are 'identical with the decision about the amount of resources to be devoted to the consumer goods industry'. As regards wage policy in operation 'it became a practice for a general wages policy, defining the general contours of the wage structure, to be agreed upon annually between the central council of trade unions and the highest organs of government in the economic system' — so that the intervention of trade unions must take place then 'and not in the form of subsequent bargains'. It became practice to secure, in the course of dispute at lower level, only 'such improvements as are compatible with the economic development of the worker State and are without injury to other sections of work people'. This is the broad frame-work in which it is presumed a wage decision in the overall is made.

A British White Paper of that time happened to deal with the same question in some detail and had this to say: 'There must always be room for the adjustment of wages and conditions, for example on account of changes in the form, method or volume of production. Also there must be opportunities for the removal of anomalies in the rates of remuneration of different grades and categories of workers, both within an industry and between different industries'. It went on, however, to state, 'The principle of stability does not mean, however, that increases in the general level of wage rates must be related to increased productivity due to increased efficiency and effort'. What these mean is that in effect and by and large, whether by market process or by planning process, we have to make a decision on some basis for the volume of consumer goods we are going to have. Once we have made that decision, the financial plan in regard to the wages budget would have the same correspondence; otherwise we are having a wage induced inflation.

This is insofar as the general wage level question is concerned. Here one could make a general observation — because this seems to be suspicion — that as far as wages in development are concerned, the controversy between capitalist economy and socialist economy is basically a controversy about the efficacy and the efficiency of control over the use of profit, or surplus value — not over the relevance itself of surplus value. Others have mentioned this point — some directly, some indirectly — in accusations against the neglect of investment by the private sector. But one of the over-riding features is the question of satisfaction wanted in this instance by the trade union movement; of satisfaction that the surplus which is ostencibly going for investment is really effectively and efficiently being put to the purpose for which it is meant — as much in terms of investment performance, as of output performance. From the point of view of labour, justice needs not only to be done, but must also fully appear to have been done.

Going back to the distinction between the share of wages in national product and the share in national income or national expenditure, we come to more familiar ground in which intensive debate has taken place in regard to the minimum, wage and related issues. The struggle essentially is for 'expenditure power'; and whether it is a certain sum of money without fringe benefits or whether it is a lower sum with fringe benefits. The thinking here is primarily not on the diversion of resources for investment and creation of future capacity to expand the

76

economy. Of course, there are a lot of arguments that can be used: that increased workers' share reduces the volume of investment because they do not save and so on. Yet these are not things that could be talked about, loosely, because there has long been acceptance among economists, starting particulary with the U.S., that investment has to be understood in a much wider sense than we had thought of long ago; that education, for example, is investment, that health is investment, that an adequate wage is investment, being investment in human capacity.

These are not as moralising but analytical positions. As is known, data has been established from American experience to show that a large share of the increase in the national product in the united States during the fifties, for example, was due precisely to this sort of investment. Another parallel was the remarkable post-War recovery of Western Europe. All the economists foretold that Western Europe after the War would never be able to recover, particularly at the speed at which it did. When the Western countries did recover, everyone sat up, like the astrologers, to see what had happened. They then discovered, among other things, that one of the most important was a stock of skilled human capital, at an adequately manageable level of remuneration, and a basis for services development. So one does need to beware of making a demarcation too easily between savings and 'consumption'.

The practical aspect of wages is a definition of what it should be, namely the yardstick by which a satisfactory wage may be identified. We have some familiar concepts, such as the ideas of the subsistence wage, the wage and cost of living, the wage and general welfare shares, wages and productivity, and wages and the building of skills. Subsistence wage, which has produced a lot of heat, has also been dealt with extensively in developing countries, including reports on various sections of the labour force. It is fair to state that there is general agreement on the fact that subsistence wage has to be a recognised minimum, that it is fairly possible to compute what sort of wage should go into this, and that irrespective of the state of the economy one should attempt to meet this. In one country, the

National Wage Policy Commission took up what it held was a realistic point of view, that one should work towards it and where an industry could not make it, one should have that industry do the best it can. But the former idea, of a comprehensive minimum, is the generally accepted principle.

Then there are questions on relative disparity in wages. We hear of plantation labour, of paddy (farm) rates, we hear of mercantile rates and so on, and one is sure that there has been a haphazard growth, that there are discrepancies and that the net result is that there are several areas where there is not equal remuneration for what may reasonably be considered equal work.[2] This is a point on which mutual understanding is necessary if we are to push any idea of common thinking on wages forward from the point where we are now. A corollary point is that the determination of these wage rates in a dynamic sense had been hindered partly by the hangover of the colonial era, using this in quite a technical sense.[3] It has also been partly influenced by the relative attitudes that now exist between the organised trade union sector and the government. There is difficulty at times of distinguishing between pure trade union demands and non-trade union demands. It may not even be a fact always, but it is a fact of psychology; psychologically, the condition has been there.

In regard to cost of living and share in benefits, there has been a lot of thinking internationally, in ILO circles, in international conferences, in publications and so on; and the relationship has been generally acknowledged that the cost of living has to be recognised in determining a wage structure by and large. But of course, in the developing context, also a context of underdevelopment, one has an increasing, a rising price situation, which has called for qualifications. We have had of late a lot of discussions about the inevitability of inflation under development. The basic point is valid; but the degree of emphasis given to it is also a matter of personal opinion. We have had the parallel in Chinese experience. It was about maintaining the prices of essential commodities, conceived not as all essential goods, but as wage goods if one might call it; holding the price line on those and allowing the prices of the others to operate at given higher levels. When we come from that to the third category, that is wage and general welfare and what a wage earner can expect to share in the increased general welfare, then one might also conveniently take up the question of wages and productivity.

One point is that productivity is again partly confused by a lot of analysis as to what goes into productivity and what does not go. On the one side, there is a claim that labour is solely responsible for productivity increases; on the other side there is just a contrary claim. In point of fact of course, the position is that there is a combination of capital, labour, motivation (that is incentives or whatever it is), management, education or skills, and technology. There are all these factors which go into the productive process and account for productivity increases. Without going into theories of value and congealed labour power in capital equipment, we may yet describe, in the productive process as we see, the factors that go to contribute to productivity. The thinking here among those who have been protagonists on both sides is that there are four possibilities on productivity and wages.

One is to hold on to a steady real wage rate, that is increase wages only up to the point that you have to hold a constant real wage. The other is to raise the real wage slightly but somewhat less than the productivity rise. The third is that you raise wages exactly in keeping with the rise in productivity. This last point is that when we do give high wages — higher than we think we can hold at the moment as an entrepreneur — there is an incentive on the entrepreneur to modernise, to make himself more efficient, and generally to see that the flow of production is more efficient. However, the broad conclusion on these four possibilities is, as one might have suspected already, the second; that is, that the wage increases should be higher than just to allow for real wage constancies; in other words, that it goes along with productivity increases but not the same extent. Here one may also revert to the question of non-wage earners. Productivity has been, in the course of the discussion, very largely conceived in terms of productivity in the factory or within the producing unit. This is true. But there are other areas in which one might usefully understand productivity; that is in addition to the factory or the unit sense, there is a sectoral sense and there is a national sense in which one might usefully understand it. The sectoral approach is that while there can be productivity increases and high wages in concentrated sectors — urban areas for instance — one could have an increasing gap between the urban area and the nonurban area. One is not saying that this is an avoidable thing. But this is a thing which must be taken care of. Here one moves on to the national aspect of productivity; which really means that productivity conceived at national level is synonymous with national development. So that we do not have productivity conceived of properly and executed properly, unless we have a programme of economic development on a national scale. How does one do this, i.e., create and divert surpluses to overall development.

Here there is the unavoidable point made that there is vicious circle in the rural areas; in fact one could go further there is a vicious circle in the whole national economy, or the economic background, in this sense. The problem, was how to break it. It is here that the largest divergence between the two types of thinking that we have had in debates really occurs. The point was by what forces, through what channels and individuals, are we to put through and implement this programme of development. There have been views about the unregulated private sector. The other point also exists, that even the public sector is bad. At this stage it is not possible to indicate conclusions unequivocally about the alternative approaches. But one should indicate the possible approach in the existing context of a mixed economy as many developing countries have. There has sometimes been a feeling that labour management co-operation is not possible, that it was a remote thing. But, this has been equally challenged, emphasising very strongly that labour management co-operation is possible and that it can be achieved.

We know from experience in public sector industry, where the management has shown itself to be efficient and also to all public appearances to be so, then the public corporation has turned the tide. One has seen situations where there have been worker cooperation, and increased output, where losses have been converted into no-losses and ultimately into profits. One could come across this type of situation both in the private and public sectors; in other words, a situation where management is prepared constantly to put itself on trial in regard to its own performances and contributions. Before mentioning possibilities of wage increases or their impossibilities, if managements in their daily operations can examine themselves in this sense and if the workers get the feeling that managements mean business about productivity activity, then, even though the whole question may not be solved, a large part of it may be.

The other part of the question lies of course with the State. On this again a number of things have been mentioned in debates about the manner in which plans are implemented and under-expenditure in budgets that, when one has under-expenditure in the budget, why abolish subsidies. Something that has to come out as evidence to the workers is that implementation is being pursued vigorously, towards discernible and agreed objectives, which are also attainable. If this approach is followed, then there is room for a certain amount of understanding in a mixed economy.

There are, thus, certain key aspects regarding relative rights and obligations of the State and workers, and relative obligations of employer and employee.

For example:

1. *The State* has a right to contain total consumption and to ensure adequate investment; but has also the obligation to maintain a minimum type cost of living; and to contain undue growth of unequal pay, and wage differential.

2. *The Workers* have the right: to a minimum wage, reasonable cost of living; minimum possible wage differential; and so on; but they also have an obligation to maintain productivity. But permit syphoning off of national income to saving, to take into account fringe benefits (not only from firms, but also from the State, e.g., in education, health, transport services costs).

3. For both the *State* and the *Workers* the precondition for accepting all these is sound development planning and sound development effort.

81

One other aspect needs note, that historically there has been — partly because of hang-over from the past — too much reliance for wage settlements on wage regulations, and too little reliance on negotiations. This has some relationship to the idea of tripartite meetings. A regulation tends to be mechanistic, relied upon blindly, and does not allow for the realistic and informal discussion which really produces in the end the picture in regard to what a particular wage level or wage structure should or should not be. In this context the idea of a tripartite meeting, whether as a National Wage Council or as a tripartite organisation, is a needed instrument. Whatever we may call it, the tripartite idea between employer, employee and the State, who are the people concerned, is the only means by which the relative aberrations in wage structures can be settled and by which closer union participation in greater efficiency, greater value for money and more productivity can gradually be made to seep into a common group which is tripartite in organisation.

As a summing up, we may perhaps recall a classification of trade unions given at an international conference several years ago where the participants included representatives of socialist and non-socialist economies. The classification as given was of *productionist* trade unions and *protectionist* trade unions. It was amplified there that when a trade union movement is productionist, it serves as an auxiliary managerial force, and it was also observed that is the case in the well organised socialist or other highly nationalistic countries. The protectionist trade union was declared to exist in economies which had or have a dynastic elite, or a middle class or colonial background either in the present or in the past; and it was felt that in this context there is a tendency, among other things, to loose sight of the objectives of productivity and growth, in lieu of the immediate, 'segment' approach in regard to trade union activity. This is not to suggest a dichotomy, but to underline the point that, in countries that have accepted the premise of a mixed economy, under that premise, and within that framework, it is still possible to go a considerable way from being protectionist to being productionist. Indeed, we could elaborate and apply that term not only to trade unions, but to management and all other agencies in the production process.

82

Wages in a Developing Economy

Notes

1 Vide *my Economics of Full Employment in Agricultural Countries*, p. 248.
2 Women's wages is one among these, even if carrying special overtones. In fact for the whole area of 'women and development' generally instead of viewing the problem emotionally, we could view this as an under-utilised and disadvantaged segment of society, much as the working class or child labour were in the last century, leading to a more functional analysis and approach.
3 e.g., flowing from the inheritance of dualistic economies.

Chapter Eight

Debts, Deficits and the Development of Developing Countries*

I

This is a study on the stagnation of developing countries; their inability to change from being 'dependent' on debts and deficits, to becoming 'non-dependent', from being developing to becoming developed; the failure of current growth prescriptions to make them developed; and the required policy approaches to development.

The prescriptions for development have been plenty, especially over the last forty years. A brief resume of these prescriptions is provided later. Yet, most countries of the world are still developing, with no indication that they will be otherwise in the foreseeable future. The irony is that a 'pattern' of so-called development and global interaction has almost come to be accepted as a permanent scene in the international landscape, the poorer countries borrowing into the foreseeable future and following export promotion as the means to change towards 'self-reliance'. In the meantime, developing countries have long begun to behave as if the export strategy so far recommended, along with borrowing, are permanent features of a global economic organism, almost a natural law. One of the latest ideas is that of an international bankruptcy law. This is all the more amazing as at least a few countries, the NICs, with qualifications for the special circumstances of Hong Kong and Singapore, have begun the process of ceasing to be 'dependent'

---

* Based on Paper, first published in. *The South Asia Journal* (Oct./Dec. 1990, New Delhi/London)

borrowers and becoming holders of large foreign exchange balances. Also, some countries like India, Brazil and China, which are half-way in the process of development, have perceived the way. Finally, Japan herself was, before the War, an NIC, not to mention all industrial countries at some time in their past. Yet, today, growth, tacitly but futilely assumed to be the breakthrough for developing countries, is identified with export, from their existing structural bases. In turn, exports themselves are seen to rest with the growth of the developed countries, as the purveyors of the markets that enable those exports. The absurd implication that developing countries must therefore always remain several steps behind the developed countries, for their own growth mechanism is the export to them, appears not to have troubled anybody. As a result, amazingly unsaid but actually a continued status for the developing countries has come to be accepted. The purpose of this paper is to unlock the true basis for growth out of 'debt dependency' to 'non-dependency', available in the experience of both the developed countries and the NICs, but needing to be brought out and implemented as policy in developing countries, in place of the usurping role currently played by export promotion (EP) that replaced the old discredited import substitution ('IS'). We shall see that exports play a big role, but not in the present theorized form.

Over the years a strong school of thought has developed which holds simplistically that what is wrong with the developing countries is that they do not export enough and have not pursued policies that make for these exports. These policies are termed structural adjustment policies, but do not refer to anything like the physical production structures. Rather, they mean simply the fiscal, budgetary and related monetary policies, designed to depreciate currencies, eliminate social expenditures, and bridge the budget deficits by reduced expenditure and increased revenue, in the process hopefully containing inflation, stimulating exports and curtailing imports. That basically was the policy stand, and the one applied to developing countries by the IMF and the World Bank. In reality these measures have had three effects. By their draconian nature they have crippled basic socio-economic levels of income availability and levels of living. By their contradictions, especially on the currency rating, they have created new inflation. By their devotion only to fiscal, monetary 'structures' they have left the particular country's export base much the same, especially in nature as it always was and, therefore, unable to meet the demands of any but a poor economy.

The gist of the issue as to what must be looked at may be restated as follows.[1]

The struggle for growth by poor countries-variously called autonomous, self-reliant, or self-sustaining growth (for which I shall use the word 'non-dependent')—has increasingly come up against chronic (or recurring) budgetary, trade and balance of payments deficits, internal and external debts of a high order, currency devaluation/depreciation, and inflation.

The struggle to contain them has taken the form of fiscal, monetary and (limited type of) physical measures-blessed, or pressed, by the international agencies concerned-that have left these countries hardly better off, often worse off. These measures, on the fiscal and monetary side, have been to rectify budgets by reduced spending, including elimination of subsidies and other supports, devaluation, fight against inflation and now re-structuring debts. On the 'physical' side, the major policy plank has been 'bland' export promotion, i.e., pumping life into an export sector which, as it is, cannot attain the scale required by the economy.

'Re-structuring' is a word often used in the process. But when it is used by the international agencies concerned, it does not refer to the physical structure, but to the fiscal and monetary structures. The former (subject to the position on the export sector mentioned) was supposed to follow the latter, though it rarely did.

In experience, countries pursuing these policies have found themselves still unable to be 'non-dependent', relying on rich partners for much of current financing support and virtually all of capital development. This is that part of the goods flow in a growing economy, not only of basic or essential nature, but representing the items carrying the greatest value added

86

component, namely machinery equipment, intermediaries and the like, covering all sectors. With all these virtually imported, albeit in the name of development, the capacity for autonomously steering growth simply disappears. For example, Arthur Lewis states in *The Case for Development*. 'In developed countries....even though external events will call for adjustments....the origin of growth is in the home market.... The underdeveloped economy with its origin of growth in exports is at the mercy of the....industrialized countries'.[2]

It would seem that a prime cause of current failures is the reliance by international policy-makers on fiscal and monetary measures, and an 'over-simplified' reliance on export promotion, in place of a strategy for the entire physical structure. The aim of the study is to pursue this prima facie evidence, and to lead to a set of policies that assure stable growth to the poor countries, the only rationale of all domestic and international actions in this field.

At the outset it seems essential, though one should have thought it unnecessary, to dispel some misapprehensions that have been allowed, all too long, to emerge around any policies other than the 'classic' re-structuring-cum-export promotion measures. First, though obvious, is that there is no such thing as being self-sufficient or self-sustaining, or autonomous as such, in the use of these words or phrases. Second, therefore, these terms do not stand for capacity to produce everything internally, in substitution for imports or as new product; but they stand for the ability to create investment and production, in a range and at a price, required for higher growth without 'dependency' on otherwise inevitable imports for nearly all of the capital goods as now. This the economies fail to afford, and then double under at present.

What the new process does create, in effect, is an enlarged domestic supply base, and in many surprising areas, a base for a different, new range of exports, whose 'value added' components are much larger than the traditional. A new Domestic Production Base (DPB) is thereby created that never existed before. (These are the cases, historically, with variations, of Japan, Korea, Taiwan and India in Asia; Singapore and

The Wealth of Poor Nations

Hong Kong too, save that they are also 'special cases' of enclave development.) It is this central characteristic that informs the 'non-dependent' structures of economies.

The policy consequence is that in place of debate in terms of IS verses EP, we shall need to be talking of IS, DPB and EP viewed together and, dynamically, leading to expanded EP, both in volume and value, adequate-along with an expanded DPB supplying the domestic market—to carry development successfully. Yesterday's 'IS' produces today's 'DPB' for tomorrow's 'EP' foundation. As of now, both domestic and international aid policies are as likely as not both to perpetuate aid and to perpetuate dependence. Under the new policy view, the issues that had hitherto been made to look 'confrontational', cease to be so.

As hinted already, the experience itself is not intricate. The countries that have succeeded, in fact, adopted these policies and none other. Their various in success could have depended partly on the intensity of political awareness or application of such policies, partly on other factors of size, endowments, etc., none of which obviously are entirely wiped away like magic by a new policy *per se*. But the evidence and the successes are clear.

II

The contention therefore is a simple one, that countries seeking change effects by export had first to institute a Domestic Production Base capable of generating, *inter alia*, a massive outturn of exports. Inevitably, this change in the domestic base (DPB) is not only quantitative but also qualitative. One qualitative change is by concentration on higher value added items. One should not, in this design, exclude agriculture. On the contrary, a textile industry depending on imports for raw material, machinery and expertise, and supplying only labour domestically, may not be higher in value added terms than several lines of sophisticated horticulture, pisciculture and so on. The other qualitative change is even more fundamental and is related to what it takes to become a developed country. The scale of imports involved in the current situation, in order to meet the full requirements of 'developed economy' satisfaction is so large that no amount of export expansion on the present economic base will come anywhere near meeting it. Let alone this end, the scale needed in the path to development itself is so large that the proposition as to current export base incapacity will remain *a fortiori*. In this, there lies a crucial link area which becomes the engine of change for growth. Development involves machines, tools and equipment in every sector and category of activity, truly the 'infrastructure' of all development. They extend over agriculture, industry, transport and other services, and all their sub-systems. They also constitute mostly the highest value added items in the economy.

In this setting, the way then to exports is not bland export promotion, but establishment and expansion of the domestic · production sector (DPB) in all the categories of machinery, equipment and tools, as feasible, in addition to the conventionals.[3] Import substitution is thus not that of decades ago, which was attacked by the EP protagonists, with superficial substitution of imports of major categories and setting up of industries, etc., themselves heavily import-loaded with little net export values. Import substitution is creation of the domestic base which will allow future larger export expansions, even as they provide the 'infrastructures' to domestic development. The exponents of EP have created an unnecessary opposition out of IS, as if they were contradictory. Properly seen and carried, they are complementary.

All this is new, or apparently so, only in abstraction and expression. This is all borne out in the actual experience of the countries that succeeded, or are in the process of doing so. Unfortunately, customary statistics have not been geared to this and only limited verification is available. While there is plenty of statistics on GDP. External Trade, etc., traditions and tasks were not geared to data collection in precisely the way we need them here for our purpose. For example, GDP was stated to be good at looking at output and faulted when looking at welfare; in fact, it fared even worse in looking at 'sustainability'. Albeit, we could make some headway by approximation, even with

89

which the evidence becomes clear enough. Before doing so, however, let us look at the essence of the growth process and what is central to it, recalling our presentation at the start of this book for a necessary integrated view at this point.[4]

It seems that development should result in the following two goals. First, an enhanced welfare basis, obviously through use of material means for the population; and second, a sustenance of the production structure, not to be mistaken with Rostowian indices, that would ensure continuation of that welfare basis to the present and future populations. After all these years, what has gone wrong? I wish to set out something that must be simple, even self-evident, but seems to lie buried in the mass of international policies, theories and refinements that have cumulated over the years. This is the invariable condition for wealth creation in any economy. In this sense, it is a simple mechanics of growth which carries universal validity. The mechanics itself does not depend on, nor does it necessarily question, the innumerable theories of development in the literature of economics. It simply points to a constant process, under growth, which goes beyond the broad factors of production—of capital, labour and so on—and the aggregates—of savings, investment and the like.[5] The marxian dynamic or the Tableau Economique, perhaps provide examples of invariables, in their light, on which development must depend; and on which governments may trace practical policy paths for growth.[6] What is therefore attempted at the outset is a simple description, fundamental to government's strategies, overlooked amidst the profusion of other sophistications, and central to the growth process.

The basis for growth, as for existence, is the environment of all of our resources. This is the 'land' (natural resources), 'labour' (human resources), combined to productive advantage by the application of capital (cumulative labour or technology or both). But the mechanics of growth itself is determined by a process and not the existence of the factors; nor of the aggregates. The combination of factors at a given time produces an output which divides itself partly into consumption and partly into investment. The production process creates a 'surplus',[7] however called, which has to be ploughed back into the process, for growth to continue. This is the cause of wealth. There is no other cause. All the rest may accelerate or decelerate the process, sometimes halt it, enhance or adversely affect the composition of the wealth created, and so on. These are, of course, many and the preoccupation of various national, as well as international, actions. But the mechanics of growth is single and invariable.

This is indeed how the process of repaid wealth creations occurred in the 19th century; while the consumer privation, exploitation, depression compensatory aggrandizements, determined the scale and composition of that wealth. But the mechanics was this. This was also the process of wealth creation later, in societies having state ownership of the means of production. In these, in contrast to the last century, there was less conspicuous consumption out of the 'surplus', less privation and exploitation of the non-privileged class, and a policy based package of low priced basic consumption goods mainly food, clothing and accommodation. Whatever the political system, where countries succeeded, the accumulation process, necessarily and inexorably, took place; and the surpluses were repeatedly redeployed into continued productive expansion.

It was the same mechanics which Third World countries, thereafter, were having to apply. It was an impersonal mechanics. But they were left without the means by which these mechanics were made to work, either of the countries that developed in the last century or of the countries that did so in this century. It was the dilemma of these countries that they had willingly eschewed the 19th century free market model, had not pursued the 20th century socialist model, and were left without the aid and trade premises which were supposed to provide the brave new basis for the undisturbed operation, in effect, of the predicated post-War Third World model. Here, we are faced with the need to see how these may be overcome, because that is the only means to growth. Some basic characteristics seem to be part of such a growth mechanics and these may be considered here.

An essential pillar in the growth mechanics has to be the consumption capacity of that part of production that is meant for consumption. In practice, these are not only the 'end goods' normally so understood, namely, final consumption goods like food and clothing. All outputs, intermediate and capital, are also consumed at respective stages and represent consumption capacity of the disbursements from investment out of the national product. However, the end goods have a special connotation, not only as the end purpose, hedonistically, of a society's productive activity. Its level and its composition will be crucial, first, to absorbing the portion of the production process set aside for consumption goods. Second, it will reflect back on the ability to market what comes out as investment goods. In other words, the set of capital and intermediate goods in an economy can only continue to sell if the consumer 'end products' they are producing, or will produce, are such in quantity and composition as will be consumed. The quantity and composition of the end goods are therefore crucial. Given proper decisions as to what these shall be at a given phase in an economy, each of the innumerable segments and items of both investment and consumption outputs will complement each other, and through this interlocking support, become each other's own market. This is not a new theory.[8] The above pattern of goods produced becomes the basic set of goods for economic movement and sustenance. If consumers in a society are seen as wage earners or workers then the most visible basic industries in developing economies are the 'wage goods' industries.

As may be inferred from the foregoing, the basic industries are not just consumption goods in the popular sense. It is these, plus a configuration of closely related intermediate and capital goods, that are involved in rational sustenance of the pattern of the planned wage goods themselves. Countries that were dependent on metropolitan countries in the past, politically or economically, typically never had this basic essential of self-reliance, or self-development. Later, in the post-War phase, the promise of aid and trade eschewed the adoption of this strategy as a basis again. Yet there was no commensurate outlet in exports to absorb the increasing production that was not in any case diversified enough for the low income domestic market to take, but had to be sold, if the pace of reinvestment and the growth rate were to be maintained. Having adopted a development style that was internationalist, it also became practically impossible later for a dependent country to find the margins to reduce imports, since these were mostly development imports. Nor could they find leverage in expanding exports, since these were practically primary, or similar goods. In any case, when it came to bargaining, the buyers knew who was dependent on whom. The concept of progressive 'non-dependence', in significant form, on imports for developmental inputs was a crucial component of the growth mechanics that was not adopted.

This 'non-dependence' was also crucial in another, somewhat interesting way. Developed countries that originally relied on colonial patterns in order to develop, did not collapse after that pattern was lost, but continued to prosper, in fact, contrary to many opinions in the early, post-War years. While advantageous inputs and sales of outputs were crucial in their early stage of development, they ceased to be important, relatively, with the technological advance and giant superiority that they had attained subsequently. These provided new competitiveness and even price advantages for their goods subsequently. In a different situation even Marshall aid to West Europe would have had to take a longer, varied course before 'reconstruction' took place.

Parallel with this, the transition 'from the first shovel to the first hydraulic forklift' proved similarly crucial. For too many cases among developing countries, the transition achieved was chimerical, since what came about was the end of the indigenous 'shovel' making handicraft industry and the beginning of a vigorous import industry for the hydraulic 'machinery'. This could be multiplied with a thousand more examples in various production lines in the history of these economies. In effect, there was no transition in which a machine or component became also a prototype to fabricate and to multiply appropriately domestic equivalent. This distinction between countries which failed to do so and those that did runs like a golden, or not so golden, thread dividing today's new prosperous countries and those still 'developing'. Japan and, in certain ways, the 'four little dragons'[9] of Asia, illustrate the former; too

93

many countries exist around the world illustrating the latter; while a few, like India or Brazil illustrate a mid-way mark.

Thus, internal 'fabricating capacity', without at all presuming that everything is to be fabricated internally, is integral to planning for wage goods industries, as bedrocks of the growth mechanics. Indeed, no country has become developed, which has not developed a highly advanced agricultural system, a meaningful industrial pattern, the range of wage goods output, and, coupled with it, the internal fabricating capacity as appropriate to each economy. If one may exclude ready exceptions, like small city states, the pattern seems invariable. Where one or two such countries have been lucky, so as to receive a much larger volume of per capita aid and foreign market opportunities than others, the pace of growth has been faster. But the pattern of the basis for growth was the same.

Yet, some of the developing countries that have so far failed must also take some of the blame. Here, we need to recall some of the things we set out earlier, particularly in chapters one and four. They have complained long and loud at, and about, the international system. All too true, but not complained enough about themselves. In that sense, so far at least as the growth mechanics described goes, the still developing countries have lessons to learn, irrespective of ideology and whether they are so-called market economies or socialist. Given those invariables we have talked about, other issues, ideas and theories, advanced from time to time, on how to develop, can find due place; but not without these invariables. That was the tragedy of the many intrusions that passed as theories: balanced versus imbalanced growth; export related versus domestic based growth; agriculture versus industry; environment versus development; social versus economic; consumption versus investment; monetarist versus non-monetarist; and others. That was also the tragedy of the international postures on aid and trade, self-reliance, even NIEO, so the developing could 'catch-up' with the developed. Such realization required in fact sound national structures with international efforts based only on these. Were the basis for 'self-sustained' growth properly established, 'catching-up' would then take its course.

94

'Non-dependent' Development: Based on Installed Machine Fabrication Capacity, for Optimum 'Value-added' Production

Stages		Production Patterns	$ million
1.	(i)	Raw material exported unprocessed	100
	(ii)	Imports of finished products of above	25
	(iii)	'Development benefit'[a]	
		('dependent development')	100
2.	(iv)	Part value added[b]	250
	(v)	Import of capital equipment for (i)	50
	(vi)	Development benefit[c]	275
3.	(vii)	Full value added	500
	(viii)	Import of capital equipment for (vii)	100
	(ix)	Development benefit[d]	425
4.	(x)	'Non-dependent' machinery fabrication	600[e]
	(xi)	Import tooling/equipment/materials for (x)	200[e]
	(xii)	Development benefit on 4	400
5.	(xiii)	'Non-dependent' fabrication based	
		development benefit[f]	or 825
			900[g]

a Defined as 'net' export earning (i.e.,(i)-(ii) plus import value). Under case (1) the 'Development Benefit' is not stable, but exists so long as the raw material lasts (in non-renewable till exhaustion; in renewable subject to degradation deterioration/synthetic substitution).
b Say light consumer stage, etc. (for 0.5 final value stage) exported.
c Capital equipment 0.5 × (i)+(ii)+(iv)-(v).
d Capital equipment (ii)+(vii)-(viii).
e Hypothetical; could be lower.
f Made up of (ix)+(xii), or (vii)+(xii).
g Being the differences in economic strength between a developed country (xiii) and a developing country (iii). Also a measure of falsity of foreign aid instead of trade, so far the outcome of current economic cooperation.

The whole question of dependent development, full value added, and fabricating capacity is so central to the creation of wealth and welfare, that they must be considered fundamental and foundational, making for the lasting differences between the rich and poor countries—tying down terms of trade, income, sustainability and capacity. Here, we give a simple illustration of its significance as an invariable condition for self-reliant growth. A look at the varying 'development benefits' in the move towards real development bases, shows how diversionary and superficial, in a sense, current aid role is vis-a-vis suppressed national capacities for surplus generation.

What comes as aid to the Third World is a small part of what would have been 'value added' resources within these countries. All countries that are developed had gone through this change first, incidentally putting them in a position of superior trading, payments, and 'aid giving' power. Not having done so the developing countries had neither autonomous growth capacity nor own created surpluses. Their concepts of growth were then beset with concessions, grants, loans and aid and continuing ways of seeking short-term relief. The real growth path for them lay elsewhere.

III

As statistical substantiation, certain groups of data are seen to be relevant. One is data on agricultural reorganization, product orientation and production. Another is the extent of wage goods[10] manufactured within the economy. The third is the extent of manufacture of (a) the machinery that produces these and other goods, and (b) the machines, equipment and tools that make (a) possible. One must reiterate, if necessary *ad nauseum,* that nothing in this is to imply that anything like all the goods in this range, even agricultural goods, are to be made domestically; but that is no refuge for not producing anything at all in these categories, particularly including (b) above. Having said this, what one sees is a linkage between these categories; and a stronger component of higher value added items, vital for economic growth, which must otherwise be imported by incurring trade deficits and debts, soon to become unrequitable. The result of this 'restructuring' of the domestic production pattern is, in addition, an enlarged base for export potential, quantity-wise, and in value added terms. Countries will trade, as experience has borne out, at such historical turning points, at rising levels of production; and regional, inter-regional and global economic cooperation, becomes more feasible.

In this paper we are not looking at agricultural data on reorganization and performance, which is well accepted. Nor are we looking at industrial production from machines which may all be imported, for which area in any case documented data can be found. We are concerned here with the critical transformation, where an economy slowly begins to turn out some of the tools, equipment and machinery that serve its production over entire areas of its agriculture, industry and infrastructure development. Neither GNP/GDP figures, nor figures of external trade are strong in this, a situation explainable only by the failure of theoretical or analytical economics to see this as the culminating key phase of economic structuring in growth; and, instead, concentrating on 'boomeranging' recommendations of EP on the basis of financial restructuring of stationary physical structures. An attempt is made, by as near direct means as possible, to ascertain the extent of inputs in machinery, equipment and tools (MTE) in selected economies, currently and in the past, as the key to their performance or failure. Without doubt, not only the analytical approach adopted here, but also a concerted drive to cull and to identify data on this crucial area in countries, in past and recent times, must be one of the gaps in the economic field—a highly recommended one for future sustained study and research efforts by economists everywhere.

As for our modest data, we have used only a limited number of countries, while conceptually classifying four types. We have selected data for several countries, all recently or newly developed or semi-developed. Unfortunately, we have failed in not including any of those that became developed in the last century or earlier. The countries which are presented are: Sri Lanka, Thailand, India, South Korea and Japan. They are all different in their own ways in relation to the stage of growth; also, broadly typifying for other countries in the world at those

97

phases of development. What the data try to elicit are the behaviour and the extent of the component of 'MTE' in the national economy, if possible, as a part of GDP, as a second best, as part of external trade.

It will be seen that neither quantities nor percentages are readily comparable as between countries. For example, the percentage of MTE in a developing country may not be too different from that in a more advanced economy. Low and high GDPs will have low and high MTEs respectively, as absolute quantities, but the percentage relationships of MTE and GDP within each could be much the same. On the other hand, within each country, the rate of increase in provisions for MTE affords an explanatory index on what has happened in these terms. It would be far better if one were able to follow all the patterns in the movements of MTE—the areas in which it developed over periods, the value added to the total product thereby, and the strengthening and widening of DPB, thereby giving sustainability to both enlarged, more wide ranging and more value added production at home, and larger and much more value added export promotion abroad. But these statistical refinements are what are not available at present, national income and production and trade data historically having been geared, as we said, to straight GDP and export/import analytical frameworks. A wide area of competent research, it must be reiterated, awaits us in this field and is a future challenge and vista for economic study and analysis. For the present, we must limit ourselves to more modest, indirect or inferred data to give us an idea of the desired MTE-DPB-EP relationships and linkage.

In setting out that limited evidence below we have looked for MTE behaviour not only in GDP but also in exports and imports, and over a time span. By way of 'grouping', Sri Lanka and Thailand, although the latter is way ahead now, may be considered as one group, of the still developing countries; India, as representative of those at the half-way mark; South Korea as the newly industrialized country; and Japan as an older industrial country, although it cannot substitute for what must be fascinating data awaiting probing for the really older industrial countries like the UK, Germany, France and the USA.

Debts, Deficits and the Development of Developing Countries

In the case of Sri Lanka, the data are as follows (see table). The figures have been extracted for a period of thirty years at selected intervals. It will be seen, on the imports side, that MTE as a percentage has doubled over the period, while of course exports of MTE are either zero or totally negligible. The industrial base under DPB has fallen dramatically over the period for which figures are available by more than half, as a percentage of the total production. While this is an index of the prominent increase in agricultural production, the increase in industrial goods in absolute terms has itself been less than

Trade Statistics — Sri Lanka Production

TABLE 1: IMPORTS   (in Rupees million)

Year 1	Agricultural Goods 2	% 3	Industrial Goods 4	% 5	Machinery, Tools and Equipment 6	% 7
1957	993,138.0	55.0	608,581.3	33.7	202,344.9	11.3
1960	947,736.8	48.4	719,097.9	31.7	297,787.9	14.9
1965	772,889.2	52.4	524,335.4	35.6	117,157.1	12.0
1970	1,185,141.2	51.8	696,812.3	38.4	406,428.3	17.8
1975	3,590,274.8	68.3	1,196,895.5	22.7	478,080.4	9.0
1980	5,680,168.1	50.1	205,526.5	23.1	8,385,428.7	26.8
1981	6,882,272.6	19.20,4	432,711.0	59.1	7,789,579.1	21.1
1982	4,909,316.9	13.28,3	399,023.8	63.4	8,581,252.8	23.3
1983	7,395,730.9	17.83,9	338,700.4	50.9	10,729,810.4	25.5
1984	6,451,298.6	15.88,3	351,199.8	60.3	11,240,231.7	23.9
1985	10,096,827.6	20.99,0	337,358.7	59.1	10,033,939.4	20.4
1987	9,539,017.6	18.80,2	210,685.4	59.2	11,606,470.1	22.4

TABLE 2 : EXPORTS

1	2	3	4	5	6	7
19571,£ 561,472.1	98.3	26,770.6	1.7	38.9	0.0	
19601,7 750,769.6	98.6	24,007.7	1.4	11.6	0.0	
19651,8 896,748.2	99.1	16,780.6	0.9	388.2	0.0	
19701,4 455,216.8	73.8	516,920.0	26.2	159.8	0.0	
19752,6 604,670.5	66.41,3 307,728.0	33.3	8,978.3	0.3		
19809,3 326,652.4	54.37,7 776,265.5	15.3	0,215.3	0.4		
19819,3 314,969.2	47.310, 1,251,316.	52.0	11,565.7	0.7		
19829,6 661,354.7	46.610, 1,950,941.	52.8	6,194.9	0.6		
198311 1,315,785.	47.612, 2,854,334.	31.7	2,319.5	0.7		
198419 9,427,148.	53.216, 6,907,290.	16.3	6,216.5	0.5		
198516 6,462,645.	48.117, 7,577,238.	51.3	8,112.9	0.6		
198713 3,327,105.	40.119, 1,538,905.	59.0	0,437.6	0.8		

TABLE 3 : EXPORTS
DPB**

1	2	3	4	5	6	7	Remarks
1957							DBP/MTE-Derived
1960							from Industrial Goods
1965							and given percentage
1970							for MTE.
1975	4,976.0	47.8	5,344.0	50.7	80.1	*1.5	
1980	3,573.0	64.5	4,646.0	34.0	69.8	1.5	* 1975, 1980 and 1981
1981	13,472.0	77.8	3,777.0	20.7	56.7	1.5	assumed as 1.5
1982	15,597.0	80.6	3,693.0	17.9	55.4	1.5	percentage.
1983	10,652.0	78.2	5,079.0	19.6	111.8	2.2	
1984	17,866.0	69.9	7,394.0	26.5	266.1	3.6	* From 1982 to 1986
1985	22,043.0	70.5	8,603.0	22.3	619.2	7.2	Actual Figures
1987	25,346.0	72.1	8,980.0	19.1	790.2	8.8	

Sources: Sri Lanka Customs.

Debts, Deficits and the Development of Developing Countries

National Accounts of Sri Lanka, Department of Census and statistics.
Table 1 'The percentage shares of nine major sectors'.
(Total manufacturing industry at current prices 1982-1986).
Table 2 'Gross Domestic Product by Industrial Origin at current producer prices, and the percentage contribution of major economic activities to GDP'.
** DBP - Defined as Domestic Production (GDP) less Exports.

double. As for MTE, some increases have occurred in internal output as will be seen from the last column, but this must be read alongside the enormous import of MTE that has been evident. Much of the MTE manufactured in the Sri Lankan case has been in the tea sector, with some of it in the coconut and paddy areas. Very negligible all-round development in MTE has obviously occurred, contributing assuredly to near total dependence on imports for both MTE and, overall, for the so-called industrial and development programme.

For Thailand, it has not been possible to elicit the type of information on MTE, even limited, as we have for Sri Lanka, mainly due to the way in which the otherwise expansive national statistics are prepared and published. From what indirect evidence is available, or is feasible, for use as a basis of judgement, it would seem that the picture has been the same. The figures below are from the *Statistical Year Book for 1987.*

Value of Imports by Principal Commodity

(Thousand Baht)

Commodities	1978	1979	1980	1981	1982
Miscellaneous articles of base metal	386,310	491,854	511,494	556,611	554,748
Boilers, machinery and mechanical appliances and parts thereof	13,737,30	16,761,63	18,089,20	22,672,63	19,425,55
Electrical machinery and equipment, and parts thereof	7,381,808	9,376,685	13,264,86	13,710,81	13,746.76

The Wealth of Poor Nations

Value of Imports by Principal Commodity (contd.)

(Thousand Baht)

Commodities	1978	1979	1980	1981	1982
Railway and transway locomotives, rolling-stock and parts thereof	28,074	13,878	416,535	339,044	60,261
Vehicles other than railway or transway rolling-stock and parts thereof	10,707,73	9,862,227	10,034,06	13,779,18	10,260,84
Aircraft and parts thereof	366,931	957,102	5,132,501	3,772,348	546,629
Ships, boats and floating structures	557,195	472,440	536,157	1,782,418	1,622,290

Gross Fixed Capital Formation By Type of Capital Goods : 1968-83

(Million Baht)

Type of Capital Goods	Current Market Prices				
	1979	1980	1981	1982	1983
Machinery and Equipment	78,003	37,944	95,155	82,137	97,421
Transport Equipment	20,676	24,170	23,433	19,818	23,243
Road Motor Vehicles	14,915	12,515	12,419	13,497	17,361
Other equipment	5,761	11,655	11,014	6,321	5,882
Machinery and other equipment	57,327	63,774	71,722	62,319	74,178
Industrial machinery and appliances	10,491	12,854	13,771	11,728	16,049
Office and other equipment	46,836	50,920	57,951	50,591	58,129
Gross Fixed Capital Formation	144,356	177,099	189,067	179,898	203,445

Debts, Deficits and the Development of Developing Countries

The data on India illustrate vividly the role played by MTE in its development progress, with its positive impact on performance in the manufacture of industrial goods. The following tables set out some of this information.

Trade Statistics

(Rupeess in Lakhs)

Year		1970-71	1974-75	1975-76	1976-77
IMPORTS					
Agricultural		27,210	85,626	142,990	96,446
goods	%	16.6	18.9	27.2	19.3
Industrial		96,739	296,680	290,029	306,738
goods	%	59.2	65.7	55.1	61.2
Machinery		39,469	69,570	93,458	97,914
tools and					
equipment	%	24.2	15.4	17.7	19.5
EXPORTS					
Agricultural		44,524	110,148	135,179	137,037
goods	%	29.2	33.2	33.5	27.6
Industrial		100,403	200,864	241,769	330,337
goods	%	65.9	60.4	60.1	66.5
Machinery		7,511	21,348	25,639	29,407
tools and					
equipment	%	4.9	6.4	6.4	5.9

Domestic Capital Formation by Type of Assets

(At current prices Rupees crores)

	1. Total Gross Domestic Fixed Capital Formation	1.2 Machinery Equipment	** Percentage
1950/51	970	241	24.8
1955/56	1,283	473	36.9

The Wealth of Poor Nations

Domestic Capital Formation by Type of Assets *(contd.)*

(At current prices Rupees crores)

	1. Total Gross Domestic Fixed Capital Formation	1.2 Machinery Equipment	** Percentage
1960/61	2,156	819	37.9
1965/66	4,132	1,772	42.9
1970/71	6,305	2,346	37.2
1974/75	11,041	5,171	46.8
1975/76	13,631	6,031	44.2
1976/77	15,774	6,810	43.2
1977/78	17,344	7,419	42.8
1978/79	19,942	8,805	44.2

Source: *Statistical Abstract, 1979.*

** Item 1.2 as percentage of item 1 in each column.

In view of the extensive nature of certain other data relating to imports and exports, although they are of much interest, they are not reproduced here.*

As in the case of India, by way of approximation, we present a table of imports and exports, including MTE, for South Korea. There is no doubt that the Korean record in terms of MTE is impressive.

Trade Statistics—Korea

PRODUCTION (in million US Dollars)

Year		1968	1970	1975	1980	1981	1982	1983
IMPORTS								
Agricultural		520	877	3,525	12,293	14,342	12,676	12,292
goods	%	35.3	44.2	48.5	55.1	54.9	52.2	47.0
Industrial		409	517	1,824	4,999	5,752	5,564	6,311
goods	%	28.0	26.1	25.1	22.4	22.0	23.0	24.0

* Tables 73 and 73A of the *Statistical Abstract,* 1979.

Trade Statistics—Korea (contd.)

PRODUCTION   (in million US Dollars)

Year		1968	1970	1975	1980	1981	1982	1983
IMPORTS								
Machinery tools and equipment		534	590	1,925	5,000	6,037	6,011	7,589
	%	36.5	29.7	26.4	22.5	23.1	24.8	29.0
EXPORTS								
Agricultural goods		117	189	923	1,667	1,924	1,800	2,070
	%	25.7	22.6	18.2	9.5	9.0	8.2	8.5
Industrial goods		314	584	3,397	12,283	14,491	13,900	14,393
	%	69.0	69.9	66.9	70.2	68.2	63.6	58.9
Machinery tools and equipment		24	62	761	3,555	4,839	6,153	7,982
	%	5.3	7.5	14.9	20.30	22.8	28.2	32.6

Source: *Korea Statistical Year Book, 1984.*

The table we set out for Japan is again similar to those for India and South Korea. As in the case of India, certain very interesting data, with detailed breakdowns are available which, in view of their extensiveness, are not set out here.*

Trade Statistics—Japan

PRODUCTION   (in billion Yen)

Year		1955	1960	1965	1970	1975	1980	1981	1982	1983	1984
IMPORTS											
Agricultural goods		225.0	198	529	926	2,615	3,327	3,499	3,617	3,539	3,796
	%	25.30	12.2	18.0	13.6	15.2	10.4	11.1	11.1	11.8	11.7
Industrial goods		665.0	1,262	2,138	5,044	13,28	26,42	25,71	26,77	24,00	25,66
	%	74.70	78.0	72.7	74.2	77.4	82.6	81.7	82.0	80.0	79.4

Trade Statistics—Japan (contd.)

PRODUCTION   (in billion Yen)

Year		1955	1960	1965	1970	1975	1980	1981	1982	1983	1984
IMPORTS											
Machinery		–	157	274	827	1,270	2,239	2,248	2,263	2,473	2,861
tools and											
equipment	%	–	9.8	9.3	12.2	7.4	7.0	7.2	6.9	8.2	8.9
EXPORTS											
Agricultural		45.00	92	125	233	225	359	382	350	330	345
goods	%	6.20	6.3	4.1	3.4	1.3	1.2	1.1	1.0	0.9	0.9
Industrial		679.0	995	1,847	3,502	7,410	10.61	11,04	11,64	10,92	11,58
goods	%	93.80	68.1	60.7	50.4	44.8	36.1	33.0	33.8	31.3	28.7
Machinery		–	373	1,071	3,219	8,910	18,41	22,04	22,44	23,65	28,40
tools and											
equipment	%	–	25.4	35.2	46.3	53.9	62.7	65.9	65.2	67.8	70.4

Source: *Japan Statistical Year Book, 1985.*

The picture, even from this limited information base, whether in terms of the type of information or the number of years covered, is quite impressive.

The performance of Japan is overwhelming in its nature in regard to MTE, both by itself and in comparison with other sectors. It has no doubt been the key factor in the purveyance of the internal domestic production capacities over the entire area of its economy, primary, secondary and tertiary. The full role of MTE in the case of Japan does not yet come out in the absence of data preceding the years given in the tables.

In the case of South Korea, it is possible to see the role of MTE performance, again subject to the overall data limitations we outlined at the outset of this paper, in building up the

* Table 6-18, 6-19 and 6-20 of the *Statistical Year Book,* 1985.

domestic production base and capability for both indigenous manufacture and export performance.

The data for India illustrate very much the contribution made by MTE not only in the portrayal of that country as an emerging self-reliant economy, but also notwithstanding the oil prices and consequential shocks of the 1970s.

In the case of all these countries it is reasonable to infer that modernization of agriculture, the creation of infrastructure and the expansion of manufactures and the consequential growth of exports depending on each country's political/economic policies owe not a little to the MTE base that was created.

In the case of Thailand, while the economy is still 'dependent', there is sufficient evidence of a build up in MTE capability which should lead to beneficial domestic and export results in due course.

The case of Sri Lanka illustrates something like a 'worst' case, with very poor MTE rating or chances of either indigenous production expansion or worthwhile export growth taking place.

IV

In Section I we mentioned that prescriptions for development over the last four decades have been plenty and that we would touch on them in due course. What will be said on this is not fundamentally new, but nonetheless something more often than not either ignored or not addressed by the professionals or by policy-makers. Often it becomes very useful to stand back and look at ourselves in order to be able to see really what we have been prescribing for others. We shall therefore set down a brief roundup of these prescriptions in this section.

The second component that may be usefully to go over in this section is a look at the already existing support of the approach adopted in this paper. The literature, both popular or academic, has not been without its own corroborations of the arguments and data so far presented. It was perhaps more a case, having set out observations or glimpses to that effect, of their preoccupations having been determined by the hitherto accepted theoretical premise for growth, of export promotion on the familiar existing, or almost similar, production structures. At the same time, as the corroborations of our presentation are interesting enough and so some citations are made in this text, using both media and professional academic sources. We shall treat the foregoing in three sub-sections here.

First, for the roundup of past prescriptions, and account of 'the models that failed' is given. From the 1940s, a broadly defined yet clear promise of rapid growth was made available to the developing economies. It was based on the theoretical foundations of growth economics that dominated the 1930s and early 1940s and drew sustenance from the aura of post-War humanity and rising expectations. It was further strengthened by the pillars of international co-operation that were built by optimists. In order to assist in this effort voluminous literature poured forth through periodicals, pronouncements and learned studies, and from many parts of the developed and, to some extent, the developing world. Many developing countries, charted their developmental course on the political-democratic-welfare-statist and international cooperation based philosophy, that was to be their guide in and after the 1940s. Thus they readily used many theories that came from the source of the expected aid and trade.

In the early years, development based on import substitution was such a theory. It was impeccable and, further, attractive to the developing countries.[11] In practice, however, this became mostly, and at best, import of machines which produced consumption goods and had to be each replaced by imports. It had little lasting implications for a developing economy in its capacity to reduce imports, establish tolerable terms of trade, reduce continual dependence on aid flows, or the ability to build up its own internal structure.

With the end of the import substitution phase as a solvent, the international cooperative community followed a new idea, of export led growth and of lead sectors. As will be seen in the previous case, as well as in this and others, none of these by themselves are false. But what has been curious, and wholly false, is the way in which international and national dialogues have got on to one or an other of panaceas as the solvent. Lead sector and export led growth were in the same category, except that each failed for its own reasons. In this case, there were two reasons. First, that internal agrarian and economic revolution was never established. Second, the so-called export lead mostly came from the same colonial type primary or quasi-primary production lines, with their own capacity to earn foreign exchange or to produce adequate local incomes quite inadequate to the demands of development.

Then there were the theories of balanced growth of a type, which said that what was wrong with the development efforts was the lack of a balance between agriculture and industry and that something should have been done with agriculture much earlier. A failure to do so explained the foreign exchange and debt servicing limits and even the capacity to produce inputs to industry within the countries. Again, there was nothing new or objectionable, but countries during a certain phase were all practically giving up everything else and single-mindedly pursuing this development as the panacea. While interest in agriculture revived, it was presumed industry was less important, whereas what was less important was the dependent type of industrialization pointed out earlier.

Then there were also supporting facets of ideas to prop up one or the other of such theories. One of these facets was a series of 'imported' policies for rural development. At one time, it was all community development. When disillusionment came upon this some years later, serious examination had to be undertaken internally to realize what should have been realized at the beginning, in order to initiate an alternative strategy. Community development—as community services and public works programmes, even with some economic and related assistance as obtained—was a thing apart from integrated resource based planning and development by the community itself at an autonomous level. In such a context, infrastructure and other support had a place and had to be given a place, but in accord with needs directly of the production resources and of production. Block development schemes in India were different from the commune in China, the kibbutz in Israel, or the shemaul in Korea, or the earlier rural programmes in Taiwan and Japan. But each shared this integrated resource based planning and production approach.

More recently, I drew attention to what I noted as a major gap[12] in thinking—and implementation—which is economic, that has in fact held back success in the past and, perhaps, created a consistent need for reassessments. This is the role of highly selective 'fabricating capacity' going hand in hand with any technological advances in consumer and 'welfare' goods. Neither increases, nor will equitable distribution of the latter, serve without the former. In just one instance, the miracle rice and the envisaged Green Revolution were said to have failed since they failed with distribution policies. While indeed so, the failure to construct, indigenously, the whole cluster of manufactures (and their related machinery and tools) in fertilizers, pesticides, agricultural equipment, or 'infrastructural' equipment, made failure even more certain. Where these were developed, it was possible even to correct errors later; where they did not, there were only debt, bankruptcy, 'backwardness' and well-nigh never ending struggle for 'development'.

The key distinction between countries can even be, not between being developed and non-developed, but between being 'dependent and non-dependent'. One could well propose a law of growth, wherein if any growth in 'consumer' output were not accompanied by growth in supporting 'fabricating capacities' and their outputs, the economy will remain 'dependent'—even more drastically, despite semblances of higher growth curves, than earlier sometimes—on indigent budgets at home, runaway debts abroad and social inequities all round. Where the two accompany one another, the beginnings of take-off are seen.

Another concept that offered to come to the rescue during these times was that of employment-intensive development, as having been the missing link and the explanation for the massive insoluble unemployment, low income, foreign exchange constraints, budget deficits, costly subsidies and many other ailments. Dazzled by its immediate chemical effect, we have largely preferred not to see where such an approach led. Along with a somewhat diffuse slogan about appropriate technology, it carried a wide charisma which became difficult to overthrow.[13] The countries that 'suffered' seeming benefits failed later to achieve self-sustaining growth.

In Amartya K. Sen's celebrated formulation bearing on quick policies for employment creation without the foundation for its sustenance into the future, 'the determination of the optimum size of total savings and that of the optimum capital intensity of investment are interdependent problems'.[14]

More recently, we have had the philosophy that what was wrong was the failure of the so-called trickle-down approach to development, whereby the massive large-scale production programmes were to have beneficial chain effects in employment and productive activity down the line, to the populations at lower income levels. It was very quickly agreed that the trickle-down theory was incorrect, forgetting that, in fact, it existed as a fact of life in the experience of the last century, even this century. What the present-day developing countries did not have were the conditions in which the trickle-down 'theory' worked, including the political, social and moral conditions thereto. The same effect, however, may be said fairly to have been simulated, partly in the socialist economies, subject to the initial provision of basic consumption goods by these economies to the population. Most other growth was highly capital-intensive and large-scale and the benefits gradually worked themselves down. It is not that the trickle-down theory is needed at all today. But from this, an alternative was next developed to help the poor countries. This is what was called the basic needs approach.

Under this concept, it was declared that the problem with non-development was the fact that the lower income deciles did not have basic incomes to meet basic needs. The meeting of these needs would be development by itself; would also be efficient and economic use of local factors of production; and would, through demand effects, generate other growth. This again was not something to quarrel with by and large, and by itself. But as a single panacea it was more a trap, like the many traps that the poor countries have had, than an adequately compulsive theory of growth. As in the employment-intensive theory, so in this too, there remained a serious question of the

111

optimal combination of factors in every production process to ensure maximum surplus creation, as well as to ensure overall full use of national resources. 'If the primary object of government was to raise the rate of growth of output, then it should maximise the rate of investment at each moment.' Subsequent writers have recognized that the level of modern sector employment and rate of investment are interdependent.[15] Even in early discussions on attaining full employment, it was noted that 'the labour intensive ideas could be pursued only in conformity with the principles of optimal grouping of factors in the unit'.[16] 'It is the capital labour ratio of the development process as a whole which has to take account of the relative capacity of the various factors and not the choice of productive techniques in each production unit'.[17] These are fundamental points of view which, in a practical way, the Chinese have questioned in international forums, suggesting that it may border on being simply another trap to be cautious about, diverting countries away from the essential strategies for lasting growth. Sound development planning will inherently have basic needs, both as benefit and as instrument for high rates of re-investment of surpluses and rapid growth.

Then, of course, there was the other set of ideas provided to the developing countries under new headings of development. For example, it was important to have social planning and provide for social changes as preconditions to development, perhaps including cultural and spiritual conditions as well. There was hardly anybody to consider the fact that social change precedes development, but also accompanies it and flows from it. Similarly, there was the concept of population planning as one more precondition for development to take place. Again, few considered the fact in history that development was the most assured solvent of the population problem. Or again, there was environment as something to be preserved and considered before development. There were few to consider the fact that environment management, as sustained resource use management, was a support and an essential support to development.

They all add up to a somewhat simple fact that there were as many theories or philosophies as there were 'disciplines'.

112

There was no integrated theory of growth which after all must be more in conformity with the realities of life. It is somewhat surprising that all these separate theories have carried weight and conviction with the developing countries; with the developed countries themselves, in times of trouble, simply prescribing more of the same. One reason at least that they did so is that they were tied to the grants and loans and the markets that were supposed to be made available by the developed countries.

As one of the final steps to advise on development, there was a dethroning of GNP, as we saw at the beginning, without knowing of, or finding an alternative. GNP itself was always a means to welfare in the end, even to the mercantilists! The change that had to be made was in the automatic inference of social welfare from economic production. But GNP was needed for welfare, and this fine thread was not really researched.

Neither the conventional financial ingredients of sustained growth, given savings and investment ratios, plus demand maintenance by incomes policy or 'monetarism'; nor the establishment of Rostowian indices, of percentages of national output and savings and so on, can, or will, assure take-off for these countries. These are indices, not causative instruments. The structural changes posited will inevitably reflect later in the emergence of Rostow and Colin Clark type phenomena, critical-mass investment ratio to GNP and thinking of agricultural workforce and population in favour of industry and tertiary sectors.

On the problems, and the havoc and irredeemability of the position created by international and domestic economic policies, there has been a plethora of writings, both in journals and the media. At the media level, the contributions by Frederick Clairmonte and John Cavanagh[18] have been among the more impressive illustrations of futility of the present policies. Their conclusion is that, simply deferring interest payments and principal to the Trans-National Banking Circuit and seeking rescheduling agreements would perhaps mitigate the bleeding and pain but it could by no means stop the haemorrhage. In the meantime, for example, the World Bank in its Report to the June 1988 Sri Lanka Aid Group, stated that 'the country's economic problems are serious' and called for structural change

113

of the economy, but meant by it only financial, budgetary, fiscal, privatization and export orientation measures.[19] In another Report of about the same period, the World Bank has conceded that China and India are the only very poor nations likely to claw their way out of poverty by 1995. All poor nations were hit during the last fifteen years by rising prices of oil, falling prices of other commodities, rising debt service costs, and cuts in aid from rich countries. But both China and India, according to the Bank, had uncommonly high savings rates and relatively low per capita external debt. While these are given as the reasons, the actual reasons for this healthy situation, which are 'structural' in the sense used in this paper, are unfortunately not touched upon. Jacques Attali, spokesman for President Mitterrand, in a letter to the Group of Seven (G-7) for their June meeting in Toronto, declared that the impoverished countries must 'make effort at managing their economies' after the debt write-off of one-third of their debts, as suggested by Mitterrand. What this management of the economies constitutes is not discussed. Meanwhile Third World countries have widely and frequently criticized the IMF for their social and political upheavals. Slogans have been common in the Third World continents. In 1984, over 50 people were killed in the Dominican Republic by riots sparked off by price increase which the Fund had ordered. In 1985, the Sudanese Government was toppled by the military after the IMF suspended loans. In early 1987 Uganda was turning to barter in order to side step the IMF requirements. Alan Garcia in Peru announced a unilateral policy in 1985 regarding servicing of its debts, limiting repayments to 10 per cent of export earnings. Even on the Baker Plan of that year, Garcia saw policies that looked much like an attempt to maintain monetarism as an official theory, whose conditions aggravated the problems from which countries like his were suffering. Even a respected source, such as the Executive Director of UNICEF, had to say in a statement in July 1988, that the strategies followed in the past six years may have brilliantly succeeded in containing Third World debt problems, but at the cost of tremendously increasing human suffering in many developing countries, and possibly some

114

millions have already died as a consequence. The Executive Director quoted Julius Nyerere, the former Tanzanian President, to ask whether African nations must starve their children to pay their debts.[20]

Nor were International Commodity Agreements any help or substitute. In terms of one Report[21] 'all the agreements which have existed from time to time covering copper, wheat, cacao, sugar, coffee, have had rough patches'. The most publicized Third World contribution that UNCTAD recently attempted, namely, the Common Fund for primary commodities, little more than falls in this category.[22] Without alternative policy, the developing countries will continue to be developing, gaps and all, losing sight of far more basic changes that they themselves must seek inside their own countries and between them. UNCTAD in its Annual Report on Trade and Development of 1984 had come to the stage of stating that lagging Third World economies would not be revived as a mere by-product of economic recovery in industrial countries. It proposed no concrete solutions but said that what was required was 'an alternative approach' linking trade and financial problems to those of employment and development. Enoch Powell, for all his other views, was right when he stated:

> When the West stands aghast at the destitution of the new countries, it is looking upon its own handiwork. With typical European arrogance, we have presumed that those we no longer govern are incapable of finding the lines on which to organise their own affairs; with typical European selfishness we have used our economic power to prevent them from doing so. Then having declined to let them work out their own salvation—a rough translation of laissez-faire—we face the spectacle of resulting havoc with no notion but to go on with more and more of the same, pouring endless aid into the gulf we are forever deepening.[23]

A leading Indian journal emphasized the inadequacy of Western policy in a forceful media illustration in one of its issues.[24] While the essential ingredients of Indian policy were round import restriction, domestic production of currently imported goods eventually resulted in elimination of all but essential imports. The intellectual foundation of this strategy had been laid by Prebisch, Myrdal and others. It was argued that only after industrialization had proceeded some way that increased production could be reflected in large export earnings. It is undeniable that 'whatever the other shortcomings, the strategy has contributed to the emergence of India as one of the foremost industrial powers in the Third World'. That some aspects of the Indian trade policy system are restrictive and outmoded has been readily granted, with the warning that one should not throw the baby out with the bath water. Most Western commentators, while analysing the success of the four Far East Asian countries invariably attribute it to the free trade policies of these governments. Very little attention is focused on the structural transformation that these economies had undergone before they launched their export drive. These include South Korea, Taiwan and Japan. Their experience proves that it was the dynamics of the internal revolution within the economy, rather than free trade policies that was responsible for their success. The Philippines had also followed an import substitution strategy in the 1950s. But during the early 1960s the economy was completely liberalized. The accent was on free trade and export led growth. There were no comprehensive land reforms or any fundamental restructuring of the economy. Consequently, during the last two and a half decades, contrary to expectations, the liberalization strategy has actually weakened the economy. Income differentials have become acute, unemployment has increased, vertically integrated firms dominate the plantation sector and the country has one of the worst debt problems in Asia.

The experience of Chile is even more illuminating. All the so-called financial and fiscal restructuring common to EP-oriented policies were adopted. But 'under the new dispensation there was no clear vision of an overall development strategy, except to rely as much as possible on market forces. The results of these policies were not long in manifesting themselves. Industrial production declined as superior goods from abroad freely entered the economy and destroyed the infant industries in the country.

116

Consequently, unemployment increased and it was estimated that between 1974 and 1983 Chile lost nearly a quarter of a million jobs in the industrial sector. Further, foreign exchange reserves were depleted and Chile was obliged to go into large-scale commercial borrowing both for current consumption and for investment. The experience of these two countries—and the examples can be easily multiplied—shows that liberalisation without fundamental restructuring of the economy will lead not only to no growth but to actual de-industrialisation....

Having noted that the Latin American countries, following debt led growth, contracted huge debts which they are now in no position to repay, the writer concludes by quoting Arthur Lewis that 'The engine of growth should be technological change, with industrial trade serving as lubricating oil and not as fuel. International trade cannot substitute for technological change: so, those who depend on it as their major hope are doomed to frustration'.

The same paper in an editorial on 1 January 1988, describes a proposed World Bank/IMF regimen on further depreciation of the rupee and its proferred benefits and calls it 'an unconcealed reiteration of the often touted concept of export-led growth' and asks whether the additions to the export earnings will be such as to make a significant impact on the overall trade balance. It notes that devaluation would aggravate the heavy burden of external debt and reinforce inflationary forces.

In a letter addressed to the Prime Minister of the United Kingdom[25] and acknowledged thereafter,[26] the present writer explained that the external contingency facility and the broader 'menu' of direct private sector lending, bonds into equities *et al.*, remained, in the former case, a palliative, and in the latter opened a door, but if tied to real growth policy. While the position at the time of the IMF/Bank meeting in 1987 was therefore one of caution, it was also one of opportunity. In the context of policies so far pursued, the present writer had stated:

all current public aid flows end up in only perpetuating dependence on Aid. Your [UK's] own prospect as a Donor, is only of ever-recurring Aid demands, in increasing

117

quantities. The policy pressed in my communication, while positing an initial Aid flow, posits its early elimination, as the all-encompassing obsession and preoccupation of the poor and the rich countries in so-called international development cooperation. If so, the traditional Aid pattern has to be stopped early and the new pattern set up, geared to a visible horizon for its tapering off.

A similar letter was addressed[27] to the US Secretary to the Treasury, without response.

As stated earlier, in the professional literature of academia, although there is an emphasis of the traditional thinking and policies, there are points at which at least the types of alternatives necessary come out. The international debt crisis itself is described mostly in standard terms.[28] Fisher, for example, concludes by suggesting that 'with sensible debt relief, countries and the multi-lateral institutions can begin to worry about growth-oriented development policies. If the debt relief does not come by agreement, then debtor countries would have to consider taking the first step'. Heller states: 'Ultimately, the international debt crisis can be overcome only by enlarging the economic pie through economic growth and increased exports by the debtor countries'. His description of the international debt crisis of 1982 is as succinct and clear as any:

> The global recession of the early 1980's and the associated fall in commodity prices produced a sharp curtailment of the earnings of the developing countries. At the same time, the real and nominal interest rates surged, straining the financial resources of the LDCs until they were no longer able to fulfil their financial commitments, thereby triggering the crisis of 1982.

Even Krueger, despite stringent views on inadequate LDCs' financial discipline, stated 'In Mexico's case, highly expansionary macro-economic policy had been financed through capital inflows that seemed warranted based on her rapidly rising oil exports. Nonetheless, that macro-economic policy was unsustainable; there could be no reasonable doubt that Mexico's debt crisis was the result of domestic economic policies.'

Undoubtedly this refers, in Krueger's thinking, to the need for more EP. It is a continuation of earlier thinking, for example, the contention that South Korea's success was simply due to its change from IS to EP policies at the time of its growth.[29] That the export expansions were via new IS product bases (industrial, agricultural, social and infrastructural) is not picked up. Perhaps the best *reductio ad absurdum* of the EP argument is offered by Hans Singer.[30]

> The question is not whether EOI (Export Oriented Industrialisation) is desirable, but whether it is possible.... A recent analysis has indicated[31] on the basis of a simulation exercise, that if all LDCs in the mid-seventies had the same export intensity as South Korea, Taiwan, Hong Kong and Singapore, adjusting for differences in size and level of industrialisation, this would involve a more than 700 per cent increase in Third World manufactured exports... This would result in untenable market penetration into industrial countries.

In a sense, the case for strengthening DPB as the basis for both internal growth and export growth, may be found in the 1930s and 1940s, in writings such as those of Allyn and Young, Rosenstein-Rodan[32] and Mandelbaum.[33] Without doubt, there were a number of other writers, some would go back to Quesnay's Tableau Economique coming down to Sraffa. Earlier, we had mentioned Schumpeter's contribution on 'The Concept of Technology and Creative Destruction' as an agent of change.

There are also, in the course of surveying specific development efforts, references to the role, if not of MTE directly, at least to its basis. Undoubtedly many examples can be adduced by others. The following are purely random citations. Dwight Heald Perkins[34] points out that China's per capita product rose three-fold between 1953 and 1985. 'Rises in per capita income of that magnitude are usually accompanied by important changes in the structure of national product and China is no exception to that rule'. 'The emphasis was on industry and autarchy. Within industry, the focus was on the heavy industry sector, particularly machinery and steel. Between 1972 and 1976, the degree of heavy industry rose from 36 per cent of the gross value of industrial output to 56 per cent. In quite a different context, discussing a continuation of the decline of the United States economy,[35] Seymour Melman observes that the number of engineers and scientists per 10,000 of the labour force in 1965 was 64.1 per cent in the United States, 24.6 per cent in Japan, and 26.6 per cent in West Germany. For 1977 the number of engineers and scientists in civilian activity per 10,000 of the labour force in the United States was 38 per cent, 40 per cent in West Germany and 50 per cent in Japan. The machine, tool and electronic industries have been important areas where the pre-emption of technical talent by the military has played a part in so weakening competitive position, as to hasten the decline and even disappearance of major sectors of those industries.

Gavin Wright[36] observed for the American South at the time of its transition that it lacked a strong indigenous community of engineers and economists. 'Here is the element of truth in the "colonial economy" thesis, and it is no small matter'. 'The fundamental problem', he observed, 'was not the small size of the economy; rather it was the historic absence of an indigenous technological community and the high set-up costs required to establish one'. And then, 'while the South continued to rely on outside machinery and expertise, Japan began to create a distinctive technology.... These developments stand in strong contrast to the relative technical passivity of the Southern industry'.

John W. Mellor and Bruce F. Johnston[37] emphasized that 'the common feature of the success achieved in Japan, Taiwan and Korea is that each country created an effective agricultural research system, a good rural infrastructure and comprehensive input delivery system and a deep and broadening educational system'. Although these countries had no communal farming, a notable feature was that irrigation systems at the farm level played a major role both in construction and use of irrigation and drainage systems. Although our prime concern in this paper has been with MTE, these were, clearly, foundations for the establishment of a proper DPB.

Finally, as a brief reference to the Soviet Union, Gur Ofer[38] states that 'the classical Soviet investment strategy first follows the objective function in attracting the lion's share of investment to producer-goods industries.... as the key to rapid growth'. The second distinction made in the Soviet economy has been between 'productive' and 'non-productive' investments. The latter included those in services as well as administration and allied fields. A perference of Soviet investors was for investment in core production processes as against auxiliary functions, left to simpler labour-intensive technology, so as to allow the concentration of scarce capital in key processes.

Obviously, all these opinions, findings or conclusions are not for copying blindly, but they do provide pointers, whether we like it or not, to certain invariable and unavoidable policy decisions for really effective and sustained growth amongst the developing countries. It is those policy decisions that have yet to be made, and researched.

V

The expressed policies for growth, distinct from the countries that have grown, have failed to lead developing countries from their 'dependent' debt and deficit laden status to 'non-dependent', self-reliant growth.

The international cooperation policies, and those of the IMF, have been virtually self-defeating, with countries that are wobbly being pulled up by their necks only to collapse again.

The thrust in these policies has been as if what was needed by the poor countries was to overcome their debt situation somehow and once this was done they had no other problem. The real situation was starkly different, namely, that the countries would fall into deep debt again because that was in their set-up and their organic nature. The need to attend to this has not been really addressed.

As a result, the great international forums and discussions on debt, for remedy of the situation of afflicted countries, have been on the symptoms, with debates on doles, deferments and waivers, and more lending, but no thinking on the basic causes of future debts.

121

The Wealth of Poor Nations

Clearly, the theory of growth of dependent countries has to change from being based on the present policies, to concepts of creating Domestic Production Bases (DPB) for domestic and export purposes, as all developed countries, old and new, did.

There is a rich field awaiting economic specialists: (a) to research the basis of DPB creation, and the role of MTE, along, of course, with the other established prerequisites to which this paper has referred earlier; and (b) by direct or indirect means, to elicit data and statistic of already developed countries in these terms in order to revise and to carry forward an alternative theory and approach, such as suggested, towards development of the developing countries.

In the meantime, the evidence of this study is strong enough to call now for a policy change amongst the assisting countries, the World Bank and the IMF, towards the developing countries. These are primarily towards addressing themselves to building MTE capacity (in addition to land reform and wage goods establishment) in these countries, in place of current stunted EP policies. Exports would follow. These changes may well entail policies, different from the present, on what is now called restructuring, without meaning merely the fiscal and financial policies in these countries.

In its import and implications for the world, the attention to redeeming the developing countries from their present impasse must, in any case, be considered to be on a par with the attention drawn to the twin threats of nuclear and ecological disaster. That is the measure of the priority that we need to give to the subject raised here, whatever the further work and effort needed on it.

Notes

1   As formulated in an exchange of notes with the Institute of Development Studies at Sussex, 1988.
2   Arthur Lewis, *The Case of Development*. New York, Washington, London: Praeger, 1973,p.66.
3   The concept is not without links to Schumpeter's emphasis on Technological Innovation and his fascinating idea of Creative Destruction.

122

Debts, Deficits and the Development of Developing Countries

See also R.D. Norton, 'Industrial Policy and American Renewal'. *Journal of Economic Literature*, vol.XXIV, no. 1, March 1986, pp. 1-40

4   c.f. Chapter II

5   For example, the Harrod-Domar model, in itself consistent and useful.

6   In another connection, I had once observed that economics had for the most part never created development, only annotated it after it had occurred.

7   A Third World writer on the 100th anniversary of Marx's death wrote: 'Marx discovered the law of motion of capitalist society through the theory of surplus value....' N. Sanmugathasan, *Ceylon Daily News*, 14 March 1983. Indeed in it was also the law of motion of socialist society, save that ownership and management of the surplus was in another segment of society.

8   A survey on its pioneers such as Rosenstein-Rodan, Mandelbaum, Allyn and Young in the 1930's and 1940's appears in the earlier books of C.Suriyakumaran, *The Economics of Full Employment in Agricultural Countries*. Colombo: K.V.G. De Silva & Co., 1957; and *Ceylon, Beveridge and Bretton Woods*. Colombo: C. Suriyakumaran, 1946.

9   A complimentary term referring to China. Taiwan, South Korea, Hong Kong and Singapore.

10   See n.8 for a very early discussion of the role of wage goods in C.Suriyakumaran, *Ceylon, Beveridge and Bretton Woods*, 1943. The original use of the phrase 'wage goods' industries in the sense applicable to modern analysis was perhaps in Rosenstein-Rodan, *Economic Journal*, June-September 1943.

11   Having had, at one time, no less a leadership than that of Raul Pre bisch, with great influence on the Third World and on UNCTAD during the 1960's.

12   In a personal communication exchanged with the President of the US Foundation in July 1986.

13   Among its well-known lead agents were the ILO Employment Studies series for various countries; and Schumacher, whose essential wisdom became diluted by its later indiscriminate application. Perhaps confusion still reigns in the environment area, with inability to discriminate between small-scale, low cost and non-waste or low waste technology.

14   Amartya K.Sen, *The Choice of Techniques*. Oxford, 1967.

15   Newberry, 'Public Policy in the Dual Economy'. *Economic Journal*, June 1972.

16   C.Suriyakumaran, *Economics of Full Employment*, n.8,p.171.

17   Adler, 'Fiscal and Monetary Implications of Development Programmes'. *American Economic Review*, May 1952. See also Yale Brozen, 'Investment, Innovation and Initiation', May 1951.

18   On UNCTAD and the US Institute for Policy Studies see Frederick Clairmonte and John Cavanagh, 'The Third World Debt Unpayable'. *Third World Network*.

19   Report of World Bank to Sri Lanka Aid Group, June 1988 in *New York Times Service, Sunday Times,* 17 July 1988.

20   Julius Nyerere as quoted in 'Best of Reports'. *Reuter and Third World Network Features,* July 1988.

21   Alec Gordon, 'Economist Intelligence Unit'. *Financial Guardian,* 4 December 1985.

22   In a notable statement Hans Singer, quoting J.E. Benham states, 'The gains from price stabilisation to the developed countries were at least three times the size of the gains to the developing countries'. Singer, 'Mutual and Conflicting Interests in Relations with the Third World'. Adam Weiler Memorial Lecture, 1982; Benham, *International Commodity Agreements: An Evaluation of the United Integrated Commodity Programmes.* Overseas Development Council Monograph no.9, NIEO Series. Washington D.C., 1977.

23   Enoch Powell, 'The Gilt Edge of World Aid Havoc'. *Guardian,* 7 October 1985.

24   'The Chimera of Export-Led Growth'. *The Hindu,* 28 January 1986.

25   30 September 1987.

26   9 October 1987.

27   8 October 1987.

28   One of such professional presentations is the set of articles assembled under the authorship of Krueger, Fisher and Heller, *American Economic Review,* vol.77, no. 2, May 1987, pp.159-75.

29   Ahne O.Krueger, 'Trade Policies in Developing Countries', in *Hand book of International Economics.* Vol.1.ch.2, 1984.

30   Quoted from an unpublished paper by Hans Singer, 'Import Substitution Revisited in a Darkening External Environment', 1986.

31   Cline, 'Can the East Asian Model of Development be Generalised'. *World Development,* vol. 10, no.2,pp.81-90.

32   Rosenstein-Rodan, *Economic Journal,* June/September 1943.

33   Mandelbaum, 'Industrialisation of Backward Areas'. *Monograph Series* no.2.Oxford: Basil Blackwell, 1945.

34   Dwight H.Perkins, 'Reforming China's Economic System'. *Journal of Economic Literature,* vol.XXVI, no.2, June 1988,pp.631-32.

35   Seymour Melman, 'Economic Consequences of the Arms Race: The Second Rate Economy'. *American Economic Review,* May 1988, p.56.

36   Gavin Wright, 'The Economic Revolution in the American South'. *The Journal of Economic Perspectives,* vol.1,no. 1,1987,pp. 167-69.

37   John W.Mellor and Bruce F. Johnston, 'The World Food Equation: Inter-relations among Development, Employment and Food Consumption'. *Journal of Economic Literature,* June 1984,pp.556-62.

38   Gur Ofer, 'Soviet Economic Growth 1928-1985'. *Journal of Economic Literature,* December 1987,p. 1807.

124

Chapter Nine

Environment and Development Management

We have seen before, how in the course of development efforts and development co-operation during these decades past, various lead ideas have been at one time or another advanced for priority attention by developing countries. Some of these ideas were also mentioned briefly, particularly in connection with international conferences organised on them. At one time, family planning would solve the development problems; at another, it is national housing programmes; or again it was social development; and so on.

This mode of approach also applies to what was contentious area in earlier years, namely social development planning, then placed in opposition to economic development planning. While social change is not a pre-condition of development, it can precede development, can accompany it and can also be the result of development. It is thus very necessary to link planning in a socio-economic frame. One may distinguish between marginal problems in social change and mass problem, in which the mass problems are often automatically overcome by development itself and it is the marginal problems that become the object of social welfare services.[1] As concluded at an interdisciplinary conference to prepare for an educational programme related to development, it was a necessary for the social planners to know how the economic machine worked and whence the resources for social programmes came, as for the economic planners to know the roles and relationship of social

125

change to economic growth. The possibility, and the need, for such integrative approaches did not relate to economic planning alone. They would extend over various other disciplines and functional areas such as policies, laws and educational patterns. In this Chapter, we concentrate on the now over-riding issues of environment and development.

A. The Environment — Development Background

I. *Environment* itself, as a subject, is still not comprehensively understood, whether by practising environmentalists or by other professionals. Despite their confidence to the contrary, it is not certain that Development too, as a term, is correctly understood, whether by development economists, or other specialists, including sociologist, environmentalists and political scientists. Much less, therefore, one must presume, may a phrase such as the Environment-Development Background, be considered to be adequately understood. As we shall see below, the whole attempt to do so, has been (a) of recent origin; and (b) still not what one might call, 'an available body of knowledge'. The numbers who have given attention to this seriously and cohesively are indeed still extremely few. Let us look at these concepts briefly.

Today, environmental concepts have edged grudgingly - grudgingly one must say — to more relevant relations with development. But in its origins, the environment content was quite different. It is very important to understand this because, it seems that factor still influences the present situation; as also influencing the attempts being made at solutions. For example, at all the stages leading to the World Conference on Environment and Development (UNCED), there were the same mental blocks in trying to find meeting grounds between environment and development.

The original concepts had two characteristics. There have been many descriptions given, but basically they boil down to two essential characteristics in their original contexts. One was, if one might use captions, as an 'esoteric', and the other as a 'specific' characteristic. The *esoteric* character was of environment as 'conservation' — an exotic of luxury, where even concepts of wildlife and the conservation of rare species were originally mooted by those who were well off, who enjoyed the luxury of looking at these things from their perspectives and their points of view. The *specific* characteristic was the old view of environment as pollution out of development. We shall come to the other pollution, out of poverty, later on. But this was the pollution out of development. It was, of course, at the time, a total irrelevance to those who never had any development to talk of.

This indeed was the old concept of environment with which the environment movement was launched. It was, therefore, only much later, out of the clash with development lobbies and with the development imperatives, that the environment definitions became widened and then the environment think tanks, or enlightened groups within environmental circles, led a new type of thinking. This came up with concepts like 'the resources of the environment are the resources of development'; that the environment is the 'source of all resources as well as the sink of all wastes'; and that pollution from poverty is sharply distinct from the pollution from affluence.

But a more interesting facet of the relationship or clash was that development too became accepted as essential. This was not something that was there before. Early on, the phrase 'eco-development' caught on. Nobody really defined properly what eco-development was, but everybody was satisfied to use this phrase because it avoided clashes between the two disciplines. A little later, the phrase 'development without destruction' emerged. Again there was no precise definition of what this development or destruction was meant to be. Finally, of course, with the Bruntland Commission, which set the whole thing rolling as of now, the phrase 'sustainable development' became 'coinage'. This, again, was never defined - least as methodology[1] - but the phrase was there. Thus, after the early beginnings, there was an approximation towards acceptance of development by the environmental thought systems, and an attempt to formulate phraseology, captions, titles, linkages which described how they had common ground.

Now the whole defect of this was that, while there was linkage, there was *no methodology*, the only 'methodology' being the Environmental Impact Assessment Tool which, as we shall explain later, suffered from serious defects.

The result was that there were *some muddled concepts* of the development concession, that is, the concession to development that environment made. One of these concepts was that development is elimination of poverty; that it is an anti-poverty programme, and not much more than that. At least, it was implied that it was not much more than that. There was a moral tag attached to the degradation of poverty, and the whole purpose of development was to eliminate poverty. So, there was very little thinking about going beyond the stage of poverty, into a higher stage of development.

There was another phrase which arose out of this concession to development, that development equals 'better' but not necessarily 'bigger'; that is, not bigger output. This, of course, is a very fine idea, because it is nice to say this. One does not have to be bigger all the time in order to be better, whether for persons, or societies, or economies. So *development* was with some self-satisfaction, conceived *as being better but not bigger*. Nobody denies that development has to make things better. But to place both these as opposites and exclusive, as we shall see later, reflects an ignorance of both these concepts.

The catch was that there is, what may best be called, *a low level equilibrium trap*. This indeed is the 'Achilles' heel' of both the concept of 'sustainable development' that the Bruntland Commission had, and this concept that development should be 'better but not bigger'. It was presumed that "sustainable development" would be an utopian satisfactory development. But in reality, and we know, from the days of Keynes, that as in economics, so in the environment-development relationship, you could have a perfect equilibrium situation in a 'low-level' equilibrium trap. That is, a *lower income level than one need have* for a sustainable eco-development situation, or an environmentally sustainable developmental equilibrium situation could be advocated *to the detriment* of development potentials and *benefits*.

It was no surprise then, that when the environmental world decided to march 'forward', particularly with the United Nations World Conference, and figure a way out to have a programme for the Year 2000, it could call it only a United Nations Conference on Environment 'and' Development, not on Environment 'for' Development. In other words, there was an *Environment programme for Conservation*; we have had this for twenty years from Stockholm. But there was *no* concept of an *Environment programme for Development*.

*   *   *

II. So much for the environment. Where does the economic view of all this stand? The classical *definition of economics*, of course, was of 'unlimited ends and limited means'; really of resources also as unlimited, and technology and capital as limited; and that *the function of economics* was to maximise productivity of the scarce factors. This is nothing new. It is all known, namely that we try to increase scarce factor supplies.

But there were some doubts that naturally entered, at a certain stage in the environment-development process, when this theory of resources as unlimited was questioned, and we think quite rightly. When the doubts entered, and resources were seen as the limiting factor, the reaction itself yielded *two* different *schools*. One was what one might call the 'chemical/ engineering school'; and the other, a school that tried to 're-define' development. The chemical/engineering school, basically, was that if resources run short in supply, science and technology could always find means of discovering new resources and alternatives, through synthetics, and so on. And, therefore, there was no real limitation. Environmentalists thus took a static view and not a dynamic view of the limitation of resources.

The second view, of course, was to take a more sympathetic attitude and, as economists, to try to re-define development. This was to see how the re-definition of development affects or should affect the presentation of economic planning as much as environmental planning.

The *traditional obstacle* that economics had was also — this is not new for those who are economists — that it was essentially 'micro'. It was, therefore, not only that 'environment', through its environment impact assessment tool (EIA) started as being micro. The classical view of the firm, as we know, was that in which ability to meet demand was determined by the capacity of the 'firm'. Supply was an externality with near infinite capacity, determined by the market and given prices, over which the individual firm had little control.

And, therefore, it is fair to say that in a milieu of economic 'constraint', when it came, it was the *environmental 'constituency'*, for all its defects, that brought to the intellectual forums of the world, the factor of what is now called *global resources*. The problem, therefore, was that the way the environmentalists formulated this very important complement to a system of thinking, created an obstacle to the economists, who naturally, 'reacted', rather than thought through the process. And this was unfortunate.

Here we may look at *something* which is very interesting. Significantly, those who are economists may not have even thought about this. As one knows, in the past, *economics* has *always assumed* demand to be subjective, and non-economic. While economics may analyse demand as a process, it assumes *demand* itself *to be subjective and non-economic*. And it had, historically, almost always reacted to such expressed externalities as *alterations in demand*, whether they were expressed through 'individual' demand (which was rare), or more likely as 'socially determined' demand, or thirdly, as 'legally inspired' conditions of demand.

For example, slavery was abolished, child labour was abolished, working hours were shortened, fair wages were introduced. We know what that means. It is that the supply of labour was reduced immediately. And by strict economic logic, this is insane! But these were changes for which there was nothing in economics to say that they had to be made, or not made. But these were socially induced changes. One could even say that the whole phenomenon of capital intensive versus labour intensive approaches to developing societies, was an externally induced prescription, which then affected supply and demand, rather than inherent in economic analysis and, therefore, a conclusion from it.[2]

130

So supply was *always* based on *this assumption,* and collaterally one has people like Kindleberger, the American economist, talking of "public goods" and Amartya Sen, the Indian, talking of "public benefits" in discussing the situation in India. It was that public entitlements and benefits are assumptions, and that the `commodity stream' in an economy should consider these things as `inherent'.

Now all this has *nothing to do with economic analysis* though *it has with social effects.* Here is a situation which has *very close parallel to 'the environmental priority'* on resource views 'as a global resource'. Thus, there should have been an opportunity for economics and environment, even at that stage when this arose, to 'meet' — that was about the late seventies or early eighties. But here again, it was the way that things were put across, and importantly, the lack of any Methodology, that created such a situation.

*   *   *

III. What is the real *situation now?* on the side of 'Environment', rather than a phrase such as 'a source and a sink', a more useful approach is to classify it under two 'Truths'. One is what may be called the 'Resource Truth'. Under the resource truth, there is no doubt of *the environmental basis* of all our living, whether from Mohenjodaro, or Mesopotamia, or now, or by the Year 2000 and beyond. One of the most telling illustrations of the Resource Truth is a little statement about the 'Plant', which a distinguished Indian scientist, once propounded on Environment Day in Delhi. 'In this whole Universe' he said 'the Plant is the only organism that manufactures its own food. Every other organism either lives on plants, or on other organisms that live on plants'. From, this flows the essential indispensability, and the fundamental importance of soil, water, air, and the related phenomena which we call the Environment. From these come all the strata of the environmental scenario — the rangelands (and forest), grasslands, croplands, lowlands, coastal areas, offshores and seas; or the oceans, deserts and global commons. So this is the heart, as inescapable as true, and it is time that we *embrace it into our economic conceptualisations and thinking.* The other is the 'Limits Truth'.

The 'Limits Truth' is best defined in a UNESCO description of some years, which still bears using. It is what are called the *four Eco-system Principles.* The first is the 'eco-sphere principle', where every element in the universe, or eco-system, is inter-related to, and inter-acting with, the other. The second is the 're-cycling principle', where every component in the eco-system is 'cycling' and re-cycling constantly. The third is the principle of 'carrying capacity', where any eco-system has a given carrying capacity, beyond which it will not be able to sustain itself. And the fourth is the principle of 'human inter-action', where human beings, perhaps more than any other, and for better or for worse, inter-act with the environment.

As for the *development* response on all this, to start with, there was a very clear recognition of the resource basis by all economists. It is simply that we cannot afford any longer to deny the very basis on which development depends. But equally clearly — and this is something that environmentalists have failed to observe — this is *not the whole truth*, especially put in that form. The reason is that *development* has, at the same time, *through history, vastly 'expanded' the available resources,* and in doing so, also, welfare. It has achieved this by technology, discovery and invention, moving us from the stone age to the wheel, and to the discovery of new raw materials and, importantly, *in the Social spheres*, to the *provision of something which never* could have *existed* otherwise, namely the welfare needs of the masses. These mean, mass needs in terms of education, health, housing, food and others. It is a *process which only development has certainly engineered and made possible.* If it is to be captioned, it has to be as having shown capacity to 'expand' resources, while still depending on the natural eco-system.

Now, this is also the means to the future, for example, in energy, through solar or hydrogen sources. For example, not long ago an Oxford University breakthrough was announced *on fusion.* It might really take fifty years for full economic use; so it is not a breakthrough yet. But the fact is, we would never have arrived at this stage if there had been no hard-nosed economic development, which provided the technology, the knowledge, the resources, the means and the education, to discover these potentials.

There is also *a lesson for the developing countries*, not very much conceded in the North. This is that 'development' is not a simple matter of an anti-poverty programme. There will be no breakthrough, otherwise, even on 'poverty', or on 'population', or environment. It is significant that a UK White Paper, as long ago as the early seventies, declared that development is the only means to meeting most, if not all, of the environmental concerns themselves. The Chinese had a nice phrase again, about the same period, that it is within the development process, and not outside of it, that solutions to be environmental problems have to be found.[3]

Yet, while saying these, let us also remember that development has produced 'careless' development. This is firstly, the profligate resources use by the rich countries. The poor countries again, unfortunately, in what is best called 'enclave' development, created poor imitations of development, in eye-sores of consumerist, mercantilist and commercial conurbations. We have cities round the world, in the poor countries, which are putrid - not out of poverty, but out of so-called 'development'.

Simultaneously, development has been guilty of non-use of opportunities. We shall come back to this later in connection with specific illustrations. We are madly producing more and more 'goods', but we are not using the opportunities for a proper view (or 'methodology') of resource use. This is the reason why environmental concepts are, justifiably, still anti-developmental; and the economic concepts reactive.

What it means is that we have an interesting feature, namely, that the environment-development *conflict now* is *not* so much one of *definitions, but of 'dynamics'*. It is not the concept any more. There is a concession, on both sides, of the

---

* The First Edition to this book had a 'Scenario' of a 'City without cars' which is not reproduced here.

development imperative and of the environmental necessity. It is on the 'process of application' of all this to reality, to mutual benefit, that there is a wall. This is really now the stage at which we are.

Let us take a few moments, therefore, to look at this 'dynamics', to round up our views as it were. Development creates a 'livable environment', but it also creates an unlivable environment. Yet, it is within the *development process* that answers to both have to be found. *Outside* it is *poverty*, the worst offender of both development and environment. It is desolate and debilitating, and will obliterate, in the end, the environment, as much with a whimper, as thoughtless development will obliterate the World with a bang. Thirdly, as we saw, *development* is not merely the *cause of resource use* or resource depletion, but also the 'means to *resource sustenance*'. Out of these, there are two things that emerge as simply paramount. That is, put very simply, we have now jointly to 'think through' the development process; and secondly, an *environmental programme*, or resources management programme, *for development* itself is an absolute necessity. The more these things proceed in isolation, the more infructious, abortive and unproductive that everything that we do in our Societies is going to be. The great threat of 'global warming' and collapse of the eco-system is no idle threat. At the heart of it is the necessity to undertake these two things.

The *great impeding factor* lies in a strange paradox that has befuddled the environmental world up to now. It is a very simple thing, implicit in what we have discussed so far, but it has existed as a paradox. This is, that of the two types of environmental management essential to a true environmental programme only one, the *Qualitative management of the environment* has been *addressed* by the Developed world. The other, which is the *Quantitative aspect of the environment*, has received little recognition, and even less implementation. By quantitative, we mean not only the question of *excessive resource* use by the North, but the *massive resource need* by the South. In other words, for the South, environmental management requires not simply less resources, nor even the same level of them, but many times the resources they are using now. But we do not

134

find this in the *'catechism' of environmental programming* at the moment; and the economists, unfortunately, have been going around with 'slogans' and not with methodologies, which, like the environmentalists, they have still to find. The reason is, of course, that the environmental programme and its ideas started in the North; and now, it has been an imposition of them on the South, to the detriment of the South. Unfortunately, no matter. Because the South is going to end up using more resources!

In the meantime, what we have had out of this past historical situation, and the neo-historical recent situations, is an *'asymmetrical' policy prescription*, one for the North and another for the South. There was, what once a Spanish writer called, *the vertical invasion of the masses* in Europe, during the industrial revolution, when Europe used, not less resources, but far more resources. Also, the population increases accompanied, or followed, did not precede as they have in the South. But now, the South is being furnished with advice which is the opposite, namely to use less resources, or to contain resource use — the 'asymmetrical' policy prescription we talked of.

Herein, therefore, is *the problematique* that we have, of the 'interaction of environment and development'.[4] Too much resources for the North, and success in Qualitative management by the North, although there is a lot more to do; but a complete forfeiture of the Quantitative side of the management. For the South, too little resources, with also failure on Qualitative management and soon, whether we like it or not, an enormous increase in resources, due by the year 2000, *without the means*, the *wherewithal* and the *intellectual preparation*, for a fusion of environment and economic management, in terms that we have seen here to be so vital.

B. The Policy Framework

I. We saw that there was a distinct demarcation between developing country priorities and those of developed countries, in the environment-development relationships. Considering the rather *disjointed presentations* often made available to developing countries, whether as policy advice, or other offerings, a clear idea of the policy framework that would be relevant to developing countries *per se*, for sound environmental management in development, becomes essential. We, therefore, set out an important presentation of concepts, definitions and content, that must guide our policy designs for Environmental Management.

The subject is extensive, and the descriptions do not seek to go into all of its aspects. Rather, we take a look here at the foundational concepts that serve as the major physical bases for organised management. These are of population, resources, and what may be 'limits to growth'. Although separately classified, they are, of course, inter-related; and the descriptions here reflect that. Let us begin with population.

*   *   *

II. Perhaps the most oft-treated aspect of human resources, *population* constitutes along with natural resources, the two foundational concepts of environment-development management and its implications in both eco-system conservation and sustainable development. We do not intend to go back to Malthus. But it does not mean that we have a balanced view at all today of this question. Population growth in the Third World has been taken up *as if* it were a *single agent* of destructive resource use. The multiple inter-relations between population, resources, environment and development are *much more complex* than that. It is quite legitimate that population be a centre-piece in any concern of outer limits management; but it is more *than counting numbers, or of* the developing *countries alone*.

People are the beginning and the end of most of our intellectual and other pre-occupations, their cause and their purpose. The problem caused by this has been with us for a long time. In some ways, it looks simple and has been even interpreted in simplistic terms, as a question of numbers: that the population question is one of the expanding numbers of people — men and women and children in this globe — whose growth has to be contained. But it is as complex, if we might say, as it is simple. Just as an example, if there were no problems of income differentials in a population structure, then there is no population problem. The best way of looking at the question itself seems to be in *terms of two time scenarios*, the perspectives for the nineties and on being the first.

The second is the 21st Century scenario, in which a very simple implication is that the world cannot take an exponential growth rate. This is simply a game of space and numbers. There has been one computation some years ago, to say that if the population grew at the rate posited at that time in many countries, by the year 2000 there would be only standing space in the world. One would not want to labour with examples like this, where it is of course easy to see the implications of such progress. One could well state one thing very clearly, namely that this sort of situation would never occur for the simple reason that people will just exterminate themselves even before it reached this point. Yet, the spectre of this type of exponential growth is there and this is the biggest factor in the so-called 21st Century perspective.

Therefore, right from now — and this is *the first component* in population strategy — every policy, every acceptable means, every break that can be applied in terms of containing the *unrestrained growth of population*, must be so applied. There is no doubt that at some time the world must realise a 'standstill' growth rate as we have it in some developed countries. Otherwise, we may simply reproduce ourselves out of existence.

But in the application of this type of family planning and policies, we need *also* to be a little cautious and be sure we look at the total picture. Are we right in assuming that straightforward, mechanical, demographic and family planning policies are the totality of tools and instruments for meeting the population problem? We could answer this for the time being in the form of a question: Is that how countries which are presently having stable populations achieved this stable rate and solved their population problems? This is a historical question with evidence right here today. Let us take this up with the second scenario, of the shorter term, that we mentioned.

137

As far as this century's[5] problem was concerned, one could not slot it into the type of solutions that are relevant for the 21st century. There are at least two types of factors relevant to this. One is what we called *the historical* question. Is there, or is there not, a lesson to be drawn from historical experience of those countries which are today having stable population growth rates or stationary rates, but which had a high growth rate in the past, say, a hundred years, fifty years, or twenty-five years ago? If they did not achieve this by what are called today family planning approaches, how did they achieve this?

The second factor is that there is an *existing* vast *population*, in any case, with a compulsive need to meet the basic needs, and more, of this population. It is nothing more, or nothing less, than the challenge of providing the resources and providing the means to development for the vast population. So, as opposed to the '21st Century', we have a counterpoise and a different type of priority for the '20th Century' - viewing, of course, the latter as going into some years thereafter as well.

As we know, world population will, we are told, by the year 2000 be six million. The population of Asia is expected to be three and a half billion by the year 2000. That is the broad canvas. Within this, we have been told that the developing countries are generally considered to be over-populated. In fact, this is considered the problem. Now if what we have been saying earlier about the immediate scenario is true, then the fact of developing countries being given a blanket classification as being over-populated, it seems, needs a little closer look. There seems to be something more than the *figures* behind the over-population *definitions* and concepts. *For example*, if we talk of density per square kilometre, say in 1977, we could take a few country cases. This density in Belgium was 325, West Germany 247, Netherlands 339, and, one more on this side of the world, in Japan 306. There are more cases. Against these, the population density per square kilometre in India was 190, Malaysia 38, Nepal 93, Pakistan 94, Philippines 150, Sri Lanka 213 and Thailand 86.

The question we may ask is: How is it that a high figure in one case is classified as over-population and in another case as not over-population? Or, conversely: How is it that a low figure in one case is not considered as under-population and in another case it is considered so? What we are thrown back on is a very important fact. As a picture of the population dimension, for the future as for social and political stability, there is something wrong with these figures or something wrong with the interpretation of these figures. The statistics are sound; so there is something wrong with the interpretation. It is obvious, therefore, that the analytical *problem* is not simply population, but *population plus resources*.

As we recalled earlier, during the *Industrial Revolution* in Europe, the population in Europe shot up, if we may talk in round figures, from 100 to 300 million. What happened at that time were two things. Firstly, alongside the enormous increase in the population, there was an increase in the harnessing and in the use of resources. This was fundamental. Secondly, when the stage of development had reached what is today called 'the take off stage' and the 'high mass consumption stage' there was *automatically a levelling off*, ending finally after the last World War, in a standstill demographic growth picture.

This was the situation and the historical experience that we had. The same historical experience stands repeated in the case of Japan, although one country cannot be compared exactly with another. Thus, if there is an *over-population problem* in most of Asia, it is also because of *a resource problem*. It is not an over-population problem *per se*. It is also because resources have not been sufficient. Such a poverty problem has an interesting *analytical meaning*, because it means that, while we are pursuing family planning policies, demographic analyses and actions, we should, equally, push for the development and the use of more resources. It has another potential value in that if we do this and raise the per capita incomes of the peoples from poverty lines, the chances are that this as much as mechanical family planning policies, perhaps more in some cases, would help to level off and to reduce the rate of growth in the population. In these situations, the 'Outer' limits are *not human congestion, but resource privation*.

If, for developing countries, the core issue in resource management for maximum growth is resource availability, then past socio-economic conditions under which resources were exploited need serious re-consideration. First, the poverty situation itself has to be reversed sharply and urgently — even in order to arrest the vast degradation, depletion and loss of vital developmental resources. Secondly, it means utilising at least twice, perhaps three or five times more resources than the population of the Third World are utilising today. The *management challenge* is not to conserve resources — as must be relevant to the developed world — but to use more resources and to find out how to tap these resources without affecting outer limits and future availability. As of now, the big resource users are not in the Third World, but in the developed countries. With anything between twenty to forty times the consumption per capita of resources by an individual in the developed world, compared to that in the developing world, one way of looking at the resource, population and limits relationship is to consider that the *population of Europe*, if say 400 million in round figures, is at least *8,000 million in resource use terms*, if not more. Beside such a figure, a population of 800 or 1,000 million in India or China, pales into relative insignificance and falls into a much better perspective. Given the historical rate of use, of world resources so far, the past centuries of exploitation of natural resources, and the lack of any signs of alternative lifestyles in the developed countries, the Third World has to plan vigorously against possible limits to resource availabilities in pursuit of undisputed growth imperatives. As we emphasised, and we need to repeat, Third World resources have been vastly degraded in poverty conditions and now they are vastly needed in enormous quantities for development.

* * *

III. It is necessary to understand therefore, that *resources* are *not* to be obtained simply by *market means, nor* by present, mostly *negative, environmental policies.* The first challenge in outer limits management for growth, therefore, is to introduce into resources planning the necessary dimensions, *a methodology* of handling, which we mentioned, but which we must set out now, recalling the foregoing discussions.

140

DESIGNS AND POLICIES *

A Policy Design for
Environmental Management in Development
(The Management Package)

I. Background

1. The Environment Concept embraces all Sectors, not any one sector or sectors. It is a dimension *in all sectors.*

2. In its Definition, it is not only to do with 'pollution' and 'conservation' (in the sense of 'preservation'), but with *all resource endowments.*

3. Poverty, and *lack of development* are causes of some of the worst *environmental degradation* and problems.

" [The foregoing may be expressed, as Propositions, in the following three elements:

— The *Environment,* is simply the totality of all our resources, literally under the sun;

— *Environment management,* is the *use* of resources,** not their non-use; and

---

* Based on a framework first done in the mid-seventies.

** There is no such thing in Nature, in Society, in Economics, or in proper Environment management, as not using resources. The concept of *destruction in conservation* — let alone natural cataclysm — *should be accepted as 'inherent'* in Management, turning our attention then to the 'nature of the resource use cycle' itself, away from negativism.

Perhaps we should recall that the greater Indian metaphysical tradition does not overwhelm itself with a negative view of 'Destruction', declaring that *Creation* itself contains *Preservation* and *Destruction* (re-constitution) each part of the other (symbolised in Brahma, Vishnu and Shiva). The profound Buddhist tradition of 'Impermanence' and 'Change' underlines the same Truth. So, perhaps, St.John in the Gospel, when he says that the 'seed' must first fall to the ground and *'destroy' itself, before it may 'create' life.* The Sufi tradition in Islam underscores this same Unity in change. And so does the, even more ancient, Tao metaphysic of the Far East.

— *Environment management for development*, is the use of all resources, *alongside* sustained maintenance of future resource levels.]"

4. Development and Environment are, thus, joint environmental goals — as they are *joint development goals* — not separate and competing.

"[The solutions to the problems of the environment must be found within the process of development, and not outside of it." (China);
" Development is in fact the means by which many, if not all, of the problems of the environment are solved.]"(UK)

5. Environmental Conservation is, therefore, not merely the *'Conservation of resources'*, but also the *'Conservation of development'*.
Conversely, development is the creation of a livable environment'. Certainly, not the 'consumerist', 'mercantilist' or 'commercial' type of development emerging in the name of development. If an Environment is 'unlivable', then there has been an under-use, over-use, or wrong use, of resources.

6. Even as the issue of Environment arises out of 'use' of resources, and therefore of degradation, depletion, and exhaustion of resources; so, the *Methodology* of environmental management is not a series of 'restrictions', but the full spectrum of three inherent functions, of Restoration (of degraded resources), *Maintenance* (of resources while being used) and Enhancement (of resources through a vast range of 're-use'/replacement strategies and technologies).

7. The resulting environmental *Plan* is a *Design for 'maximum' development with assured Eco-system balance, and Policies for their sustenance.*

142

Environment and Development Management

8. The Framework of such a Plan rests:

(a) on four Eco-system principles, namely,

— the 'Eco-sphere principle', in which all the elements in the Eco-system are related to one another;

— the 'Re-cycling principle', in which all the constituents in the system are continuously 'cycling' and re-cycling among themselves;

— the 'Carrying Capacity principle', in which a given Eco-system of land, water or air, has a natural limit to its capacity to sustain itself; and

— the principle of 'Human inter-action', in which human beings, more than any other in the system, can alter the environmental configuration, for better or for worse; and

(b) on four *Management Tools* (also cited at the end) namely:

— Comprehensive Resources Balance Sheets (for all major resources);

— Integrated Environment-Development c/b presentations (in place of EIAs);

— an Expanded System of National Accounts ('SEEA' in supplement of SNA); and

— Environmental (Green) Audits (as supplement to Financial Audits).

143

II. Guidelines for Plan Formulation

In a search for guidelines, the following broad indications are set out:

1. In the *first Group* are problems which may be loosely termed 'Micro' (meaning specific. 'Unit' type, similar to the 'Firm' in Micro economics) and are essentially *Qualitative* in nature. These share the 'classic' view of Environment as 'pollution' and 'conservation'.

   Typically, these are about *'fragile eco-systems'*, such as:

   (a) watersheds,
   (b) rangelands,
   (c) forests,
   (d) grasslands,
   (e) croplands,
   (f) genetic resources,
   (g) endangered species,
   (h) habitat (the basis for (f) and (g), both natural and human),
   (i) mangroves,
   (j) coastal areas; and island eco-systems; *and* the *'classic' pollution* source (solid, liquid, gaseous) such as :

      (i) soils (fertilizers/pesticides, etc.),
      (ii) water (run-offs, eutrophication, etc.),
      (iii) wastes (agro, industrial, fisheries, transport, human settlements),
      (iv) 'disasters' (siltation, epidemic, starvation, 'Bhopals', 'Chernobyls'),
      (v) 'apocalypses' (Ozone, Global Warming, Sea level rise, and others).

2. The *second Group*, by and large at the 'Macro' Level, is *Quantitative* in nature, *not hitherto reckoned in the Environmental 'catalogue'*. This is the sheer need for *enormously more resources* than are being used now, or

144

are 'available' for development. *No* sensible Environment *Plan* can escape this responsibility. In this category are —

(a) forestry sources ('expansion' through social forestry, wastes conservation; and not merely anti-felling laws),
(b) soils (fullest use of potentials),
(c) waters ('additionals'/alternatives),
(d) food grains (strains and yields),
(e) raw materials (types/volumes),
(f) energy (expansions/alternatives),
(g) renewable and re-usable resources and wastes conversions (all sectors),
(h) minerals (utilization 'scales', 'added values'),
(i) transport ('alternative' systems),
(j) urban/rural human settlements (expansions, 'linkages').

3. Both these, the so-called 'Micro' and 'Macro' issues and needs must be met by *positive* environment-development *relationships*; not negative, anti-developmental, or 'one-track' solutions.

Plans and actions must be 'productionist' not 'protectionist'. *Laws* need to change from being merely 'punitive' (especially on poor polluters) and emphasise conversion of 'wastes' as economic products (not as residue to be 'disposed' of 'on pain of offence'). *The 'apocalypse' type issues* should be of great concern, but should not mislead; their solutions lie essentially with their creators, namely, the rich countries.

III. Outline of Action for Plan Formation
(A summary 'sequential' presentation).

1. Identify and catalogue a first *list* of *major Areas* of both environmental stress or *needs*, and environmental *opportunities*.

2. Prepare short *operational Notes* on each of them, with outlines of *designs and policies*, based on positive management approaches, in particular the expected resource needs of development.

3. For *major resources*, prepare *Resource Balance Sheets* (separately for Renewable and Non-renewable resources) that set out availabilities, carrying capacities, potentials, and needs of restoration, maintenance and expansion — distinguishing between 'physical' supply, and 'effective' supply.

4. On a selective basis, schedule certain *natural resources as capital stock* providing for sensible rates of use, depreciation, re-equipment and even later 'substitution' (given new discoveries, technologies, etc.).

5. Also *for select resources*, establish *Resource discounting* systems, with future values at higher level (contrary to normal accounting of financial/economic assets).

6. Allow all E.I.As *(environment 'impact' assessments)* for projects *only where 'resource balance sheets' have been* first prepared.

   ['One could have perfectly sensible E.I.As on a project basis, which are equally nonsensical on a national basis'.]

7. Progressively, replace EIAs with an *Integrated Environment/Economic Cost Benefit System*, making for *joint decisions* in resource management and economic development.

8. Flowing from these, *draft* Designs and Policy Frameworks would result, enabling the formulation therefrom of systematic *Area and National Plans and Programmes*.

9. The *foregoing* are all *'ex-ante' actions*; and precede any formulation of designs and policies, or plans and programmes. However, having got there, sound management must foresee a follow-through with an *'ex-post' set of actions* that will, (a) *ensure* the essential *monitoring* of and intelligence on, performance, and (b) *yield* outstanding *feedbacks* to the benefit of the successive pre-planning phases of environment-economic management and development which, after all, is a continuing process.

   Two major instruments belong to this Group.

10. One is the development of an *expanded*, integrated, environment-economic system of *National Accounts*, reflecting 'true' GNP values, as well as losses and gains of resource stocks and uses.

11. The other, at the micro level, is what is known as *Environmental (Green) Audit* of all production activities, yielding better management, a better environment, and even better profits.

A Note on Resources Balances and Materials Balances

Resource balance sheets in national accounts and in national planning are a type of qualification of effective supply which, it was certain, would greatly assist economic planners to introduce environment management into development planning.

Pertaining to the perspective and medium-term planning stages this concept would yield concrete benefits in terms of national decision on rate of use of critical resources, long-term policies for their maintenance, substitution and expansion, and policies for science and technology assessment and application in relation to them.

Such a macro context is essential to any valid project level exercise, since there could be: (i) an alternative project to

147

achieve the same goal; (ii) an alternative source of resource supply for the same product; (iii) an input of a re-usable resource — all of them possibly more development supportive than the original project design; also once a choice is made; (iv) concomitant restoration projects; (v) protective activities to stabilise the resources tapped; (vi) additional projects based on residues created producing end products, or inputs to other industries.

As we saw, a key concept in this integration exercise has been the idea of the use of resources balance sheets for key natural resources. There has been before this, a concept of materials balances* which, while representing a stage beyond the earlier marginal and incremental analysis at micro level, is still self-limiting. From the point of view of integrated macro-level development planning, some observations may be made[7] on the materials balances concept in relation to the resources balance idea.

The increasing clarity about the relevance of the wider view of environment for developing as well as developed countries leads to a reappraisal of received economic concepts in the context of environmental management. The materials balance approach is a concept based on the consistency method of national accounting and emphasizes residuals generation as affecting environmental quality. As an approach, it bears only superficial resemblance in nomenclature to the resource balance approach, which has more fundamental connections with factor supply-extraction, production, distribution — and environmental management, especially in relation to development planning.

Beginning with a common property problem of resource misallocation and resulting externalities, the materials balance approach maintains that the class of externalities arising from residues (waste) disposal due to consumption and production activities must be viewed differently. Three reasons are advanced in support of such a viewpoint: residuals do not disappear but are matter in a different form; the waste assimilative capacity of

* With acknowledgements to Dr.R.Bharadwaj, Professor of Economics, Bombay University.

the environment is scarce; and it is a common property resource even though operative decision units are decentralised. In order to assess the external costs associated with residuals discharge or even their technological transformation into different forms, an economy wide materials balance is suggested. Further, the interactions increase when environmental pollution of one medium, say, water, has effects on other media. Sometimes different weightage has to be given to waste disposal by incineration affecting air quality or by dilution affecting water quality. In effect, waste disposal is not an isolated problem nor a final outcome of any activity; it is an intermediary activity in the materials flow. Whatever the methods of residuals disposal, the disservices flow back to the consumers and producers who initiated the process; thus control of pollution must have a materials balance perspective for the entire economy. The focus is on the 'consumption' angle where materials exist and render services but do not get used up or destroyed. According to the advocates, the better the energy conversion and material utilisation, the lesser will be the requirement of new materials for a given quantum of production and consumption. Nonetheless, it is maintained that technological external diseconomies increase with population and production levels disproportionately.

The residual material balance is thus a definition and a concept. In order to render this physical process operationally meaningful from the economic point of view, it must be viewed in conjunction with a general equilibrium framework, to examine the inter-relationships and welfare considerations. Here the concept gets bogged down with the assumptions that necessarily go along with the models used and carries the reservations that are expressed about a neo-classical framework.[8] Certain other drawbacks follow as a fixed coefficient assumption is made to arrive at the balance model. The model concludes that material flows from the environment minus the recycled products would be equal to the sum of residuals from the intermediate production and final consumption sectors. However, the recycle time frames have varying ranges and may not coincide with the production period in the dynamic case. The recycled augmentation of raw materials would not be balanced in a given

149

time period. On the contrary, if recycling is assumed away then there would be no basis to assess the changing waste-assimilative capacity of the environment. Also the aggregate nature of residuals flow does not discriminate between lethal and harmless residuals or yet, changing materials balances due to changes in waste assimilative capacity. Even when, to comprehend the above factors, the relationship are expressed in terms of inequalities, they do not have empirical meaning unless the equalities hold. Thus, the more important aspects of recycling in materials balance in fact get left out of consideration.

In terms of the earlier discussion, the resource balance is an approach, and not just a concept, to formulating and assessing the physical and effective supplies of environmental factors. We call it a methodological tool as it differentiates resources by category — renewable and non-renewable — and by process. This approach, as earlier mentioned, is a system of sequential and schematic linkages forming the core frame for environmental planning in the various phases and stages. It aims at approximating the effective supply of non-renewable resources to the physical supply by activating the parameters of rate of use, and existing re-use alternatives, also allowing for changes due to R & D application. In the case of renewable resources, the approach emphasises restoration, maintenance and expansion processes along with their improvement through R & D possibilities. This forms a basis for national resource accounting, with a perspective of sustainability in resource supplies. The resource balances, therefore, naturally subsume the residual materials balances more meaningfully, in that use of raw materials, by products and recycling are also considered. The resource balance sheets constructed after such a total environmental assessment would help development planning, especially for developing countries. The actual use of all the resources depends on a cost/benefit estimation extended to include the relevant environmental characteristics in each case.

The two views have a point of tangency, implying a whole line of departure. Both the views take special cognizance of the recycling and residual assimilative capacity of the environment. Whereas the materials balance concept begins and ends there itself, the resource balance approach is a stream of thought beginning earlier and continuing further. First, conceptually, the resource balance approach is a general equilibrium macro framework which aids development planning. The materials balance concept is a tool which has partial relevance only to the inter-relationships of residuals and has static implications. Secondly, the former approach helps disaggregation as it deals with special focus on renewable and non-renewable resources. The latter is a hold-all concept for all forms of residuals. Thirdly, resources as factors of production are differentiated from the concept where residual and renewable resources as a process of consumption are emphasised. Empirically, the approach is fitted to assess changing supply positions and arriving at operational balances for each category of resource and process. The materials balance concept on the other hand is constrained by the very mechanism of balance and fixed technological coefficients. The premise and methodology of the resource balance approach seem to be the only reasonable manner in which environmental management could be integrated with development planning, while being able to subsume the materials balance objectives.

NOTES

1 Long before, from around the early seventies, some of us had already used the phrase, "use of all resources alongside sustained maintenance of future resource levels", and outlined the beginnings of a *methodology*, but were not placed to attract World attention! (see esp. UNEP/APDC, Environmental Assessment of Development Projects. BKK/KL. publ.1983,) We shall be referring to this later, as well.

2 c.f. *My Economics of Full Employment in Agricultural Countries* (KVG de Silva & Co., Colombo, 1957) & A.K.Sen's *Choice of Techniques*, (Oxford, 1967), for a more 'economic' analysis of these, and for references to other writers of the day.

3 At the same time, readers must be reminded that the Chinese had taken one of the most enlightened world views on environment and development, when they emphasised recently that they do not see, or intend to see, every Chineses having a car, for that would be the end of the world! How many others have anything like this to show, amidst their 'profound' studies, statements, views and "movements"?

The Wealth of Poor Nations

4   A phrase introduced and developed in the early Eighties by Philippe de Seynes, former Under Secretary-General for Economic and Social Affairs of the United Nations. As he says, "ecology became a concept of such philosophical breadth that as soon as it gained the right of city in the political arena, it expanded into a comprehensive, though vague and not very coherent, system of values pertaining to the most important aspects of Society."

5   For convenience, shall we say up to ten years or so, of the next century.

6   For a detailed presentation of all these (the 'centre piece' of Environment Development Management) see writer's *The Methodology of Environment and Development Management*, CRDS, 1993.

C. Issues and Options — International

Chapter Ten

Return to Growth — New International Decisions

The international world today is beset with problems that seem to be notably different from those preceding. The differences, which are not only of scale, seem to be also fundamental qualitative differences, that bid fair to be more than temporary and which must make the emergence of mutual commitments between countries much more vulnerable. This seems a strange situation at a time when, on the surface, recent years have perhaps been the most active in terms of intentions to hold, and the holding of, international dialogues between the developed and developing countries. Most of them seem to be rather the product of an old momentum and instincts generated by the post-War philosophy of a new international world. In other words, it would seem more that the motions of cooperation are prominent, while its content has long begun to erode. Further, this may not be even explicitly realised, at least by some on both the developed and developing sides, during the engaging in these parleys. Hence the pious agreed declarations, still, at conferences that all should get together in full partnership and to work out solutions to the world's problems.

The fact is, for one reason or another, the main pillars of international action, namely truly liberalised trade and adequate aid, seem never to have been really instituted. It does not mean that there cannot be new sound perspectives, given sound long-term political decisions. But the indications are there may not be. The reluctance, in actual practice, of the developed countries

155

to fulfil the post-War declarations of partnership is an old story, such as with not fulfilling declared aid targets as percentages of their GDPs, not dismantling a host of non-tariff barriers and so on. But during the seventies, new big factors emerged. Oil prices shot up, at a time in fact when growth and budgetary policies in the developed countries had also attained, or almost attained, their peaks and were ready in any case for inflation. Secondary structural inflation in these countries, through the multiplying of their export prices of manufactured and other goods, set the world on quite a different inflationary plateau, in which both developed and developing countries struggled for a new equilibrium. The latter of course more than ever before, needed opportunities for export and for acquiring needed foreign exchange resources.

Meanwhile, from about 1974, the growth of world trade, which was about eight per cent per annum in real terms for two decades preceding, began to fall down nearer to four per cent. Simultaneously, regional integration took a big jump in the developed world, with the advance of internal trade within EEC and, in certain ways, within the OECD group.

These began to show in international relations. By the early eighties, the United States was categorical enough to advise that no amount of aid can produce progress, but that the developing nations must put their own financial and economic houses in order. Simultaneously, the IMF was calling for what it termed in its own light, realistic pricing of exports, slashing government spending and adjusting currency and interest rates, without stopping, for example, to look at realistic pricing of imports or the distinction between palliatives and permanent solutions. However, the IMF made sure by declaring that there is no other path to follow. There were, of course, also other similar declared positions, of which the above are two prominent examples. Already the volumes of aid and trade flows were not comparable at all to what was required to carry countries to development. The new situation needed either inconceivable, sudden change in the developed country attitudes; or, as must be more certain now, categorical, well-defined, major change in the growth strategy to be adopted by the developing countries.

Return to Growth — New International Decisions

It seems therefore, a good starting premise that the growth philosophy that we saw proclaimed in the early years after the War was never really implemented. True, the deck was cleared by agreeing to drop some old barriers. For example, the comparative cost argument based on factor endowments was recognised as no more valid. There was an early emphasis on a new division of labour based on skills, which was actively fostered and had its uses, but also limitations. When exports began to surge out of the developing countries based on these skills differentials, there were sentiments of protection against them by the developed countries on the ground of cheap labour costs in the developing countries and, therefore, unfair competition. These too have largely disappeared as active arguments. But the most important fact is that in terms of hard trade barriers, tariff and non-tariff, the discriminations have simply continued, making nonsense of the concepts of trade instead of aid. It represented a full turn around from the nineteenth century advocacy of free trade by the developed countries, to a practice of protectionism by them. The symptoms seemed to be as much psychological as factual, when the developed countries through the sixties and seventies dismantled their barriers to each other's trade while increasing those to the developing countries. To give again an illustration from Arthur Lewis, imports of manufactures from the developing countries to the developed were by the end of the seventies, only two per cent of the consumption of manufactures in OECD countries. The trade barriers betrayed an exceptional sensitivity in treating this minuscule flow. On the other hand, there was a lack of sensitivity, in that the developing countries (even excluding the OPEC) were taking twenty per cent of OECD exports, and it could hardly be in OECD interest to force the developing countries to discriminating against OECD sources.

From the sixties if not earlier, the developing countries have allowed themselves to be led into beliefs of salvation by some specific trade and aid promises of international cooperation, including related stock-in-trade such as price stabilisation, international buffer stocks and so on. However, their record turned out to be one of marginal benefits. Even more dangerous

157

was that these limited benefits, appearing sizeable in absolute dollar terms but minute in relation to fundamental needs, kept diverting developing countries away from the essential policies and actions for their own salvation. In one sense, they were not to blame. They had been brought up through colonial type economic conditions in a dependently structured world economy. It seemed the first course to try out, when ushered into promised advantages of negotiations.

An early report of the EEC to its Council in 1972, itself came out openly against those industries in highly developed countries which sought protective measures, giving low wage rates in developing countries as an excuse. 'Contrary to still fairly wide-spread opinion, wage levels in an exporting country are no valid justification for specific protection measures on the part of a more highly developed country'. The fostering of agricultural and industrial sectors in the developing countries, was in fact underlined by the Commission Report as 'an irreversible and desirable process of development' and an advantage to the Community. It is interesting also, that at the level of the private sector, about the same time, one of the leading metropolitan banking organisations functioning in Asia had to say: 'For their international trade, and in fact for their livelihood, these young nations are still too dependent on the policies, which usually means politics, of the industrial countries. It is difficult to see an easy solution, for prices of commodities are governed by the law of supply and demand, though industrial countries are responsible for quotas and tariffs designed to keep out the exports of emerging countries. It is not recompense to exclude a country's goods and then give aid, often tied — and trade not aid is still the genuine desire of most Asian countries.' An OECD report published about the same time on Japanese support to its industry, noted, *inter alia*, the use of subsidies, loans, fiscal measures and special depreciation rates. A particular point of interest which it recorded was that Japan found it useful to apply restrictions to foreign imports for time periods determined necessary to the development or rationalisation of given sectors. Meanwhile, the Indian delegation, obviously echoing many others, lamented at UNCTAD III in Santiago, that the EEC had abolished all internal tariffs among themselves and have raised a common external tariff against all outsiders including developing countries.

As for the much hoped for relief through the Generalized Scheme of Preferences, we noted it proved to be marginal. In 1964, largely as a result of the efforts and inspiration of Raul Prebisch, the United Nations Conference on Trade and Development was convened in Geneva with special emphasis on raising the material wealth of the developing countries through trade rather than aid. The most favoured-nation treatment extended by industrial countries to themselves or others in the past (MFN) was to be extended on a unilateral basis to all developing countries without countervailing concessions for them. This was the Generalised Scheme of Preferences (GSP). Innumerable assessments have been made of this and it is not the purpose to analyse all these.[1] There is unanimity, however, on the net results. Essentially, GSP was restricted to some commodities only and moreover hedged in by additional factors such as low quota ceilings, tariff barriers and other restrictive measures, leaving developing countries practically where they were. In specific cases of commodities or countries, for example, agricultural commodities for India, exceptions were not offered by EEC or at the most they were for marginal reductions only. The position was similar in various categories of manufactures and semi-manufactures with low annual ceilings, such as in cotton and textiles, or as in barriers on finished jute and coir products, but not for their raw materials. Generally for developing countries, one might say that something like two-thirds of the exports originating in them were simply outside the scope of the GSP. In any case, it became clear that when industrialized countries get organised into a vast common market, preferences given to developing country exports become virtually meaningless.

The effects on developing countries from the other mainstream of trade liberalisation, namely GATT and the 'Club of Ten' inspired Kennedy and Tokyo Rounds, were not different. The Kennedy Round of Multi-lateral Trade Negotiations was inaugurated in 1964, according to President Johnson, 'as a

159

proud chapter in the history of international commerce'. At the end, however, as the London Economist concluded, it remained 'a rich man's deal'. There were some concessions to some developing countries, who were not active participants in the negotiations any way. The basic situation was that those product groups for which industrialized countries were the main suppliers benefited more, namely the advanced technology and capital-intensive groups. In agricultural and tropical products, the results were modest. On non-tariff barriers, apart from some in agriculture and chemicals, practically nothing tangible was achieved. As one review put it 'the gap between declared intention and the actual performance presented a sordid picture' and in a joint statement at the close of the Kennedy Round on June 30, 1967, the developing countries declared that 'the most important problems of most of them in the field of trade remained unsolved'.

The Tokyo Round in 1973, was bigger and more ambitious and advertised as holding greater opportunities for the eighties. In the end, as in the Kennedy Round the developing countries were largely presented with a final package on a take it or leave it basis, with much similar limitations. As one opinion concluded, most of the proposals made by the Tokyo Declaration regarding developing nations remained paper promises, with the preferential tariff rates yielding limited inputs. For items such as textiles or footwear, non-tariff barriers effectively neutralised the trade expansion effects. Much the similar situation prevailed regarding liberalisation in agriculture. An UNCTAD preliminary evaluation of a few years ago considered that the MTN seemed unlikely to result in substantial gains for developing countries. A world trading system increasingly unfavourable and unresponsive to developing country needs, remained perpetuated. It came to be further reflected in the actual growing protectionist tendencies of the developed countries and proliferation of new trade restrictions.

The Uruguay Accords are so recent for us that, more than their details which are widely known, are the difficulties of forecasting their implications. These refer, again, more than to areas like the Multi Fibre Agreement extension, to the more subtle adverse potentials of the decisions on Intellectual Property Rights and Services and originating from the Earth Summit on Environment and Development, of the Bio-diversity Convention, Environmental Standards and others all of which affect the trade and growth prospects of the developing countries. As for net benefits of the Uruguay Accords there is general acceptance indeed, that by far the greatest share will be to the rich countries.

Thus some new international decisions had to be made; or, otherwise, will get made by circumstances. Perhaps some of these have already got entrenched and a belief in the old premises may be already illusory. Aid has not at all reached the one per cent of GNP target that was proclaimed in the seventies to be provided to developing countries. Nor do intentions of strengthening aid at special points, such as for least-developed countries, answer the overall question. Aid as loans in the future, it seems, has to be against committed offtake of developing country exports. As was remarked on one occasion, tied aid must be against tied exports, identified in advance and obligated by the lending countries. This is on the expectation, which unfortunately seems to be valid that aid will never come up to the capacity levels of need for developing countries to rely on the premised system of the forties for their growth. Precisely those countries which had to keep out, or keep down imports, could not do so. In turn, countries which could import, kept out the imports; controlling, to boot the import prices of such as they imported (save oil now) and their own export prices of manufactures.

Any ability by the developing countries to limit and manage aid in these terms will depend on their trade needs. Given the expectation that the developed countries would be against tariff dismantling and liberalising on the scale required, developing countries have to make decisions gradually to limit their imports on a development needs basis. It has to be hoped that the developed countries will not retaliate by excluding established developing country exports. In principle, the developed countries need to accept that position. Perhaps also, in practice, this may happen, considering the raw materials dependence by

161

the developed countries in trade. Further, thanks to long import dependence by LDCs combined with oil price escalations, the developed countries virtually faced prospects of debt repudiation by LDCs. It was even sufficient to attract a special CIA study which found that, by 1970, total (non-OPEC) LDCs[2] (medium and long term) external debt was over $250 billion (of which $150 billion was to foreign private banks, etc., and not to governments). While seventy per cent of this was accounted for by ten countries and some having 'excellent growth prospects' it was clear that lenders had a vital stake 'in finding a sensible solution' instead of 'the whole of the Third World debt' sitting on their heads. It noted that more than a dozen major creditor countries are adopting official relief measures such as cancellations, conversions to grants, or retroactive adjustment of loan terms.

As for developing countries, apart from technical dependency considerations, there is also a psychological situation. It is one thing to say that a wasteful or meaningless preference for imported articles should be resisted and that austerity should be carried to all forms of less essential consumption. But where countries have tried to do this, or have done this, the climate of world opinion — not only economic, but also social — has been anything but realistic, or helpful. The privations of a population are pointed to, simply because they go on bicycles or because cars will not be manufactured in quantity; whereas the basic low cost provision of food, clothing, shelter, as the initial foundation of transiting from the 'shovel to the forklift stage', is overlooked. In the democratic market economy countries that are developing, as one discussion concluded, 'a more or less thorough overhaul of social and economic structures' is required. Whatever be the pattern of trade decisions for developing countries for the future, it must be in terms of imports that help wage goods to be established, and foster machinery and inputs for building up fabrication capacity.

Thus, the big international decision for developing countries is to embark on constructive and creative regional trade and development programmes, accelerating their trade with each other. Most would agree, as Arthur Lewis has reiterated for instance, that this is necessary. As he said, this is also possible. Experience has not been encouraging so far. This we shall consider in a later chapter.

Such a development needs national import policies, yet also implies that bases can be found for meeting large-scale requirements, particularly of intermediate and capital goods. That scope lies within the developing countries themselves as a group.

Also of deep concern and relevance in such a future pattern are, naturally, the nature of international mechanisms and arrangements for trade and monetary cooperation that should exist, especially compared with what has existed. At the same time, during recent years, some old and some new globally gestated concepts of concern to development have emerged. Among them are population and health, resources and environment, water, food and energy, unified development, wages and employment, cultures and conflicts, and the power of information systems. These too we shall try to consider in the ensuing chapters, in relation to our own concern of self-sustaining growth in poor countries.

NOTES

1 Sources used here include UNCTAD documentation, UNCTAD/GATT International Trade Centre Issues, EEC Reports, London Economist, Eastern Economist, Far Eastern Trade and Development.
2 Covering about 100 countries (excluding 'Communist').

Chapter Eleven

The International
Cooperation Institutions

The symbol of international cooperation institutions is the United Nations Organisation. There have been global organisations much earlier, some like the Universal Postal Union (UPU) and the International Telecommunications Union (ITU) being very old. Others like the International Labour Organisation (ILO) were already in existence when the League of Nations was organised after the First World War.

But the coming of the United Nations Organisation, since popularly known as the United Nations, marked an entirely different turning point for countries and peoples. It was born in the atmosphere of post-World War hopes and expectations that we have repeatedly referred to in the preceding chapters — for which it created a special Security Council — not simply to keep the peace but to achieve wealth and welfare for future generations in peace and well-being. This aspiration was expressed in the setting up of an Economic and Social Council. The United Nations thus emerged as a multiple system, concerned with economic development much more than any predecessor institutions were, also setting up concrete instruments for development, in particular the World Bank and the International Monetary Fund, as means to achieve world goals in cooperation and development. It also installed an arm which concerned itself with questions of resolving problems by constitutional means, through an International Court of Justice. It further established a Trusteeship Council, of great significance to the Third World, under which the process of decolonisation would be speedily effected.

Finally, as a practical result, the various other specialized agencies gradually developed working linkages and a relationship with the United Nations, making the whole something near to a unified world organisation for peace and for development. These were the expectations. Part of the purpose of this Chapter is to consider the realities for the attainment of the development goals that the poor countries entertained.

Perhaps one may begin by trying to understand what seem to be *four* distinct *characteristics* in the Organisation as it developed. They relate to its *origins,* the *attitudes* to it, its *effectiveness* and, perhaps even its *relevance*.

First despite the proclaimed origins as mentioned, certainly true to that extent, the United Nations was essentially a creation by the victor countries of the Second World War, though hopefully for the benefit of all. In certain crucial aspects, concerning matters of war and the nomination of the senior-most official of its Secretariat, it still remains so. It also remains so in regard to the controlling management of the major financial institutions namely the World Bank, the International Monetary Fund and the United Nations Development Programme. Meanwhile, with progressive decolonisation, as well as acceptance of the defeated countries, the membership of the United Nations continued to expand, from an original number of 51 to the present figure of 185. Thus while the founding group, popularly known as the Big Five, continued to maintain its position in the Security Council, which considered matters of war and peace, the members dominated in the General Assembly, which normally met once annually, on an agenda that was unlimited but whose implementation was not entirely in its hands.

With such credentials, it was natural that the attitudes of the developed and the developing nations, as also their notions of what the United Nations could or should be, varied increasingly. To some, it was a convenient flogging horse when something they wanted could not be achieved. To others, it was a red herring which could be trailed across to divert from a real issue.

165

In many ways, it was a sop to both and a refuge to neither! The confusion in expectations was also added to, in no little measure, by the general pretence that the United Nations had power to solve either security or economic problems, but was not being efficient about it. The fact was it had no power in a sovereign sense, unless all countries concerned on an issue agreed within the United Nations on the matter. When they did not do so, as was mostly the case, there were not a few who were only too happy to put the blame on the Secretariat, although the latter could be no more than a mirror of the memberships determination, or otherwise, to accomplish a thing. But the Secretariat too contributed its share to the capacity to be ineffective.

This was the third characteristic. It had more than one side, as may be expected. One was its somewhat leviathan growth and consequent tag of easy inefficiency that became attached to it. We shall revert to this later, particularly in considering the contribution of the United Nations system in the regions and countries in practical terms for development.

In terms of basic character of the United Nations, there was another prior factor that is worthy of note. This is the concept of the Secretary-General as the Secretariat of the United Nations. As envisaged, the United Nations may be said to be composed of the following three constituent elements: namely the Membership, the General Assembly, and the Secretary-General of the United Nations. As envisaged in its founding, the Secretary-General is the head of the Secretariat of the United Nations and in fact the Secretariat. All others employed within and working for the United Nations simply derived their obligations, responsibilities, duties and authority from the Secretary-General. The position of Secretary-General was as unique and as important for a complete functioning of the United Nations concept, as the others. While being the servant of the General Assembly and therefore of all the countries, he was no servant of any one country or group of countries. While implementing the decisions and directives as decided only by the General Assembly, he carried a Charter right and duty, to undertake his own initiatives, within the limits of existing authority, in order to bring issues before the General Assembly, or other organs as he thought fit, as occasion demanded and on any occasion, in the cause of peace, as of other major issues affecting the welfare of peoples, anywhere.

Secretaries-General have interpreted the extent of capacity or willingness to use this initiative variously, with consequences to the world situation or to the functioning of the United Nations that again may be judged differently by different people. Yet the fact remains that the role of the Secretary-General is visible and creative, in any maximum contribution from the United Nations as a whole. The second Secretary-General of the United Nations, Dag Hammarskjold, believed fervently in this obligatory role of his position on behalf of the membership, as well as of the General Assembly or its other key organs, namely the Security Council, and the Economic and Social Council. Of another, it has been said that he avoided the charge of doing too little and was almost never accused of doing too much, presiding without leading, rarely giving his multitude of masters cause for genuine offence. Obviously, these bore on the work and limits of the United Nations in the world at large, whether in economic or political matters and issues. In some cases, they also bore on the capacity of the United Nations secretariat, at the centre or outfields, to fulfil their expectations. A danger, fortunately not common, but one which certainly occurred, has been the sacrifice of priority or quality to narrow political expediency, to a point where the organisation is reduced to incompetence and erosion — economic, political, or both. Too high a price to pay, indeed, in the name of any principles of expediency, the present condition of the United Nations System is not a happy one indeed.

Thus, if we may look at all the composites that make up what is called the United Nations as a whole, we may begin to get a better idea of its effectiveness or its ineffectiveness and in some respects even its relevance at all. Again as remarked, the world gets the United Nations it wants, all its fissures replicated in the Security Council and General Assembly. And the Secretary-General is everybody's man. On the problem of what the United Nations can do to help the Third World to rapid growth, these questions have to be asked, particularly whether what is being done, despite looking impressive, is only marginal after all. For example, before the United Nations ever existed, there were countries that became developed countries. Also there were countries, after the United Nations was created, for example the Socialist countries including the Asian republics within the USSR, which developed in one or other, without the involvement of the paraphernalia of United Nations systems of technical assistance, seminars, conferences, training programmes, institutional loans and so on.[1] We do not intend to, and one cannot obviously go into, all their details, but it would seem necessary to look at two aspects of this role so far in the efforts of the developing countries. One is the ineffectiveness that the United Nations has created for itself by multiplying organs and by not decentralising actions. The other is the role played by developed countries in actual practice when United Nations bodies or developing country groups took serious steps for development in international forums, particularly down at the regional level.

The multiplying of the United Nations system was not an issue in the early years. On the contrary, many steps helped towards a rationalisation and an impact at ground level, nearer the regions and the countries. The existing specialized or newly created specialized agencies — Food and Agriculture Organisation (FAO), World Health Organisation (WHO), International Labour Organisation (ILO), United Nations Educational, Scientific and Cultural Organisation (UNESCO), World Metereological Organisation (WMO) and others — slowly agreed to harmonise and in many ways to orchestrate their development assistance programmes round the world with the United Nations. As in many things in life, it was a process that was made easier by money, namely technical assistance funds deployed by the UNDP into the country and other programmes of the specialized agencies.

Also, at a certain stage in the development of the United Nations, the General Assembly decided that there shall not be more specialized agencies. Any new specialized or sectoral needs which may call for special institutionalisation were to be

168

met by creating special bodies within the United Nations system directly and under the authority of the General Assembly. Thus emerged the United Nations Industrial Development Organisation (UNIDO), United Nations Conference on Trade and Development (UNCTAD), and the United Nations Environment Programme (UNEP), among others. Meanwhile from early on, the United Nations set up what it called Commissions for certain subjects, such as the Social Commission, Population Commission and so on. Their functioning mainly took the form of annual meeting of country delegates in these fields held generally at United Nations Headquarters, but with the Secretariat being essentially part of the United Nations Headquarters Secretariat. A particularly interesting creation early on was the United Nations Children's Emergency Fund (UNICEF). And there was UNDP to which we referred earlier.

Along with these, beginning late forties, a set of Commissions for economic development were set up, one for each of the four regions of Europe, Asia, Latin America, and Africa. The Economic Commission for Asia and the Far East as it was called, began in 1947 in Shanghai, after that for Europe had been set up in Geneva. The Economic Commission for Latin America was established in Santiago and subsequently that for Africa in Addis Ababa, with one for West Asia later in Beirut. These were the Regional Economic Commissions as they came to be known. In Europe and in Asia, their first targets were to assist in reconstruction by providing a politico-economic forum to evolve common programmes of various types and in various relevant fields; just as the World Bank was called the International Bank for Reconstruction and Development, providing capital funds for those purposes. In Europe, the Economic Commission served the unique purpose, until recently, of being virtually the only body that spans East and West Europe in its membership and operation. In actual working, the tasks of economic reconstruction and restoration were rather accomplished outside, by the Marshall Plan for West Europe and by COMECON for East Europe.

As mentioned, while the early rationalisation of arrangements with the existing specialized agencies and the

169

attempt to limit new agencies was entirely right, the process of rationalising work approaches could not be said to have proceeded very much further than establishing linkages within the system for discussion and exchanges. One or two consequences took their course. The size of each of these organisations expanded freely. Secondly, while in recent years the General Assembly was talking seriously of rationalisation of United Nations structures, it was ending up simultaneously with setting up new bodies. For example, one for Human Settlements was set up, and it was moving to elevate another body, UNIDO, to independent specialized agency status. Thirdly, all agencies and bodies of some size saw reason to develop programmes and sub-programmes in various sectors and sub-sectors outside the mainstream of their own responsibilities. Theoretically, it was never difficult to justify this. After all, as just one example, there is always an industrial aspect of agriculture and agricultural aspect of industry. These examples can be literally multiplied hundredfold. The result has been that in each sector or sub-sector or category, there was a criss-crossing of programmes simultaneously going on among almost all agencies and in almost all the countries which were supposed to be assisted by the United Nations system. Needless to say, they added not a little to confusion if not to development. In some agencies, for example, such as UNESCO, the perfectly valid academic position that all sectors are proper purview for research and education has been carried to fullest limits and into field programmes in sectors where there are other agencies. In the case of UNDP and, largely, of UNEP, their function being to help conceptualise and provide fund support to the programmes of agencies, the issues of system relationship were not the foregoing.[2]

It is not that a subject must not be studied from the angle of various disciplines. For example, population is in the programme of virtually every agency; and innumerable others. But the problem is that each subject is pursued zealously and separately within each agency, with only superficial administrative coordination, and no collation in the conceptualisation or implementation stages. The result is there is obviously a lot of duplication, leading to highly ineffective products for the countries, and of course unnecessary duplication of staff in the system. It is these ramifications and inordinate growth of the United Nations, supposed to be taken care of under the principle of rationalisation, pose the most serious efficiency threat within the United Nations system as well as for the countries seriously looking for development.

It would seem that the stage has long come when a complete reorganisation can and should be effected, resulting in one United Nations Organisation under a coordinating authority which can, then, as much identify separate departments for important sectors as ensure optimising work, staff and results. Without appearing irreverent, one might even recall the made up story of how half the files in the government of a country were burnt down by mistake and neither the administration nor the country were the worse off for it. The United Nations has, under pressure from its membership, instituted internal management teams of sorts, inspectors as they were called and, of course, inter-governmental groups, all to improve efficiency and to rationalise. While some of the studies, for example, of the inspectors have made very good reading, none of them have made an approach which is anything more than marginal in terms of fundamental need.

The ramifying growth of the UN Secretariat should not be wrongly understood. It is not, as some would make out on occasions, that enormous sums of money were drained into financing the United Nations Secretariat. In the early seventies, when this accusation gathered momentum, it was pointed out with truth that after all the entire budget of the United Nations proper was less than that of the Fire Department of New York City. Thus we have also a problem of the postures of the developed countries regarding the United Nations. It is not a question of being able to afford, but of being willing to contribute, a situation which emerged strongly in the eighties with the increasing vocal power of the developing country majority in the General Assembly. So the two should not be confused and have to be kept quite separate; namely, the question of rationalisation and efficiency for the sake of the developing countries and everybody else equally; and the question of essential financing of a rational United Nations system. As of now, both seem to have settled for irrationality.

Then we come to the question of decentralisation of functions of the United Nations to the regions in order that the purposes of the United Nations and the needs of the developing countries may be better served in the economic and social fields.

The Regional Commissions are not development financing agents. They were not even, essentially, pre-investment funding agents. The regional offices of the Agencies, with possible exception of WHO, were perhaps even worse off. These were the functions respectively, within the United Nations system, of the World Bank and of UNDP. But unlike any other in the system, the Regional Commissions were the voice of the developing countries on economic policies, programmes, and priorities in their own areas. The instrumentalities of their functioning were, thus, by building up arrangements and confidence among the countries: for getting together on well-defined issues and objectives; for agreement to develop common study and research programmes; for chalking out lines in which they may contribute ideas; and, progressively, for agreeing to set up concrete cooperation programmes and activities. In the early years, the fact of getting together and exchanging information and contributing material for a common regional survey or report, were themselves acts and symbols of cooperation, in a world where none had existed before. Later and, gradually, as confidence grew under leadership of the Commission Secretariat, more concrete and varied programmes emerged. Programmes around a particular natural resource, like a river basin, emerged, of which the outstanding United Nations example perhaps was and still is, what is popularly known as the Mekong Project, serving the four Indo-China countries of the Lower Mekong Basin. Another type was in infrastructures, of which again a good example was the establishing of the Asian Highway Network, replicated later in Africa. A third type was around the idea of institutions, where under the leadership of Raul Prebisch in ECLA the first Institute for Economic Development and Planning (ILPEs) was

172

established, followed thereafter in ECAFE and in Africa. Then followed arrangements such as cooperation round commodities, led by an Asian Coconut Community[3] and later a Pepper Community which was also to include Brazil. The next advance was in the creation of programmes for cooperation in trade and financing. Examples were LAFTA in ECLA and later an Asian Trade Agreement, and an Asian Clearing Union in the ESCAP region. As part of the trade and finance package, the Asian Commission had earlier established a development institution, the Asian Development Bank (ADB).

Some of the Commissions even pioneered ideas, based on their obvious economic expertise, of improving the United Nations system of 'country programming of technical assistance', much before the Jackson Report and the later UNDP attempts to change from cataloguing to development plan related programming. For instance in the early sixties, and Asian workshop on national coordination of technical assistance considered a system for technical assistance programming within economic development planning. By the time the Jackson Report was done, the Secretariat had enough basis to outline a clear integrated country programming system which, on hindsight, reflected the direction in which efforts later really evolved.

In their preparatory work and in creation of all these, the Regional Commissions had to rely on pre-investment funds from sources within, such as UNDP and special trust funds within the United Nations, or from extra-budgetary contributions from interested countries. There had also to be greater concentration of United Nations energies at the regional level, along with increasing acceptance as the level for action. This indeed did occur in one important way. From the late sixties, the General Assembly and ECOSOC adopted a series of resolutions on decentralisation of functions to the Regional Economic Commissions. It implied decentralisation of staff as well, but that was hardly implemented. As a result, decentralisation of functions also suffered, especially as parallel functions continued at Headquarters, which suffered from distance and continued to do so. One Asian remark during the sixties was: 'They call us the Far East and forget about us: and the words Far East simply meant far from New York and east of nowhere'.

It is hardly that the Regional Commissions themselves were without blemish and this was obviously pointed out. Sometimes for lack of concrete initiatives, sometimes as victims of a large-scale United Nations style, common to Headquarters and the Agencies, the Regional Commissions too were packed with meetings, seminars and reports and with repetitious advice, often general, to countries on various matters. One could compare also different phases within the same Regional Commission. For instance, when a number of concrete regional cooperation activities were being forged or when nothing feasible was happening, the tendency to solve problems by meetings and paper-work was obviously the hallmark in the latter type of situations. Thus, tied to the problem of decentralization was also the obvious need to install a tightknit, highly practical and action-oriented system within the Regional Commissions, as much as others, before one could think of solving either the problems of proliferation or of coordination. In the meantime, developing countries occasionally had benefits and occasionally none. But also, for reasons of high principle and noblesse oblige, they went along in public expressions of deep appreciation.

Alongside, in whatever the Commission or others were able to do, it was not only these limitations which hindered results. There were serious problems of postures of developed countries themselves, which were sometimes even more serious as an issue than the health of the United Nations system. An apparently continuing trend of East-West, North-South, or whatever relations, it would seem profitable to look at some of these problems and postures, as they actually materialised, in the course of attempts by the United Nations to serve the cause of development.

Since the illustration will be mainly from the Asian region, it is necessary to give a brief background of the development of this particular Economic Commission. At the time of establishment, all the Regional Commissions in the developing regions had also certain non-regional developed countries as full members. In fact, there were originally hardly any regional members in ECAFE just four. The other countries were members on the ground, nominally, of being responsible for the many dependent countries or colonies, but also, de facto, reflected the Big Five basis in the establishment of the United Nations. Thus as full members were also the United Kingdom, France, Netherlands, the United States, and the Union of Soviet Socialist Republics.

The Asia and the Far East region did not originally include the South Pacific, namely the islands of the South Pacific and Australia and New Zealand. There was another, non-United Nations, colonially established Commission for that area, called the South Pacific Commission (SPC). Gradually, as the membership of the Commission increased, with the majority becoming genuine Asian countries, a move developed to give expression to this in meaningful terms, so that decisions may be made by the developing countries for their benefit.

By a decision in 1951 at a Commission Session held at Lahore, Pakistan, what came to be known as the Lahore Convention was established, whereby the non-regional member countries agreed that in matters pertaining to the regional countries, the decisions of these countries would prevail. About this time, the two developed countries in the South Pacific, namely Australia and New Zealand, decided to take advantage of the full membership arrangement that had come along with the Regional Commission structure and, therefore, applied for membership of ECAFE. At the time of application, they made it very clear that it was not their intention to determine the course of decisions or development of the developing countries of the Commission, but only to assist them. On this basis, they were admitted as full regional members considering their location vis-a-vis the region. While this was the background, the experience was slightly different when the developing countries tried to forge or to institute cooperative programmes. It was a fairly consistent history of postures in this regard, which perhaps became something like a 'record of the rich' within the Commission vis-a-vis the 'aspirations of the poor'. Some of this record may be cited to illustrate this genuine problem.

Minor indications appeared early on in the fifties when, for example, what was then a single International Trade Division in the Secretariat, also dealing with industry, was suggested to be separated, with a distinct Division for the emerging regional priority sector of industry. The idea was finally carried, but not without some objections and reluctance from the developed country sources. When the Lower Mekong Basin Project was to be initiated, there was similar reluctance to see the Economic Commission as the instrument for its development, it being suggested that it was purely agriculture and therefore just a matter for a sectoral agency, namely FAO. Events of course have shown the emptiness of these viewpoints.

The classic instance was the setting up of the Asian Development Bank and its aftermath. It remains perhaps one of the most vivid illustrations of the problem of developed country assistance. It is a matter of record that, at the time of moving to set up the Bank, it was categorically opposed by almost all the major developed countries concerned, particularly Japan, Australia, New Zealand, USA and U.K. It was actively argued that there was the World Bank, which garnered the resources from the world's financial markets and there was not more than an Asian Bank could do; a view which naturally appealed also to the World Bank authorities. There was no accommodation given to the developing country point of view that the concept of the Asian Development Bank emerged out of, and was linked to, the movement for regional trade and economic cooperation and that the assistance in this was a key contribution from such a Bank.

Chapter XII, below, is devoted to this and the subject is, therefore, not pursued for its details here.

An instance of a different type, of the polarisation between the developed and developing countries was when the Third Council of Ministers was convened in December 1970 at Kabul, to adopt a declaration instituting a payments scheme, a clearing union, a reserve fund, a re-insurance scheme and certain other sectoral programmes. The declaration was indeed adopted and became, de facto, the charter for regional activities of the

176

Commission during the seventies. But the postures of the developed countries vis-a-vis the aspirations of the developing were no augury for the type of mutual cooperation and support required for full implementation. In fact, one of the undocumented side-effects of the Kabul charter was pressure to have a new regime succeed the leadership of the Regional Commission, as in fact it did, with slowing down of programmes, or retaining them in cosmetic form. One of the interesting related facets was an attempt by the developed group to put forward one of their candidates for the top echelon in the Commission Secretariat, a move that was finally thwarted only by strong developing country representations to United Nations Headquarters to cancel the accommodation that had been given to this viewpoint.[4] An index of what the developed group found desirable may be seen in a remark, informally addressed to a Secretariat member about this time by a senior member of the United States permanent representation to the Commission, that the Commission should become action-oriented. A highly praiseworthy point, indeed, and when requested what it meant he bluntly stated that there is a need for more knowledge in the region and the ECAFE should concentrate on holding seminars, workshops, training programmes and the like.

A final, different, type of illustration may also be recalled. The region was, as mentioned, known as Asia and the Far East, a nebulous term but an accommodating one under which Australia and New Zealand has the ability to become members, within the boundary of the Commission. Countries that were slowly becoming independent in the South Pacific were, somewhat naturally, looking to others than their former trustees or masters for development advice and assistance. Thus initial contacts began to be established with ECAFE which led to some of them becoming members. While this was one strand in the process, another strand was the great enthusiasm shown by Australia and especially New Zealand in espousing new members from the South Pacific into the Commission. This was no problem because there was no controversy in any quarter about it and the membership increased. But two features were notable. One is that these new member countries remoteness from ECAFE Headquarters — it could take as long to travel to some of them as to Europe and by virtue of their very limited financial resources just could not participate directly in the Secretariat's activities.[5] Thus virtually most of these countries were represented, for Secretariat purposes and even at meetings under special arrangement, by Australia or New Zealand and, where they were still colonies, by the United Kingdom or France. The second point was that the South Pacific, a very large area occupying one-sixth of the globe's surface, had its own South Pacific Commission which gradually became more decolonised. The independent countries also set up a South Pacific Forum which excluded the colonial countries. Thus not only was there a focus and medium for cooperation and development, but as a matter of fact and, perhaps, rightly, the territories resented over-active involvement by the Regional commission Secretariat located in Asia in their programmes and affairs. They were prepared to receive assistance, but as and how they needed it. As a distinguished South Pacific leader put it once: 'We want these people on tap, not on top'.[6]

When the third Director-General of FAO, Boerma of Holland, assumed office, he visited the other organisations, and mentioned to the head of one of them what he felt was a simple, but powerful, truth. He said that if only all these organisations could get together and work jointly, the United Nations could be one of the most powerful forces for Third World development. In a sense, we are going back in this to what we started with earlier, namely the problem of rationalisation of United Nations structures and the problem of orienting them to action closer to the field. The record of the United Nations system has varied. It was not intended here to evaluate this, but only to illustrate. Also, it must be made clear that the virtue of ineffectiveness was not a monopoly of the United Nations system. There are other inter-governmental organisations performing similar economic and social tasks — the Colombo Plan, the Commonwealth Secretariat, OECD, EEC, COMECON and others. Many were themselves hardly redoubtable successes in assisting development activities if judged in hard basic terms. Doubtless, all of them, including the United Nations systems, had their points and their value.

Within the United Nations system, it seems the agencies with more technical targets did better for the world than those concerned with economic and social development. Examples of the former are UPU, ITU, and WMO which have rather well defined and specific purposes. A creditable record belongs to WHO, best exemplified in its eradication of smallpox and, on its past, giving hope of achieving its target under the Health for All By the Year 2000 Programme. It must be admitted that bodies concerned with economic affairs are more subject to political controversy. In fact, where a similar sentiment intruded even among the technical bodies, progress was slowed down. Quite irrespective of one's views on the matter, there has been the case of the WHO campaign for breast-feeding, implying a condemnation of artificial foods sold worldwide by multinationals, in which full developed country support was not possible.

One function of the United Nations activities generally may be worthy of note. Almost all agencies had the failing of acting as if they could readily answer the problems with which countries came to them. The fact is they could do so in some, and definitely not in others; but they could all go through the well-known United Nations motions of appearing to solve problems. This is the system of giving a problem the tested treatment of a study, a seminar and a report, which gave satisfaction to the agency and left the country slowly to realise that the problem had yet to be overcome. The main malaise was that each agency would not recognise its own character — derived from its structure — and take up problems only for which it was originally built. For example, the regional commissions were uniquely fitted to forge cooperation programmes, to provide a springboard for specialized agencies, to work out systems for programming by the United Nations and so on. The UNDP was fitted for leading country pre-investment programmes, but using all other expertise; and so on. But the regional commission cannot replicate for UNDP, or the World Bank, when a country's problem was investment; and vice versa. Sometimes a regional commission has been wanting to coordinate others without even fulfilling its own work or internal coordination.

Thus, there seem to be four compounds concerning past, or future, effectiveness of international organisations in their role in support of rapid development. To recall, they are the inordinate, disorganised growth of the international system; the totally inadequate orientation of action programmes nearer to the field; along with inadequate appreciation of each agency operation, competence and limitations; and the posture of the developed countries within the system.

The posture of the developing countries is also sometimes a question mark, as seen in many polemics in the General Assembly. Perhaps, they should set about their own development more. Yet, it might also be said that the resolutions and the pressures for programmes and funds are themselves by-products of the illusion coming down from the founding days of the United Nations that aid, trade and development support were unquestioned part of the international cooperation mechanisms. In a previous chapter, we referred to the observations of a minister from a developing country upon his participation in the General Assembly. 'We of the less developed countries', he said in continuation 'delude ourselves into believing that our perorations, admonitions and resolutions are influencing the course of world events. the reality is otherwise. Maybe some of us have been prevented from facing up to this harsh reality by the formal equality accorded to us. In theory we are all equals in this Assembly. We are also prey to yet another mythology, the mythology of equality of nations.' Meanwhile, the General Assembly, president's inaugural address at the time, had observed that 'The World Body' had long been addicted to the 'Mythology of achievement'. Echoing this, the Minister drew attention to a likely significant fact that the developed countries were growing more interested in financing their own second Industrial Revolution, than in initiating the first in the less developed countries.

The United Nations has certainly contributed in certain things, in some reasonably, not for our detailed evaluation here. It has helped de-colonisation on economic and political conditions already established for it by the War. It helped keep

180

some international conflicts as issues for discussion, perhaps thus mollifying the extent of secondary conflagration. In all matters, and to almost all members, it gave a forum to meet when otherwise there may not have been any. It greatly assisted in giving recognition to economic targets — of growth, of aid, of trade — even if marked by more lapses than achievements. But its future capacity, and use to Third World growth, depends entirely on changes that must occur, but may or may not.

In contrast now, the changes beginning with the end of the Cold War; the dominance of the US; the 'readiness' of the Security Council; and the somewhat confused, if not conscious, roles of the Secretary-General, have left the issues of Economic and Social organisation unserved and unattended, smothered by the ready profusion in UN peace keeping — sans 'peace-building' — and left 'development' to the World Bank System, the new GATT-WTO machinery, and others, all closer than ever before, to the North than to the Member Countries as a whole.

NOTES

1   It is neither that they grew out of thin air, or that they have now 'arrived' fully as developed entities; but that their development was not by being provided theories and programmes, say, first on community development, then social development, then employment intensiveness, health, housing, environment and, when still without result, basic needs. It is not that development can take place without capital assistance; these entities received capital infrastructures, basic industries, and purchase of surplus produce.

2   Their problem was, e.g., when UNDP used its financial strength to assume the mantle of professional competence over an agency that knew better but which depended on its funds. In UNEP, it was a case of virtual surrender of programming to agencies without serious conceptual thinking of its own, so that its very small funds were wasted, or supported agency activities that were ongoing in any case. Meanwhile, some remarkable catalysing, such as of the developing sub-regions in cooperative programmes, suffered acutely; as also many other major ground level resource management potential programmes.

3   At its establishment, it drew sufficient fears for major developed country lobbies to try to arrest it at UN Headquarters level; and for a large multinational to fly out a representative to the Commission Headquarters. In actual result, perhaps they were not needed. The Community, while

The Wealth of Poor Nations

achieving something, did not fulfil the fears, thanks to developed country coolness and developing country desire to go along with the former.

4 To the great credit of Canada, as in other instances of one or two other developed countries as well, it must be said that its Foreign Minister immediately withdrew an application for membership it had made in the late sixties (based on the presence of U.S. and others) when it realised that presence was itself an anachronism. Canada continued as a steady support of United Nations activities in the region.

5 Earlier, about 1964, when Isreal, and Saudi Arabia, applied to be members, the Commission, Australia and New Zealand fully supporting, agreed that the area under ECAFE was already quite large and further expansion should be carefully considered.

6 The developed countries active in the Commission, however, succeeded in making even some of the others believe that ECAFE had neglected the South Pacific, leading these countries to believe that a substantive advance was being made when the name was changed to ESCAP. (The P for Pacific and S for Social, had de facto, been already well introduced in ECAFE). Meanwhile, both ECLA and ECA, as well as ECE and ECWA, continued as before through all this; and the South Pacific countries themselves got no particular new development benefit out of the alphabets.

Chapter Twelve

The ADB Story

I. ESTABLISHMENT

It is probably necessary to recall at the outset, that the Asian Development Bank (ADB) was set up — about thirty years ago — by the United Nations Body in charge of Asia, termed the Economic Commission for Asia and the Far East (ECAFE). This Body was basically the United Nations Headquarters for Asia, based in Bangkok after its shift from Shanghai in 1949, and was known in popular parlance at that time as the 'Parliament of Asia.' In its functioning, it was the Regional 'springboard' for the various Economic, Social and Technical Co-operation Programmes of the entire United Nations family and the source of Economic Expertise for its own as well as other United Nations Agency Programmes in the region.

As the Regional Arm of the United Nations, it had been generating quite a number of major Regional Projects as well, such as the Asian Highway, the Lower Mekong Basin Development Programme and others. U Nyun, as Executive Secretary of ECAFE at that time, the latter proposed in 1963 in a Resolution, 45 (xix) at its Annual Session in 1963, the setting up, among other things, of a Regional Development Bank for Asia. As we shall see, despite steady opposition from various non-Regional and some Regional quarters, thanks to the vision, steadfastness, the sense of mission and the honesty of purpose

---

* Based on an Invitation Lecture delivered at the Sri Lanka Association for the Advancement of Science.

displayed by U Nyun the idea of a Bank never flagged - as it may well have, looking back now, in the course of its progress towards final establishment. Eventually, the Bank got established also managing to retain in its Articles of Agreement its prime purpose, that of promoting Regional Economic Co-operation and Development. For this purpose, the Articles further emphasized the importance and special place of ECAFE and the need for the Bank's co-operation and co-ordination with the former. These purposes are enshrined in the very first Article, as Article 1 and in Article 2 under (ii), (iii) and (v), as follows:-

Article I

Purpose

The purpose of the Bank shall be to foster economic growth and co-operation in the Region of Asia and the Far East (hereinafter referred to as the Region) and to contribute to the acceleration of the process of economic development of the developing member countries in the Region, collectively and individually. Wherever used in this Agreement, the terms 'Region of Asia and the Far East' and 'Region' shall comprise the territories of Asia and the Far East included in the Terms of Reference of the United Nations Economic Commission for Asia and the Far East.

Article II

Functions

To fulfil its purpose, the Bank shall have the following functions:
(ii) To utilize the resources at its disposal for financing development of the developing member countries in the Region, giving priority to those Regional, sub-Regional as well as National Projects and Programmes which will

184

contribute most effectively to the harmonious economic growth of the region as a whole, and having special regard to the needs of the smaller or less developed member countries in the Region.

(iii) To meet requests from members in the Region to assist them in the co-ordination of their development policies and plans with a view to achieving better utilization of their resources, making their economies more complementary, and promoting the orderly expansion of their foreign trade, in particular, intra-regional trade.

(v) To co-operate, in such manner as the Bank may deem appropriate, within the terms of this Agreement, with the United Nations, its organs and subsidiary bodies including, in particular, the Economic Commission for Asia and the Far East, and with public international organizations and other international institutions, as well as national entities whether public or private, which are concerned with the investment of development funds in the region, and to interest such institutions and entities in new opportunities for investment and assistance.

Regrettably, once the Bank got established, these requirements were allowed to lapse quickly and became more observed in the breach. The reasons for this astounding development and the related genesis and history during the formative period of the Bank, as well as a brief analysis of the Bank's record after its establishment, are the purpose of this paper. It is not written to adduce praise or blame. Out of this, it is hoped that, even at this late stage, the beginnings of some return to the original purposes of the Bank will be made and will take place for the sake of the Region's developing countries, for whom after all the Bank was set up.

II. GENESIS

While we noted the first explicit step on the Bank as being in 1963, in one way the genesis of the Bank may be traced to some of ECAFE's activities at its Headquarters at

'Sala Santitham' — 'The Hall of the Abode of Peace' — from late 1950s. Under the leadership of Professor Jan Tinbergen, a series of Expert Working Groups on Programming Techniques in Development began to be organized, with the help of some of Asia's promising Economists and Planners. These and related activities led to the outstandingly successful First Asian Planners' Conference, held in September 1961 in New Delhi, attended by leading Economists and Planners from Asia and outside, and inaugurated by Jawaharlal Nehru. That Conference, at which this writer had occasion, as a delegate of Sri Lanka (then Ceylon) to present a key Statement on the Nature and Rationale of Regional Co-operation, in fact anticipated the 'Dependency' situation of later years and of today, among many Third World Countries, caused by their limited, low value-added exports, total inadequacy of internal manufacturing capacities and the absence of a Regional Production and Trading Market.

In this setting, as well as the background of important work that had been initiated by ECAFE in the Trade area, the idea developed of constituting a group of Asian Ministers for Regional Economic Co-operation. Thus it was that ECAFE decided in early 1963 to convene the First Ministerial Conference on Asian Economic Co-operation. In pursuance of this step, not only a series of Ministerial Conferences, but a set of Working Groups and similar activities took place for the purpose of setting up the Asian Development Bank, beginning March 1963 and ending November 1966.

One can perhaps count fourteen steps between the ECAFE Annual Session in 1963 and the Final Inauguration of the ADB in 1966. The first step was, as mentioned, the 1963 ECAFE Annual Session and the second was the Working Group of Experts on Regional Economic Co-operation in September 1963, which recommended a number of far reaching measures both in the Trade and Banking fields.[1] This Group felt that the Bank should be primarily for Regional Trade Liberalization and Co-ordination of Economic Development Plans and foresaw the Bank as an 'instrument of co-oriented economic planning.'[2] The third step was the Preparatory Meeting for the First

Ministerial Conference, and the fourth was the Conference itself, in December 1963, which adopted an important resolution for the promotion of Regional Economic Co-operation, and linked the need for practicable programmes in Intra-regional Co-operation with the setting up of the Bank.

These four, out of the fourteen steps referred to, constitute something like the first phase, where the positions of the various countries for or against the Bank were clear and the 'battle lines' drawn accordingly. Among the countries strongly supporting were Afghanistan, Ceylon (Sri Lanka), India, Indonesia, Korea, Laos, Nepal, Pakistan, the Philippines, Thailand and Viet-Nam. By and large, the rich countries simply opposed the Bank and, as it happened in due course, this group included the World Bank as well. Japan formulated its position with the usual mixing of its character as an Asian country and a Western European Economic Group Member. It talked of "recognizing in principle" the need for countries outside the Region to support and its readiness to co-operate fully with the regional countries in the examination of the proposal.[3] Australia, while participating in the discussion, emphasized that nothing it stated was to be regarded as a commitment on the Bank and that the 'need and distinct role' for a Bank has yet to be established. New Zealand gave support at that meeting, although it was soon to oppose it.

Of the other ten steps, steps five to nine which followed, were formative and important. These were: The ECAFE 20th Session in Teheran in March 1964; The Expert Group on the ADB in October 1964 at which Australia declined participation, Japan decided to accept and to support the idea positively, and the IBRD declined; The ECAFE 21st Session in New Zealand in March 1965 at which the rich countries, including the IBRD and the Netherlands and France, began slowly taking up positions geared to their own interests;[4] The Consultative Committee set up by the ECAFE Session of March 1965, which sat from June–December 1965 and saw also the UNDP finally agreeing to give technical assistance support to ECAFE, as also partially the IBRD under a reluctant Mr. George Woods; and The Preparatory Committee on the ADB, which met in October 1965 with

187

IBRD participation for the first time, and which finalised 'the entire text' of the Legal Instruments establishing ADB.[5]

III. FROM OPPOSITION TO SUPPORT

It will be interesting to see how from a position of opposition, the rich countries as a whole went over to support of the Bank. Some exogenous circumstances happened to coincide, leading to this change; and with it, some endogenous factors were found to be feasible, enabling the rich countries eventually to go all out in support of the Bank.

The Viet-Nam War was taking its tortuous course and, as it happened, on 7th April 1965, President Johnson made an important announcement in an address at John Hopkins University. He expressed the readiness of the United States Government to contribute one billion dollars 'for the Economic and Social Development of South East Asia' and invited the countries to join in a greatly expanded effort. He also invited the Secretary General of the United Nations to use his position and prestige 'to initiate, as soon as possible... a plan for co-operation in increased development' in the area 'And I would hope', he said, 'that all other industrialized countries, including the Soviet Union, will join us in this effort'. He named a special team headed by Eugene Black, former President of the World Bank and, having talked with him subsequently, he added that the ADB 'would be of considerable value in promoting Regional Development in Asia' and that 'the United States would wish to participate, if such a Bank can be established.'[6]

Despite the ignorance of the statement in not being able to distinguish between the Asia and South-East Asia, obviously due to American obsession with Viet-Nam, this new position of the United States changed the whole picture in the rich countries, as far as the ADB was concerned. There was no question as to support, afterwards, by Japan, Australia, New Zealand and of course the IBRD and the UNDP.

Just prior to this stage the situation was so tenuous that the whole Bank idea could have, in fact, collapsed, as is evident, to take one random citation, from the passage below,[7] upon conclusion of ECAFE's 21st Session.

'At the conclusion of the session, even after the unanimous adoption of Resolution 62 (xxi), there remained considerable uncertainty about the participation of the developed countries in the Bank, largely deriving from the U.S. position and its likely impact on others. Uncertainty concerning the United States participation, the cautious and non-committal attitude of Australia and New Zealand, and the keen desire and even insistence of Japan and the developing countries of the region to have the participation of the developed countries in ADB as an essential condition of its success — all these contributed to this uncertainty. Nevertheless, the Commission decided to go forward with determination with the necessary consultations designed to accelerate progress by the end of the year'. But as we said, President Johnson's statement changed all that.

Not only here, but right through, at all times of faltering, lack of vision or courage, the role of ECAFE's Executive Secretary, U Nyun was inspiring and outstanding, in complete contrast to the lack of recognition within ADB circles to him later, as we shall see. The above writer states[8] 'In all this U Nyun, the ECAFE Executive Secretary, merits the highest praise for his faith in the project and in the Asian cause, his leadership, his determination, his indefatigable patience and his contribution to the negotiations.' Even Watanabe, who was Consultant to ECAFE earlier and who became the First President of the ADB, could not help conceding the contribution made by U Nyun, in his book *Towards a New Asia*,[9] published by the ADB in 1977, notwithstanding the general suppression of his role in his accounts.

Initially, the rich countries began to 'ration' their interest in exchange for this support that they would now give the Bank. There were two formats. One was to strengthen their internal position in the power structure of the Bank, particularly through the Voting pattern and the Presidential arrangement. The other, of an external nature, was in de facto limitation of the Terms of Reference, which could not, as we saw, delete the Regional Co-operation priority. But it saw to its stymying, by over exploiting small countries' natural temptations for direct country loans to country projects, notwithstanding the smallness of these loans in total, or that other sources could have furnished these loans. It was the Regional Development priority that other sources could not have met, and for which the ADB was so much first thought of.

The 'Asianism' of the Bank was, from the beginning, handicapped, with Japan, Australia and New Zealand in any case being within the region. What happened, between then and later, only made the situation worse. This was the crucial stage at which the transformation may be said to have occurred, from opposition by the rich countries to limitation of the Terms of Reference, in a keyed response, then to support of the Bank proposal and eventually their 'take-over' in the running of the Bank. Once the rich countries supported the Bank, naturally, they wanted it to be as they saw it and not as others saw it.

Before we outline the other details of this transformation let us, for the record, set down the other five steps which finally led to the Bank's setting up. These were — the Second Ministerial Conference held again in Manila in 1965; the Conference of Plenipotentiaries on ADB in December 1965; the ECAFE 22nd Session in March-April 1966 in New Delhi; The Committee on Preparatory Arrangements for the establishment of the ADB, January-November 1966; and the Inaugural Meeting of the Board of Governors in November 1966, held in Tokyo. As stated, these five steps came subsequent to acceptance of the Bank idea by all the countries, including the rich ones. Certainly, these five steps marked important professional, even if non-controversial, activities which culminated in the setting up of the Bank.

But two 'newsworthy' items may be observed. One was that Iran, which had offered a greatly increased contribution compared to its allocation, and was hoping to have the Headquarters there, opted out once Manila won the location. It was a matter of such great importance that when Japan lost the competition to Manila for the site of the Bank, Watanabe contemplated 'stepping down from further participation in ADB work.'[10]

190

The other bore on omission of the Bank's relationship with ECAFE, which had initiated the whole idea for a particular regional purpose in the earlier formative stages. But the matter and the issue were renewed. It was felt that a formal and contractual relationship need not diminish the autonomy of ADB. On the other hand (it) 'could be mutually beneficial and the possibility of this should be further explored.'[11] In the end, Article 2(v) was revised, recognising the special position of ECAFE, considering that it was to originator of the whole project and secondly, because it was the member of the United Nations Body concerned with economic Development in the region to be served by the Bank.[2] But the question of the Executive Secretary's special attendance, say at the Bank's Meetings, was jettisoned subsequently; and the ECAFE objective in setting up ADB began to be eroded.[12]

The other endogenous factors revolved round the arrangements of Voting power, and on the President and Vice Presidents. At a certain stage in the finalisation of arrangements, it was agreed that a basic Voting strength of twenty per cent to all countries would be allowed as equal basic votes. However, the USSR and other Socialist countries refused to participate in the Bank, particularly on the ground that the Voting strength should be distributed entirely on the basis of equality among its members. In the final result, as seen from the ADB Annual Report of 1984,[13] the Voting powers of the regional countries, less Japan, Australia and New Zealand became forty two per cent, and of the non-regional countries, plus Japan, Australia and New Zealand fifty per cent thus effectively reflecting the distribution of the power structure in that regard. The issue was of such concern that Malaysia for instance suggested that additional non-regional capital contributions beyond the original $ 400 million should be by 'B' type capital stocks, while Philippines suggested Associate Membership; and so on.[14] In a purely hypothetical way, suppose the Bank had been first set up as a Regional Institution by the regional countries, say with the available increased potential contributions from Iran and others, and then the non-regional countries had been invited, the purposes and character of the ADB may have been better secured.

It is not that the Bank's credibility and financial viability is secondary. On the contrary it is paramount. But in the course of final arrangements on the Bank's set-up, rich country dominance was equated with stability and viability.

As for the President and Vice-President, as of now the Bank has the President from Japan as before, two Vice-Presidents who are non-regional and the Indian Vice-President. The Bank started with Japan and India as President and Vice-President.

With these steps the effective 'hijack' of the ADB, both in terms of character and of its operation, by the developed countries was completed.

IV. SOME CONTEMPORARY OBSERVATIONS

In this connection, it may be of interest to quote from certain contemporary and related records. The first is an internal ECAFE Note that was prepared at the time of convening the First Annual Meeting of the ADB in 1968 in Tokyo, when the Bank had just got into operation and was establishing its style and function. This is what that Note had to say, with of course the Bank not necessarily sharing those ideas or desires.

'The First Annual Meeting is unique in an extremely important sense — it is something that occurs only once in the life time of any body or institution. It is a time when most initial processes for operation have been completed, even certain first steps taken in pursuance of the raison d'etre and objectives of the institution, and the potential for the material fulfilment of its mission awaits the important task of being laid out with thought and foresight... Where the ADB is concerned, its First Annual Meeting is occurring at a time that is heavily loaded with auguries as well as challenges... In a situation that is mixed with all these foregoing elements, the task of setting a proper course for and defining the mission of an institution like the ADB indeed involves as very high responsibility... While it would be hardly necessary... to dwell at length on the problems of investment in relation to development, certain observations arising out of matters with which ECAFE has been closely connected may be in place. These matters would also be of deep relevance to the same problems that would address themselves to the guiding hands of the ADB...

'In the first place, it may be of interest, at this First Annual Meeting to spell out and to recall some of the original intentions that were so much in the minds of the authors of the ADB at the time when the institution was being formulated. The second area of interest could be a view of some of the pressing specific developmental problems as they are seen from the side of the Commission itself. In regard to the former, it will be recalled that the charter of the ADB sets out the main objectives which were sought to be attained through the ADB. ... At the time of framing of the draft provisions of the charter, the authors were also acutely conscious of another problem, which in some ways even dominated their minds. This was the problem of regional co-operation. While countries were making every effort in terms of retaining and expanding their markets in the developed world, it was clearly felt that a basic answer to the problem of scale in *marketing* lay in expanding their own *markets with each other* in a dynamic and regional sense. Indeed, when the question of the very need for another Bank was raised insistently in the early stages of our making the proposal, it became necessary to be very clear for ourselves on the justification for the ADB. ... The main distinguishing rationale for the ADB was that investment finance for promoting regional co-operation in investment and trade was essential to the economic success of the region and that these were something which only a separate regional Bank could perform with understanding and with an adequate sense of priorities. It is this background which lies enshrined in specific articles of the charter referring to regional co-operation. The present international economic difficulties on the one hand and, on the other, the strong and conscious voice now being raised for regional co-operation among the developing countries of the region, make this occasion of the First Annual Meeting most appropriate for providing a strong start and the financial backing for various fruitful regional co-operation programmes and schemes. By doing this, the ADB would likely become responsible for one of the most important

193

contributions in this region towards Asian prosperity. The time is, therefore, opportune for developing a policy and operational frame for financial participation in regional co-operation. It is earnestly hoped that this frame work will now begin to evolve at this time when countries themselves are looking for guidance and assistance.'[15]

A second record was when this writer, in the course of work on causes and prospects of Third World stagnation and development, looked at the contributions made by International Organizations and, in that connexion the ADB. The following is what it had to say. It is quoted in full although the openning lines are also in an earlier Chapter.

'The classic instance was the setting up of the Asian Development Bank and its aftermath. It remains perhaps one of the most vivid illustrations of the problem of developed country assistance. It is a matter of record that, at the time of moving to set up the Bank, it was categorically opposed by almost all the major developed countries concerned, particularly, Japan, Australia, New Zealand, USA and UK. It was actively argued that there was the World Bank, which garnered the resources from the world's financial markets and there was not more that an Asian Bank could do; a view which naturally appealed also to the World Bank authorities. There was no accommodation given to the developing country point of view, that the concept of the Asian Development Bank emerged out of, and was linked to, the movement for regional trade and economic co-operation and that the assistance in this was a key contribution from such a Bank.

'As the subsequently adopted Articles of Agreement had it, the first pre-ambular paragraph called attention to the importance of closer economic co-operation for accelerating the economic development of the region. The first Article, which was on the purpose of the Institution, stated that it was to foster economic growth and co-operation in the region. The next Article referred to priorities as regional and sub-regional in addition to national programmes; assisting countries in the co-ordination of their development

194

policies and plans, making their economies more complementary; and promoting, in particular, intra-regional trade.

'The Secretariat was told that it would never collect the U.S. 1,000 million dollars initial capital that it had proposed for starting operations, of which more than fifty per cent was to be from within the region. When this was collected, even slightly exceeded, it was insured in the name of high banking principles that ECAFE would not be represented on the Board. As quickly as it was established, it became, appearances notwithstanding, an institution controlled by the developed group with a de facto permanency for Japan, as the Bank President. As if to make sure, the Regional Commission was simply accommodated with all the other agencies at the rear of the halls when the Bank's annual meetings were held. Needless to say, there is a notable absence of written or physical record or evidence in the Bank's headquarters of the leadership and struggle by the Regional Commission and in particular its Executive Secretary at that time, to create the institution in the teeth of opposition of those who were now determining its course. The Terms of Reference had it that the Bank was to collaborate particularly with the Regional Commission, a provision observed to the minimum extent possible and, as time passed, perhaps more in the breach.

'But all these were not the main act of omission or commission whichever term used. It may be recalled that a singular purpose in establishing the Bank was to further regional economic and trade co-operation. Hence the Terms of Reference that a prime function of the Bank shall be to assist countries, regional and sub-regional, precisely towards this purpose. By what it moulded for itself and by its general distance from the Commission, it perpetrated a vacuum and perhaps even, a constitutional lapse, which could not be made good. It was the countries that were failed in the main developmental support that it was to have given. It has largely functioned as a minor replicate of the World Bank. It is easy to get misled by the capital assistance that the Bank was giving to countries; many countries that get assistance may not themselves individually realise the inability for them to have made a break through, for want of a strong regional catalyst at the propitious times. By the late sixties and the turn of the seventies, many Asian countries were receptive to practical ideas of co-operative industrial development. Powerful support — in fact drive and initiative — from the Bank that the region had created for itself for this purpose, could have well given conviction and form to this dimension. Events, of course, kept unrolling. Asian countries advanced slower, but all the same, towards closer co-operation. There were talks of clusters of industries to be shared for development on ASEAN scale. Finally, when it came to seeking the essential capital funding to translate these ideas into reality, ASEAN had to go, in October 1980, to the European Economic Commission (EEC)[16] and not to the region's own institution, whose purpose it was to have in fact led countries into this growth.'

A third record is from a contemporary, and particularly apt, U.S. source. As witnessed both in the preparatory groups that preceded the establishment of the Bank and by contemporary workers intimately associated, the rationale for the Bank in its formative phase was clear enough. The Group of Experts of October 1964 considered three directions of importance: one was possible attraction of additional funds; the second was the financing of projects and facilities not adequately financed through existing sources or agencies; and the third, allied to the second, was that of acting as a focal point for and stimulus to Regional Economic Co-operation measures which were then being considered in the ECAFE Region.[17]

The Consultative Committee that followed (i.e., June-December 1965) foresaw the application of a collective yet acceptable judgement on the problems of co-ordinated economic growth in the Region. It saw the Bank as particularly well suited to perform such functions. The Bank would contribute more effectively to multi-national and sub-regional projects, the aspirations of the Asian countries for co-operation would be encouraged, and increased self-reliance promoted, acting for each country, as a spur to its own economic development. The

196

The ADB Story

ADB would be a symbol of Asian Regional Co-operation. The speeches made by high ranking members of Governments at the Ministerial Conference in December 1965 and at the Inaugural Meeting of the Board of Governors in November 1966, fully bore out these statements on the rationale and objectives of establishing the ADB. Of particular interest in this setting were the observations of a high ranking non-regional source on the advantages of establishing the ADB. They were a most succinctly summarized U.S. Treasury Department Special Report on ADB, presented to the U.S. Congress in January 1966.[18]

'The Asian Bank, can as could no institution either with extra-regional concerns or of sub-regional size, accomplish the following objectives:

— Bring an explicitly Asian viewpoint to bear on the problems of *complementary growth in the region*.

— Satisfy the widespread desire among countries of the region for an institution attuned specifically to meeting Asian economic needs.

— Point toward that *peaceful co-operation in Asia* which is the region's most pressing need.

— Offer an institution with its own tangible and constructive purpose to serve as a *nucleus around which broader forms of economic and possibly political co-operation* could grow. Asia as a whole enjoys no history of common political institutions comparable to the Organization of American States in Latin America. *The political infra-structure must be built out of positive acts of economic co-operation such as the Bank would provide* in its daily operations.

— Elicit significant amounts of capital from the Asian countries themselves for use elsewhere in the Asian region, with a concomitant assumption of the responsibility for sound fiscal operations.

197

— Stimulate a flow of public and private capital into Asia from outside the region.

— Provide an administrative channel through which Governments interested in national and *regional development* in Asia as a whole, *or in specific sub-regions of Asia,* could make *potentially large sums available* for special purposes or on special terms. A major contribution to South-East Asian development by the United States and other capital-providing countries, for instance, could be *administered by the Bank*, giving an appropriate Asian imprint to the funds thus provided.'

As repeatedly observed, therefore, the ADB founders envisaged an important role for the Bank in promoting economic co-operation and regional and sub-regional projects. At all stages of consideration of the ADB Project, the contribution which it could make to regional co-operation was well recognized and was in fact considered to be one of the major justifications for the establishment of the institution.[19] On the eve off the Bank's establishment, since national projects was also quickly emphasized, this too was added as a priority on behalf of the smaller developing countries, while embarking upon regional projects and co-ordination efforts. Provision was added, as seen in Articles 2(iii) and 14(iii) whereby the Bank's role 'in the co-ordination of countries' development policies and plans' would be to provide assistance in response to requests and with the approval of the member countries. Somewhat standard provisions, these were later exaggerated in the Bank's administrative mind, as we shall further see, to become an excuse for not undertaking any initiatives on regional co-operation. In all such instances, for that matter, it is not a question of 'powers', but of 'dynamism' and 'lead' from the Bank to its countries. As we shall see, the Bank has indeed chosen to point to needs and to call for action in certain areas, thus vitiating its own profession of inability to use its position in the matter of 'stimulating and promoting' regional co-operation for development.

198

V. THE BANK RECORD

The Bank began its operations in November 1966 and has a record now of activities spanning a period of over twenty years. Its Annual Reports, apart from other sources, as in the case of similar institutions, give the scope and highlights of its work from year to year. On its importance as a lender to countries in a global context and on its record as a Regional Bank, these Reports and other sources provide enough evidence. For one thing, as a proportion of lending by the World Bank to the Asia Pacific Region, not to mention the world as a whole, it is still a minor proportion of the totals. As an instance, in 1984 the World Bank (IBRD and IDA) lent to the Asian Pacific Region a total of $ 7,002.6 million.[20] The comparable figure for 1984 for the ADB (OCT + ADF) would be in the region of $ 2,171 million.[21] We could take the figures for Sri Lanka for instance. According to the Review of the Economy — 1984 issued by the Central Bank of Sri Lanka, the World Bank (IBRD + IDA) gross lending was Rs.2,034.2 million.[22] The equivalent for the ADB was Rs.875.5 million.[3] Sri Lanka's 'Performance — 1986' report issued by the Ministry of Plan Implementation gives under Agreements signed for foreign aid for that year the following:[23] The World Bank/IDA (Rs.4,055.1 million) $ 143.4 million; The ADB (Rs.761.6 million) $ 26.9 million.

This made the World Bank not only a five times larger lender, but also found the ADB lending to similar types of projects as the World Bank, or almost so. At the time that the ADB was being established and the World Bank was opposing it, its President in particular considered that the latter would be competing with the IBRD for funds in foreign markets.[24] The ADB itself saw one of the points in its rational as attracting considerable additional funds. The real rationale for ADB was not in the additional fund resources, but in its *qualitative* character, of being able to promote with those funds the regional co-operation which was so repeatedly emphasized in the formative stages. This, the Bank totally failed to do or to consider. In an informal communication to the current President of the ADB, I had occasion to indicate that the ADB could still

199

play a big role as envisaged at the time of its foundation, that truly it was at present only a miniature of the World Bank, as it would be, say if it had come about simply as a Branch of that Bank.[25]

It was natural that developing countries, especially the smaller ones, would look to loans for their domestic projects and there was always the danger of being misled by some lending of that type as a full rationale and justification of ADB. The Asian developing countries themselves at least as represented in the Bank's Meetings, after a time, forgot that there was a role for the Bank in regional co-operation assistance, a process undoubtedly made easier by the way the Bank failed to take any initiative in that regard. What is not seen is not known. The countries began to equate performance with the minimal 'duplicative' type of country project lending of the ADB. In reply to my letter, the President of ADB pointed out, in addition to the polite acknowledgements, that success in the directions we were discussing would depend on the policies and programmes adopted by the developing countries themselves,[26] taking recourse in a 'negative propriety'.

The 'Blurb' in the inside cover of the ADB Annual Reports, states that 'The Bank's principal functions are (i) loans for economic and social advancement ... (ii) technical assistance programmes ... (iii) promote investment of public and private capital ... and (iv) to respond to requests for assistance in co-ordinating development policies and plans of member countries. In its operations, the Bank is also required to give special attention to the needs of the smaller or less developed countries and give priority to regional, sub-regional and national projects and programmes which will contribute to the harmonious growth of the region as a whole.' Even in quoting its obligation, the Bank Management found it difficult to put priorities in the order of their stating in the Terms of Reference, as between regional co-operation and assistance to smaller countries! As for implementing, of course, it has implemented the latter; with the other left severely alone!

The way the Bank treated regional co-operation is seen in its own documentation. For instance, in 1984 it spent a poor sum of $ 3.7 million on regional activities. Even of this sum, only $ 160,000 was spent on what could marginally be called regional co-operation activities.[27] But there are more glaring instances in the same report. For instance, under inter-agency co-operation,[28] there is no mention of regional co-operation contacts, or of ESCAP (the successor of ECAFE). Certain research activities of the ASEAN economies and activities on ASEAN economic co-operation are mentioned. Remarkably, the ADB was able to come out of all these, without any involvement in them. Instead it was the European Economic Community which found itself supporting ASEAN co-operation. EEC founded the ASEAN Timber Technological Centre at Kuala Lumpur with six million dollars (out of a total cost of eleven million dollars) as its contribution for the first five years.[29]

Worse still, the ADB Report recounts details of the ASEAN Economic Ministers' Industry Programme, with no indication of support given to it. Certain ASEAN Industrial Projects are reported as operational. In 1983, there was the UREA Project in Indonesia, the first to become operational under this Programme; then came the UREA Project in Malaysia in 1985; the Copper Fabrication Project in the Philippines and the Hepatitis Vaccine Project (on a non-preferential basis) in Singapore. The Economic Ministers in 1984 also adopted the first phase of four Private Sector Industrial Joint ventures for ASEAN: a Motor Cycle Electrical Parts venture; a Silica Base Material for Ceramics Glazing proposal; a Mechanical and Power Steering Parts venture; and an Automobile Constant Velocity Joints proposal. The Ministers of Agriculture and Forestry agreed upon a Co-operative Programme for Management of Fishery resources, that is, in addition to the Timber proposal earlier mentioned.[30]

After its initial ASEAN Agricultural Survey, ADB started a Regional Transport Survey in 1967, to provide a basis for the co-ordinated development of Transportation in the region, and an investment programme for regional projects, underlining possibilities for progressive economic integration. Designed for South-East Asia, there is still no evidence of a particular drive or achievement by the ADB in these directions.

Following on the establishment of the Bank, ECAFE convened further Ministerial Conferences — later titled 'Council of Ministers for Asian Economic Co-operation' — and the Second Council, at Kabul in December 1971, adopted a foundational Declaration that laid the basis, hopefully, for a number of regional co-operation measures, such as an Asian Clearing Union, Trade Expansion Programme, and 'Commodity' communities for coconut, pepper, etc., from all of which the ADB kept aloof. ECAFE (ESCAP) since had to function as if it had never created ADB!

Further, when the South Asian Co-operative Environmental Programme (SACEP) was established in 1981, with Headquarters in Colombo, becoming the first Inter-Governmental Community Organization for South Asia, the ADB was invited to participate, but has not come forward with any initiative, support or assistance in any activity in this very important area, so contrary to the expectations richly described in the U.S. Statement, at Part IV above. Since then, SAARC has been established (South Asian Association for Regional Co-operation), and while that has not gone yet into hard co-operation areas of Trade, Industry, Agricultural Production, Payments and the like, the Bank interest, if at all, seems extremely minimal. The South Pacific Forum for the South Pacific Area in 1984 took initiatives for Regional Trade Promotion and allied developments.

Amidst all these, the Bank almost did nothing. As we mentioned earlier, it is not that the Bank cannot say things to countries. It has done so on more than one occasion, strongly criticising country performances and policies.

The letters exchanged between this writer and the President of ADB, mentioned earlier, themselves arose out of such a Statement by the latter at an ADB Conference at Manila in March 1987. The Asian Agricultural Survey and the Regional Transport Survey in 1967 yielded many ADB viewpoints, conclusions and recommendations. ADB country missions perform innumerable, unpublished, critical appraisals. What was lacking was not lack of capacity to be 'critical', but lack of the 'dynamism' and 'lead' — or inclination perhaps — to pursue regional market expansion and co-operation as a mandate. In recalling his past, Watanabe did concede once that he intended 'to further exert efforts to explore and identify good projects for the Bank to assist.'[31] A little later, in 1970, he also referred to 'three areas where the ADB should make further efforts: assistance to national development banks, tourism and education.'[32] The Bank, on its own record, was not going to touch Regional Co-operation!

VI. THE FUTURE

The prescriptions and policies of self-reliance of countries require much change from the 'dependency' type of economic structures that most of them have now in the Third World. Some of the facets of these were briefly mentioned earlier in this papers. The prescriptions are not uniform for each country. More backward ones have to lay basic foundations, while others may proceed to the next stage, and so on. But there is, certainly, little doubt that at some stage — and that stage is progressively reached for all countries — the types, ranges and scales of internal development in agro-industry, industry and infra-structures are such that sound regional co-operation amongst the developing countries of the region became absolutely essential, in the face of the wide gap between the highly developed and the developing countries. If this was not done, there would be continuing massive debts, deficits and stagnation, the best proof of which was the present situation of Payments and Debts within the Third World. In this background, the ADB has been seriously remiss with itself, by-passing regional funding, incurring management wastages, and relying on the short term attractions of country loans to the developing countries.

The question is can this lost area be recovered? All will the ADB begin, even at this late stage, to honour its charter obligations to stimulate, to promote and to support regional co-operation for development?

Technically and economically the answer can be, yes. Managerially and politically, the answer is still difficult to

203

foresee, particularly so as the Bank, which was started as a Regional Institution, run by the region for the region, is de facto a non-regionally owned and managed institution.

It is not that the developed countries are enemies, in this instance, through the Bank, of the Third World countries. Their positions, while carrying self interest, are mostly matters of perception, often bona fide. It is this that makes one hope, encouraging us to stimulate and to question, as this paper set out to do. One must hope that the rich countries — and the poor — will try to see that they have done so far; what they should be doing; and what steps may be taken in those directions. If that were to be achieved, then the hopes and the aspirations of the founders of the Bank, among whom are also the non-regional countries, will have been fulfilled.

One may perhaps best conclude with a quotation from (Sir) Arthur Lewis[33] in his discussion of the development Process.

'In developed countries the engine of growth is in the home market, that is, most entrepreneurs invest first to meet domestic demand and regard their export trade as an extension added to a sound home market. The economy can therefore go on expanding on its own momentum, even though external events are unfavourable. There are limits to this situation; any economy, however large and developed, can be brought to a standstill by a persistent excess of imports over exports. In this sense, all economies depend on foreign trade to some extent and are likely to be adversely affected by a decline in exports. Yet, the differences of degree are wide enough to be qualitative. The developed country will have to adjust its imports and exports to each other, but its engine of growth is in the home market, and this gives greater independence of movements in the world economy. The under-developed economy with its engine of growth in exports is at the mercy of the movement of demand in industrialized countries'.

The day the Third World countries establish strong and diversified domestic production bases, including manufacturing capacities of all types, they would move to 'self-reliance'. The progress towards that day is greatly assisted by concurrent, mutual, market expansion of developing countries one to another, in a process of 'regional co-operation for development'. That is the process that the founders of the ADB envisaged for the Bank and which awaits returning. It is no exaggeration to say that the way the ADB finally developed and functioned, determined in a significant way, for developing countries, the stature of their growth, their foreign debt burdens, and even the style and strength of their international relations, within the Region and outside.

NOTES

1   *ADB - The Seeding Days* by R.Krishnamurti; p.3, ADB Manila 1977.
2   Report of the Working Group of Experts, pp 65-67 (ESCAFE, E/CN, 11/ 641, 1964)
3   As it happened, when the subsequent consultative Committee attempted a draft of the Chapter, Watanabe, then Leader of the Japanese delegation, stated he 'stayed away from the deliberations (as) this might later bind my Government's hands; a situation that was strange as there was in any case no commitment on any Government at that stage. It must be judged more as a decision not to commit oneself to make any definitive statements of firm support on the Bank idea itself (Watanabe, *Towards a New Asia*— p. 13).
4   At the ECAFE Session at Wellington, New Zealand, March 1965. (ESCAFE, 21st Session, Summary Records, E/CN 11/709)
5   Krishnamurti - p. 29.
6   Statement by President Johnson, White House Press Release, dated 20 April 1965.
7   Krishnamurti - Page 19
8   Krishnamurti - Page 20
9   Krishnamurti - Page 21
10 Krishnamurti - Page 86
11 Preparatory Committee, October 1965.
12 Watanabe, in his reminiscences, recalls that ESCAFE 'was the organisation responsible for the birth of the ADB' and that ADB was on ESCAFE's Annual Meeting Agenda. This writer, was in those years directly in charge of the ESCAFE Sessions, sitting at the Rostrum with the Commission's Chairman and recalls the process of pure 'formality' to which this relationship was reduced by the ADB (c.f.Watanabe - p. 77).
    On this topic perhaps an inner feeling was betrayed in Watanabe's remarks in his book later that 'we rejected the idea (as) ADB's operation should not be influenced by decision of an organisation which, by its

nature, could not be apolitical' (Sic!). Eventually, as seen, there was a link, only it was not respected by the Bank. For another, it was ESCAFE, considered unwelcome 'by its nature', whose work created the ADB. Thirdly, in all this quibbling, it was the countries and the Region that lost, for the sake of a dubious 'rich countries' posture (Wanatabe, Ibid, p. 15).

13 Krishnamurti - p. 78
14 Consultative Committee, Working Paper No.13 (1-9) 'Comments and Suggestions' of ESCAFE Countries of 9, 16-17, 21-22 and 26 June 1965.
15 Note prepared by the Writer in Official capacity, for the Executive Secretary, 12th March 1968.
16 As reported particularly in the ASEAN Countries' Newspapers of the time, including the Bangkok Post.
17 Krishnamurti - Page 36
18 Agreement Establishing the Asian Development Bank (89th Congress, Second Session, House of Representatives) Document No.361, p. 45. (Underlining added).
19 At the Opening Ceremony of the ADB at Manila in December 1966, Wanatabe himself in his 'first address in the Philippines.....stressed the urgent need for co-operation among countries for the development of Asia ....The speed with which the ADB grew from a dream to a reality serves notice to the World that the spark of regional co-operation exists. It now befalls the Bank to kindle that spark with the fuel of international insight, until it becomes a raging fire of collective endeavour.' (Wanatabe, Ibid - p. 47. underlining added)
20 World Bank Annual report'85 - pages 100 & 106
21 ADB - Annual Report'84 - p.p 74 and 86
22 Central Bank Report - p. 258
23 'Performance' - 1986 - p. 242
24 Consultative Committee Report dated 5th August 1965 on meeting with Mr.George Woods, President of IBRD on 26th July 1965.
25 My letter dated 11th March 1987.
26 His letter of 23rd March 1987.
27 ADB Annual Report'84 - p. 131
28 Ibid - p. 35
29 Ibid - p. 17
30 Ibid - p. 17
31 Wanatabe, Ibid - Page 59
32 Wanatabe - Page 67
33 *The Case for Development: Six Studies* (Praeger,1973) - p. 66

Chapter Thirteen

Trade and Development Co-operation

In a world situation, the steady growth of national production in one country should also enjoy conditions for steady growth of trade with other countries. The self-reliance that was emphasised so far is not autarchy; conversely, the growth-trade relationship for poor countries is not uniquely related to unaccountable dependence on the growth of advanced countries. If equitable world trade, involving fair terms and access to developing countries as much as to developed, continues to elude, trade exchanges have to be sorted through other means, particularly at the stages of early growth of economies. These are typically intra-regional and allied arrangements. The growth mechanism that we discussed before involves marketing of some portion of the surplus abroad, so as to convert them into re-investment inputs with suitable developmental capacities, whether the inputs be internally non-available raw materials, intermediate goods or capital goods. In the still inadequate structures of growing economies, it cannot be expected that domestic demand will absorb the entire or even major part of national output, even though normally there are only a few select lines of production. This, indeed, has been the experience of presently developed countries in the past.

As seen, the Aid and Trade climates have been anything but healthy. Undoubtedly, trade is incomparably more important than aid, but this presumes that trade flow can really take place. On top of the records of the past, the Third World has been

207

recently presented with an exhortation to go to the market place for the capital flow required. Much can be written, but one feels enough has been said in preceding pages to convince that, initially, fair and legitimate trade bases — not even concessional — should exist to start with. If they did, there would be much less pressure on aid demands and much less need for alternative prescriptions such as in favour of the market place with countries free to choose their own options.

On the trade side, the market place concepts have not been applied even in the developed countries. Here again, there is voluminous material; but two popular examples may suffice. The recent Japanese export boom to Europe and U.S.A. was essentially an exploitation of national market places to which the reactions in those countries have been only increasingly fierce. Years earlier, to the alarm of some of the countries outside Europe, the European Economic Community began accumulating butter mountains, apart from others. It is difficult to imagine much weaker developing countries being able to prevail even in normal trade terms and to hope for market placed solutions until totally radical changes are openly effected in the developed countries under mutually equal relations with the developing countries.

The developing countries have tried to seek refuge in commodity and stabilization arrangements and other marginal palliatives. We have referred to the inadequacy of such solutions to the basic problems of obtaining sustained fair terms of trade and resources for investment for development. An FAO study[1] done in connection with the first World Food Day, October 1981, pointed to the host of problems being faced by the developing countries especially in the face of restrictions by the developed nations, and to the dramatic decline in their share of world earnings from agricultural exports in the preceding five years, apart from their high instability. It noted the efforts at commodity agreements as having been a slow and painful process over the years, with few signed agreements, and of those done, few lasting long or with economic provisions operative for any significant periods. That position is not going to change, notwithstanding the undoubted good intentions of some. Even such arrangements as may develop in the future cannot stabilise incomes to developing countries on a scale at all commensurate with the requirements of re-investment for development.

The special case of oil, beginning 1974, is known and too well documented to need outlining now. On occasions in the past, developing countries tried to formulate similar schemes, though obviously on a more modest scale, which would have yet brought some sizable advantage. We referred in an earlier chapter to the Asian Coconut Community and an inter-regional Pepper Community of Asian and Latin American countries. The case of pepper, though a small segment of world economy, is interesting. At the time of gestation of the Pepper Community in the Economic Commission for Asia and the Far East (ECAFE) in the late sixties, world trade in the finished product was controlled by a handful of business houses situated outside the developing countries. The gap between the floor, or ex-farm, price and the finished product prices was at least ten-fold, if not more in a smaller form, reminiscent, of the more notorious gap in the narcotics trade, between its floor and street prices. There was no doubt that an effective commodity community arrangement for pepper at that time could have transformed the industry, as well as changing the economic condition of the population involved.

Elsewhere, in a study prepared for the South Pacific Commission countries in the late seventies on possible price stabilization programmes, it was interestingly suggested that it were better to call such a proposal grower returns stabilization, on the ground that market prices are somewhat mysteriously, even morally, determined by what were called in the study 'central primary market centres'. It was explained that these were places where the forces of supply and demand have their effect.

This, of course, is quite different from reality and must have been, intuitively at least, the reason for countries to have looked to commodity communities arrangements even if, with the exception of oil, they may not have succeeded brilliantly. However, this remains an area for intensive study by the developing countries as a high priority, with obvious benefit to them, if carried with due consideration for linkages with world prices and production structures as a whole. In many of them as in several other matters, developing countries have a market disadvantage simply by being weak economically and not being able to modulate production, when it is often badly needed for sheer subsistence, let alone development.

We mentioned earlier and in a preceding chapter, that the present logic of world economy compulsively implies the best possible development in regional trade co-operation arrangements. Ironically, it is the developed countries that have so far instituted them more successfully, in the two parts of Europe. The developing countries perhaps went into their philosophy earlier. ECLA was a leader in the Sixties, thanks particularly to rural Prebisch, Executive Secretary of ECLA. ECAFE, through a series of councils, set up an array of regional co-operation infra-structures and programmes which we have briefly outlined earlier.

In the late sixties the Economic Commission for Asia set out in some detail, in view of its obvious importance, what, for developing countries, must be the essentials of such organization for regional trade co-operation. It was based on accumulated past experience of efforts. The work was itself the product of several minds, several years and several countries. The ECAFE Secretariat, under directive of a Council of Ministers meeting in December 1968, formulated a Strategy for Economic Co-operation and considered a set of Principles for trade expansion among the countries of the region. Up to then, there was a mental conflict of clear enthusiasm in principle and in intellectual doubt as to the scope available for trade co-operation, in which a Western type tariff dismantling approach was dominant. Obviously an impasse for developing countries, it represented an 'up-side-down', situation which had to be turned 'right-side-up'. The efforts in the early seventies stopped short of success, since they could not proceed to this stage as they should have.

The brief account[3] below provides this additionality of a right-side-up approach, which was essential for acceptable co-operation. Whatever its shortcomings, it is, perhaps, the only basis for the future. The strategy consisted of:

210

(1)   The strategy and aims of the commodity flow exercise;[4]
(2)   The basis and content of the commodity flow exercise inherent in the strategy;
(3)   Note on methodology;
(4)   A comment on possible obstacles;
(5)   Stages of work in implementing trade expansion;
(6)   A tentative proforma data sheet as primary basis for co-operation;
(7)   A draft statement of principles for trade expansion.

The foregoing were detailed fully in the First Edition of this book. Their principles and content are described for our purposes later at Chapter XV under South Asia Regional Co-operation. However, the core content of the concept and the exercise as reflected at (2) to (5), along with a brief idea of (7) above, are reproduced below.

Basis and Content of the Commodity Flow Exercise

A brief amplification of work for the Commodity Flow Exercise is set out below for better clarity of the approach. So far, indeed, no real progress has been recorded in this type of work. The main shortcoming in preceding work was the failure to take from the sum total of past experience, the main essence, which was, that broad tariff approaches are either impractical or highly problematic in the present context. Apart from other global examples, there were at least three High-level Expert Group Reports on regional trade expansion which could not carry the process forward.

It should be clear that any tariff approach would run up into two or three problems straight away: 1. At governmental level, the country would encounter an 'unknown' balance of payment threat. 2. In almost all cases, there will be 'pressure groups' of local producers which will tie governmental policy in the opposite direction to import relaxation. 3. There would be some marginal movements that could easily be mistaken for real success. Even

211

so, the tariff approach under the present production structures would very soon exhaust its own potential even where supported by credit holding assistance (i.e., payments arrangement), since it would not be capable of creating *new* complementarities based on *expanded* production. Without this, the whole importance of regional co-operation itself as a big 'theme' also dissolves. Nearly sixty to seventy per cent of total trade has been extra-regional and awaits tapping through suitable methodology for concrete attainment of regional co-operation; even a fraction of import diversion and export expansion in this sense would provide impressive results.

Note on Methodology

Objective

Essentially, the commodity flow exercise would identify current and potential export surpluses and import requirements in all feasible sectors and construct matrices of intra-regional commodity flows, initially for a number of major commodities, in such a way that a wide enough base is available for suggesting mutually beneficial exchange between countries. Thus, it would also be the aim to induce production and trade flow in accordance with patterns which may not yet exist. The exercise, while being long-term in its basic sense, would initially attempt to develop interim possibilities of mutually beneficial exchanges.

Some Assumptions

The exercise is based on the assumption that, in the present circumstances, regional level integration, or complete harmonisation of development plans, is not quite feasible.

It is also presumed that across the board tariff dismantling procedures would be impractical, particularly given the differing levels of development of the countries of the region.

The current imports of the developing countries from outside the region provide a constructive starting point for developing mutually beneficial exchanges among regional countries.

Thus, on the import side, the study could be conducted for the start, largely as a static exercise, providing only for obvious

212

expansions in, or new requirements of, import elements for development.

On the export side, the approach would be more dynamic since by definition the regional countries are not presently providing themselves with these imports. The aim will, therefore, be to identify possibilities of production in any of these lines - either as new production proposals or as expansion of current restricted production programmes, as the case may be.

Since the practicableness of co-operation will depend on the mutuality of benefits derived by exchange between countries, the readiness to expand exports to regional countries will become relevant only to the extent of readiness to meet import requirements through regional imports. While both types of information are naturally complementary to the exercise as a whole, the extent to which co-operation arrangements could be developed in practice would depend critically on countries' indications of import items they are prepared to meet from within the region. The readiness to import as such is not considered problematic since by definition the imports are being made in any case and most of them will continue to be. The decision to be made is to import from the regional countries themselves and to assure quality standards.

Therefore, while the potential export picture would serve to provide countries with an idea of potential import possibilities, firm indications of potential import acceptance would be a key element for success. At the same time, the offer of production and export expansion to countries would serve as the appropriate *incentive* for them to enter into co-operation arrangements.

The identification of preliminary exchange feasibilities would expectedly involve more than one round of contacts with countries, since in the first round complete information may not be available to each country, of other countries' exportable capacities. However, once such feasibilities have been identified for certain countries and certain commodities, these countries could meet jointly to take up further the next stages of clarifications involving tariffs, transport costs, payment arrangements, investment arrangements and so on. Mutual

213

benefits accruing to the co-operating countries could also be assessed in terms of gains in capital cost, unit cost of output, re-investment surpluses accruals and foreign exchange accretions.

It is implied for the success of the programme that suggestions involving closing down of existing production lines should be avoided; that commitment for commodity exchange arrangements would be in terms of given time limits; and that the export capacity of a smaller or less developed country would constitute the limit of import possibilities by that country.

Methodology

Based on the import pattern of the countries of the region, a list of major commodities of regional interest for export and import will be prepared by a secretariat to serve as a working basis for each country. Each country will itself be free to modify or expand its list in terms of its special requirements and possibilities.

For each of these commodities, data would be compiled in terms of an agreed format.

The critical portion of the format relates to data on planned or expected production for export, and planned or expected import requirements, both to be supplied for specific time horizons. Also to be indicated for exports will be an idea of pre-investment needs, including financing needs required for realisation of expectations. A third portion of this information will be in the nature of certain assessments, such as likely markets in the region for the potential exports and likely suppliers within the region to the countries concerned of required imports.

A supporting portion of the format relates to necessary historical indication of exports and imports for a typical preceding year.

The presented picture of potential regional co-operation in terms of specific commodities will also be assessed in the background of other available historical data, overall future growth trends and related indicators.

Out of these would emerge a pattern of export surpluses and

214

import requirements for each country by commodities. For example, for any given commodity, a table of the following type would become available. These tables would provide the initial suggestions as to which countries could come together for production and/or trade negotiations.

Countries	Commodity-A Export-Surplus	Import-Requirement
1	E	—
2	E_2	—
3	—	M_3
4	—	M_4
5	E_5	—
6	—	M_6

On a provisional basis also, some matrix of commodity flow among the countries would then be formulated for each commodity in the following way. This matrix would, of course, be subject of later modification, arriving out of policy decisions of countries to take up the trade possibilities.

Commodity-A

Exporting Country	Importing Country				
	1	2	3	4	5
1					
2					
3		(Trade flow)			
4					
5					

Stage B: The details of this are not being spelt out here as the immediate work on the exercise will be on Stage A. However, upon the availability, through Stage A, of preliminary feasibilities which countries concerned could accept as providing *prima facie* basis for co-operation, a group of countries (two or more) could get together for the next stage of confirming mutuality of benefit, arranging trading and transport facilities and providing for pre-investment and investment activities. These would constitute the beginning of Stage B.

Neither of these stages is, of course, a once-and-for-all process. They will be continuing in nature, although for practical purposes, initial rounds in each of these stages could be undertaken at the right times. In the long run, the programme for co-operation could go into an increasingly widening dynamic approach, involving concepts of integration or harmonisation of plans.

Concurrent activities

The activities in other connected fields, such as payment arrangements and infrastructure development, will continue concurrently. Work in the industries and similar fields for example would be utilised as resource information for the commodity flow exercise itself. Also at the appropriate stages, infrastructure development would reflect some of the needs for co-operation as brought out in the exercise. For example, shipping and ports arrangements, would be a case; as a reflection of future needs in economic co-operation, efforts should be initiated to work out suitable schemes for developing joint shipping facilities and services to handle inter-island, coastal and regional carriage. In regard to clearing and payments arrangements, of course, the highest priority should be given to seeking an agreed solution that could meet minimal needs of such a trade expansion.

Comment on possible obstacles to country acceptability in elements of the trade expansion proposal; and advance formulation of a flexible set of adjustments in order to meet situations on the spot.

1. The trade expansion proposal as here framed is a bold and positive one with a high degree of self-consistency.
2. The acceptability of these at technical, governmental and central bank levels is not, however, entirely predictable. In

216

the event of some intractable situations arising it would be essential (a) to consider before hand the nature and extent of the adjustments that may be offered; and (b) to do so within the concept, framework and merits of the scheme.

3. The basic premise of the offered scheme is that increased exports to whatever market in the world will involve a commitment to import from within the region. While the positive secondary and tertiary effects of this are clear enough, there could be serious hesitations based on very real considerations. For example, developing countries are already committed conceptually to maximum import limits, which are formulated in development planning contexts and which themselves are in the context of payments deficits financed by aid. The first reactions to additional export gains will, therefore, be (apart from feeling that these gains do not depend on regional co-operation) to reduce the payments gap and the burdens of external debts (in any case the debts created by the current pattern of developmental imports). Additionally, imports from the region which are not within the frame of the developmental plan of a country can meet with only reluctant obeisance to the logic of a long-term or indirect mutual benefit.

4. Such or similar limitations are indeed recognised in the present proposal — through provisos for low-reserve countries and for utilisation of only a percentage of export gains for regional imports.

   At the same time, however, the logic of the proposal has led to a counter proviso that the preceding provisos be not applied during the first phase of operation. In the same vein, the stipulation about quotas and tariffs which once liberalised up to a point shall not be changed later, may be something to emerge in practice later, but an insistence now may not be feasible.

5. At the same time, a further recognition of the difficulties earlier mentioned has led to a useful opening in the proposal. This is the arrangement to get the process involved in the basic proposal *started*, namely an exercise in itemising and matching export capabilities and import requirements 'if

217

they had the means'.

6. Arising out of these is a set of flexibilities which could be considered *beforehand* for use at negotiations as necessary.

7. The basic proposal, of exports to any market in the world as tied to increased regional imports may be considered as an 'indicative' idea for acceptance in principle, even if not necessarily for immediate full implementation.

8. The idea of 'increased' imports in the sense of an increase in total national imports could be varied to mean increased total 'regional' imports. This means that regional imports will take place in substitution of identified *current* extra-regional imports (in practice potential imports could, of course, be relevant too). By this means, a country's total import level will not be higher than it would otherwise be or determined by developmental policy needs, while its exports (by opening up markets within the region) will increase.

9. A more difficult matter relates to the proposition envisaging only the developing countries of the region as coming within the scope of the proposal. For one thing, there is the marginal point that one or two presently developing countries could soon become classified as developed, affecting fundamentally the concept of regional co-operation. The other point is the exclusion of the present developed countries in the region. On the basis of the variations on the application of the concepts such as briefly mentioned, it would be feasible for the developed countries also to be in the scheme and thus for the proposal to be fully regional. Somewhat like what are now accepted international postures concerning non-reciprocal preferences, these countries would have a qualified benefit, but all the same a clear benefit. If they are able to import, for example, a given additional quantum from the developing countries of the area, they would receive in return an export benefit to the developing countries to an agreed proportion of these additional imports which they would not otherwise have had. (Note that under the proposal itself developing countries, through aid, will have to be importing capital items from developed countries outside — later on, this

could include non-capital items as well according to the scale of export potentials created among the developing countries.)

Stages of work in implementing the Trade Expansion Exercise

Round 1: This will have to be conducted in the countries on the spot with National Units so designated.

1. Specification *by countries* of commodities whose production and export could be increased (existing categories); and new commodities whose production and export could be initiated.

   This is the basic offer to each country in the trade liberalization nexus to enable the country to participate.

   In order to assist the countries in preparing this list of potential export commitment, the secretariat could furnish   (a) a list of items as known to it based on surveys, etc.; (b) a list of items with large-scale economy potential based on a study of total regional trade; and (c) a list of the main imports now being made from outside the region and of such future imports.

   The list of commitments by each country should not, however, be restricted by the foregoing information provided by a secretariat which should only be supplementary assistance information.   Basically, each country should examine its resource availability and potential and simply set out the major items of its possibilities.

2. List as *provided by the countries* of significant import items from outside the region, (a) which are capable of *diversion* as intra-regional import if intra-regional exports are available; and (b) having any problem of such intra-regional diversion due particularly to imports being tied to aid.

   This offer to divert imports[5] (not to add some additional unnecessary imports) is the *only 'price'* of mention which the country pays *in return for the benefit of additional export* offers on some basis of mutual benefit.

Round 2: Exercise to be conducted back at a secretariat level with members of National Units visiting as required.

1. The raw data from Round 1 will be checked on the basis of

demand supply projection as well as techno-economic and resource endowment feasibilities and other relevant considerations.

2. A first pattern of complementarity development will be formulated in matching export potentials on the identified items with import diversion items similarly identified.[6]

Round 3: To be conducted in the countries.

The complementarity matrices will be further improved (a) by rechecking on country capabilities — import and export; and, (b) where insufficient complementarity exists, by further probe into possible resource endowment and development by eliciting this additional complementarity.

It may be noted that while wage/cost differentials as between countries, tariff structures and so on are relevant considerations in trade flow, yet this particular exercise while benefitting from streamlining and relaxation of these, could still go forward even in a context of such differentials and structures. The reason is that the exercise is a commitment by countries to import and export given commodity items by quanta[7] on a mutually beneficial basis of f.o.b. values.

Round 4: To be conducted initially in the secretariat as in Round 2 and subsequently in identified out-fields.

1. Groupings as far as possible of countries having considerable number of common commodity interest (countries may figure in more than one group).[8]

2. Delivering the results to the countries in these groupings for getting together in one of their capitals for the first phase of negotiations.[9]

Round 5: Mainly at country group levels.

1. Finalisation of negotiations into agreements, somewhat like current bilateral procedures but conducted on a 'dynamic' basis and in a multi-country setting (tri-lateral, quadri-lateral or more).[10]

Draft Statement of Principles

The Draft Statement of Principles for trade expansion

among the developing countries of the region, adopted in the Kabul Declaration in December 1970 by the Council of Ministers for Asian Economic Co-operation decided that an inter-governmental committee of the interested countries should be established in order to examine and suitably modify, where required, the Principles set out. The Principles then before the Council of Ministers had developed from the first drafts arising out of the Triffin/Uri Mission on trade and monetary co-operation in August 1970. They were finalised at the Meeting of Central Bankers and Government Officials in September 1970 before being submitted to the Council of Ministers.

The resounding merits of the Principles placed before the Ministers at the Kabul session, as they had evolved since the Triffin/Uri Mission is that, perhaps for the first time anywhere, an escape was made from conceptual or theoretical frameworks essentially derived from past, or different, economic systems, and an approach deliberately formulated to be relevant to the present situation of the developing countries of the region. The result was that for the first time, the terms for co-operation in trade expansion were expressed as physical commodity relations in country production and trade, and not as tariff relations.

The core of the Draft Statement of Principles so formulated in Article 2. It required countries registering over-all export increases to increase the share of regional participating country imports. The singular merit of this formulation was that it provided for automaticity in the operation of the system once it got started. Automaticity in the case of import commitment relied, however, on export performance, which could in most cases be extra-regional and independent of this particular scheme, especially in the early rounds of implementation. Hence, principally, the discrepancy between actual commitment to an agreement, and the high self-consistency and logic of the scheme itself.

This may be considered the broad background against which to view the decision of the Kabul Declaration to undertake further examination of the Draft Statement of Principles through an inter-governmental committee in order to launch a programme speedily. In keeping with the physical commodity approach as envisaged by the Council of Ministers in 1968 and endorsed by the fourth session, but taking care of the problems

221

in the Draft Statement of Principles as it now stands, an alternative formulation of certain Articles may be set down. The main intent of the alternatives is, therefore, not to offer a fundamental change. (It is assumed that the fundamental change has now been made.) The main intent is to overcome the acceptance problem in Article 2 and, utilising the thinking so far, to develop a self-consistent set of alternative elements to certain clauses of the Draft.

These alternatives do not carry the automaticity reflected in the earlier Article 2 of the Draft Statement of Principles. In return, what they carry, *inter alia*, are, equitable benefit; import commitment only within the context of plan development; import commitment only to the extent of additional export development (so taking care of the small *vs.* large country question, reflected as an aim in Article 7 of the Draft Statement of Principles); and removal of commitments of indefinite duration on export/import arrangements. What these mean is that, among other things, (i) there will be an assured mutuality of benefit; and (ii) a country's total import level will not be higher than it would otherwise be or than that determined by developmental policy needs, while its exports (by opening up markets within the region) will increase.

The operation of both the Principles will require continuing machinery and processes, including a continuing system of commodity complementarity exercise.[11] It will also remove dependence on tariff relaxation as a pre-condition for commodities to flow (thereby also removing impracticabilities and uncertainties as to the outcome of tariff negotiations). Thus, it could speed up action by commending and ensuring implementation.

On the premise that no participating country can lose, but only gain, it should be possible to implement them with provision for review at a stipulated time.

NOTES

1   There have been earlier studies as well within the United Nations system on the same lines.

Trade and Development Co-operation

2   Particular mention should be made of Pierre Uri who established the initial break-through in discussions with countries in ECAFE, outlining a production-related trade expansion scheme. The draft principles appearing in this chapter are virtually based on his thinking, except for one basic change at the outset offering countries an export opportunity rather than requiring an import commitment.

3   For a very early prognosis of potential for such co-operation, see my *Economics of Full Employment in Agricultural Countries*, pp 274-277 (1952, published 1958).

4   Dr. W.Rasaputram, later Governor of the Central Bank of Ceylon, was of direct assistance in their formulation. The responsibility for the text herein is mine.

5   In actual operation, the exercise of such import diversion can also refer to items never imported from outside the region but expected to be, on the basis of future increased demand. It can also refer to goods which are obtainable only within the region (physically or practically) but whose import will imply necessary diversion of foreign exchange from extra-regional imports unless matched by intra-regional exports. The existence of under-utilised industrial and agricultural capacity in the countries has a place here.

6   It is at this stage that the first meaningful country and commodity profiles, from the point of view of the exercise itself, would really emerge.

7   The test of the feasibility of this approach is that whatever the out come of the Commodity Flow Exercise, countries will *still* be *importing* the commodities concerned — only they will be doing so extra-regionally and without the benefit of additional exports.

    Three basic principles should be observed in this connection: 1. Import commitment by a country will be only up to the extent of its export capacities on the offered items. 2. There will be no request to a country to give up an existing production line or items; ideas of not expanding certain production lines further may, however, be a consideration.   3. Any commitments by a country could be assured as valid only for a given number of years, say, about five years.

8   It is this stage that what has been sought as a Trade Plan in terms of this exercise would emerge.

9   At this stage mutually assessments in terms of established criteria, assessment of pre-investment and investment needs to ensure export performance as well as, in some cases, even proposals for resource surveys and applied research would be relevant.

10   Clearing and payments arrangements for this agreed area of co-operation will easily follow; this of course is different from the wider-scale payments arrangements being sought at that time and which went on as a worthwhile attempt.

    Also emerging at this stage would be the elements for drawing up a practical code of trade liberalisation that would really be applicable since it would be based on the experience of actual negotiation.

11   At least for a first phase until countries have worked with the system; a somewhat more automatic procedure may be feasible later.

Chapter Fourteen

Monetary and Investment Co-operation

I mbalances, where they are more than temporary, require more than temporary solutions. Means and facilities for holding deficit obligations over a sustained period become crucial, more so when heavy financing is involved. There is nothing controversial in this and this has been recognised. It was the reason for setting up one of the key post-War instruments of international economic co-operation in the form of the IMF.

Deficits on development account in reality merge into liabilities on capital assets, being, thus continuously related to the balance of trade and payments. Questions of capital inflow are, therefore, an integral part of wider monetary co-operation. World Bank and private lending both come within this frame of co-operation and management. We have seen the global attempts to try to attain a consensus on the volume of such lending by the developed countries. The original target of GNP, since watered down to 0.7 per cent, has been discussed in the last decade as, still a target to be obtained. It is of interest on this context to find, for example, that British foreign investment during the fifty years before 1914 was 4 per cent of its GNP and 7 per cent during 1905 to 1913. Capital inflow, as a proportion of net capital formation, was over 40 per cent in Canada from 1901 to 1920, about 11 per cent in the USA from 1869 to 1878 and fifty per cent in Sweden from 1861 to 1870, reaching 79 per cent from 1881 to 1908.[1] It is amazing how the world has got used to expecting the developing countries today to do with much less, or, worse still, to faulting them for not doing it all themselves.

In the meantime, the question of international liquidity was being approached with palliatives rather than solutions. Under normal trade conditions, the need for liquid assets being mainly a measure of trade oscillations, one may say that the larger the trade volume the larger the oscillations and time adjustments and hence the need for larger liquidity. But in the case of the developing countries the need was, additionally, much more endemic in character and, in fact, largely a measure of capital inflow against short-fall in export earnings resulting from various trade barriers. So the real liquidity gap for the developing half of the world, based on development requirement, was quite different from the casual and operational factors that determined the quanta required for developed countries. Thus a liquidity gap, leaving aside inflationary gaps, may well have been met for developing countries either as interest free loans or payment in 'local currency'. Either way, offtake of produce, or new investment, has to be tied to use of the 'liquidity' loans or equivalent resources held by the developed countries.[2]

For the developing countries, the financial crisis may be considered the result of a package somewhat as follows:

1. In a reversal of post-War premises, the developed countries abolished the fixed exchange rate beginning early seventies.
2. While the primary produce exports were not fetching any multiple of their prices as of the forties, exports from industrial countries, including many primary exports, were annually rising and were a multiple of their original figures as at the forties.
3. Oil price structures changed beginning mid-seventies, creating severe crisis for the developing countries. They were not isolated phenomena, but an addition to the constantly rising prices of the industrial countries' exports; the oil prices became a heavy direct burden to the developing countries; soon, they also carried a serious second-round inflation of industrial country exports to the developing countries.

4. While the oil prices may have reached a plateau, however uncomfortable, the second-round industrial export prices continued upward, without commensurate primary produce export prices.

5. The energy costs of development, in the stampede for alternative energy sources amidst attempts at accelerating development, came home to roost as a semi-permanent phenomenon for the developing countries.

As a review put it, the inexorable rise in industrial prices in the post-War period was cost induced and had virtually nothing to do with excess demand. It was a consequence of the increased concentration of economic power, of both capital and labour, and thus of both monopolistic industrial pricing and militant trade unionism.[3]

The financing of international trade, based on deficit countries fighting to export and surplus countries resisting imports was a clearly 'upside down' phenomenon which had someday to be set 'right side up', if a world order were seriously contemplated.[4] In this case, it relates as much to the developed world as to the developing. The needed approach to financing of international trade was considered closely in many quarters during the late sixties and early seventies when these same concerns were already very much present. The rest of this chapter presents a framework of approach to a needed system of such financing, derived from the thinking and needs as practically encountered from those years.[5]

The subject of international liquidity has a long bibliography which had in fact intensified in the recent years.[6] No attempt is made therefore to list such references, even though in the discussion of current patterns, certain points clearly derive from already published contributions, and some others are widely known.

The concentration in the argument is in leading to the idea of 'local currency' settlements (wherein the globally deficit countries' currencies made out to the surplus countries in trade balance settlements, constitute the resources for the 'international fund') and the corollary arrangements relevant to

226

such a scheme. This idea, implying automatic creation and adjustment of the required foreign exchange media for settling the net dues of international trade, is of course different from policies for quota contributions based on gold or for commodities as a currency base or for revaluation of gold, etc. (whether with or without a world currency). It has links, however, with the multilateral clearing or pool clearing idea advanced in the past, e.g., by Schumacher as long ago as 1943 [7] as also in some ways with the Bancor scheme. It is an interesting commentary that after all these years, the directions for resolving the problem of international liquidity should still lead substantially that way, though with adjustments in the light of years and new experience.

International trade has now moved on to a stage when a number of financing problems seem to assail it with increasing force. True, finance has always been at the core of international commerce. The struggle for command over a universal means of exchange has been more at the root of the trading practices of nations than the exchange of goods itself — whether they were the practices of the mercantilist period, or of the heyday of laissez-faire, or even of current twentieth century liberalism. The past contradictions arising out of a mutual struggle for possession of 'gold', which led to so-called Keynesian and post-Keynesian thinking and the attempts of recent years to reconcile national employment and development objectives with stable international commerce, are of course well-known and do not call for recounting here.

The starting point for a discussion of solutions to current problems may conveniently be said to lie in two phenomena that have existed and continue to exist today in the field of international trade and trade expansion. One of these is the alleged state of inadequate international reserves for the satisfactory finance of international trade. Although often described in a generalised way, it is essentially a feature that is of relevance among advanced countries. The gradual supplementing of gold with strong currency media, primarily dollars and sterling, has led to a situation where the stability of international finance is now dependent on the internal stability of the economies whose currencies are being used as international

227

money. During the seventies, pressures on sterling and the dollar led to intricate swapping arrangements among central banks of advanced countries, aimed at sustaining the strength of the economies concerned and the stability of the international media used. Since the swapping arrangements do not constitute an addition to international reserves, but really a reserve creation mixed with a reserve transfer, they do not bring a lasting increase in owned reserve. In the process, a new manifestation emerged as to the meaning and content of reserves. In the meantime, those advanced countries which had begun using Euro-dollars in massive proportions, had themselves very large owned reserves of international exchange media. These countries, and particularly those of the Common Market, had still not developed an international currency of their own. Perhaps if this occurred, the apparent shortage of international currency reserves now felt would ease. It is still an open question, however, whether this is the proper basis for future financing arrangements as well.

The second phenomenon referred to belongs to the developing countries. To these countries, the problem of finance in the international sphere is not one of an inadequacy of reserves but one of its total absence. Their requirements do not get met by a mere accretion of 'gold', for the reason that any such increase will be fully spent. The inadequacy of the present nature and levels of international assistance from the point of view of developing countries' need, is therefore not even an open question; it is well nigh self-evident. Thus, we have the insistent pressure from under-developed countries for primary product prices to be determined by considerations outside pulls of supply and demand, and for preferential zero tariffs on their raw materials and manufactured goods. The same situation has led to the increasing use of foreign grant and soft loan arrangements to meet developing countries import requirements. It is also worth nothing, on the side of certain 'surplus' countries, and presumably many more in the future, that these countries have problems of surplus production useful to developing countries in certain sectors, for which it is in their own employment interests to seek export markets. Normally, in the

228

absence of international reserves among potential importing countries, such export of surplus output should be rendered impossible. So they still are in respect of some of the surplus output in many sectors; but need not be, if the methods of international financing did permit it. While developing countries have been driven to ask for better primary product prices, yet one cannot escape the feeling that such approaches are no more than asking for free income transfer from advanced countries to under-developed countries,[8] since the total requested incomes obviously exceed the economic value of their products, under normal international trade. The fact that the terms of trade for raw materials vis-a-vis manufactured goods have been against the former is, after all, no more than a manifestation of economic pressures. As for absolute falls in the terms of trade, while opinion is not necessarily uniform on this,[9] the relevant issues are rather of strengthening the economy or using OPEC style measures, if feasible.

We have, therefore, within the limits of these two phenomena in world trade, what is essentially an unnatural limitation on the scope of such trade imposed by the volume of monetary reserves available in the case of strong countries, and by the volume of international income transfer decided upon in the case of weak countries. In either case, the import potentials or export possibility is not determined by the internal economic capacity of the countries concerned, as would evidently be the case in the matter of trade between areas within one country. Clearly, the important missing factor at international levels is the absence of a single currency. To achieve this or, more correctly, to re-outline financing methods in a way that would approximate to this, would be the ultimate problem for solution. Vigorous thinking has undoubtedly gone on, on this, particularly since Bretton Woods and even, as some would claim, since the time of fixed exchange rate systems. What follows is an attempt, in the light of the doctrinal bases in current international financing, and in the light of what countries were in effect practising or working towards, to isolate the realities of trade finance.

Let us try to go over some of the basic elements in international financing even if, in a way, they may be known

well enough. As in many other spheres, the simpler elements in
a process tend to be over-shadowed by the complex operational
features of a system, and as such tend also to be lost sight of after
a time. Under present systems, there are, despite claims made
for fixed exchanges as approximating to unified currency,
important distinctions between national and international
economic transactions. In the one case, the media of exchange
are always the currency (or quasi-currency) and not reserves
whether they be real or fiduciary. Reserves within a national
system may, of course, be adjusted in an intra-bank sense, but
the total structures of 'money' remains the same and is influenced
by other factors and by conscious government policy. The limit
to transactions by income holders is, therefore, their income
itself (or producing capacity) and not the position of gold or
'near gold'. In the other case, i.e. at international level, 'note'
against 'note', or more properly book entires, will function as
the media of exchange under a situation of equilibrium
transactions. This is also the same as saying that the transactions
take on the form of goods against goods. As soon as the trade
flow ceases to be equilibrating, the foregoing does not hold
good and settlements will then need to be made in gold or
internationally accepted media, whose availability within
national economies is determined not by national income (or
money in circulation) but by the goods tradeable for such gold
or allied media; not goods that could yet be produced internally,
but only such lines as could be exchanged for gold, dollars or
sterling. In other words, the limit to international trade is set
not by national income or producing capacity, but by the
proportion of international media directly or indirectly available
in total income. Viewed from the surplus country side, the size
of the market in international trade is determined by the volume
of media available in exchange and not by total income and
productive capacity of the physical market area concerned (i.e.,
the importing country).

Now, essentially international trade is not trade in gold or
other similar media but in goods. And so, if one may elaborate
in terms of an example, it is financed, say by the U.S. importer
from Sri Lanka lodging his local currency (i.e., dollars) to the

Monetary and Investment Co-operation

Sri Lanka exporter's credit in New York, and the Sri Lanka importer lodging his Rupees to the U.S. exporters' credit in Colombo. Giving this implies a U.S. importer and Sri Lanka exporter (and vice versa) in the scene to equivalent value, the two holdings are extinguished by using the funds created in the transactions. If this were followed now by a transaction, where there was only a Sri Lanka importer (without a U.S. importer), Rupees to the U.S. exporter's credit will emerge in Colombo, which conceptually the U.S. exporter has to hold on to (because of course, no Rupees will be sent to the U.S.), or more realistically the exporter's bank will hold on to, after paying the former a dollar equivalent. Under present international arrangements what obligations now emerge for Sri Lanka? Either there must be an exporter who could send an item of equivalent value to the U.S. or the country must stop its import obtained in the earlier equilibrating trade mentioned and settle the outstanding debt. If the U.S. bank is, however, prepared to hold on to the Rupees created in the second one-way transaction (incidentally, the basic process of an international currency) there is no further debt and Sri Lanka's import limit is determined by the global demand for goods equivalent of its internal money income. Whether rupees are so held or whether they are requited by Sri Lanka exporting goods or gold, the U.S. exporter himself receives dollars from his bank and there the transaction for him is complete. When the U.S. finances an export beyond the equilibrium point, the financing system within the U.S. economy remains the same; it is only that the U.S. does not receive goods or gold or equivalent, but holds Sri Lanka Rupees. The position, therefore, is that internally exports are dollar financed (as always they are under any system) and externally in this case, are rupee financed.

It is worth noting that if the U.S. does not wish to adopt a system such as this in the case of a developing country (or even an advanced country placed in a similar position) the only course open to it is to cut down its own export and thereby depress its own employment and income levels; or, in the case of countries helplessly dependent on U.S. commodities, to maintain exports at the high disequilibrium level and create

231

dollar repayment obligations by deficit countries sometime in the future. From the point of view of financing, this is the same as the U.S. holding rupees, except that, unlike under a unified currency, interest costs have to be met by the deficit country till such time as the latter exports adequate goods to wipe off the debt. Internally, within the U.S. economy, the position is the same whether the export surplus is paid for and received in rupees or is made out as a dollar loan to Sri Lanka. Dollar payments are made out to the private American exporter by his government in either case. Under either system, an imbalance is created within the U.S. economy between goods and money, with a consequent price pressure on national product, which is larger by the amount of the exports unrequited by corresponding commodity imports. How far the U.S. as a surplus country would keep exporting beyond the equilibrating point would, of course, be determined by the capacity of the economy or more properly by the U.S. budget, to husband surpluses or run deficits for exchanging dollars for the rupee holdings of its banks. The parameters to trade are thus the economy's financing capacity on the surplus country side and the government and private income holders buying capacity on the deficit country side. Even under the present context, therefore, the availability of international reserves are not the limiting factor in trade for most deficit countries. The question is whether this should be pursued to its logical conclusion and a system accepted where 'local currency' holdings constitute payment in settlement, with the possessor of the currency using it as part of its international financing reserves. For the developing countries, the question is whether they should go on asking for higher prices for their primary product as what is essentially charity, in the face of other economic determinants, or press an alternative possibility of a payments system which gives all countries the chance of being in the same position as those that now have large gold and allied reserves.

In a situation where trade is between the U.S. (assumed for the present to be a surplus country) and another industrial country (assumed to be in deficit with the U.S.), the trade disequilibrium has to be settled ultimately either by an increase

232

in imports by the U.S. or by suffering a cut-back in its exports. The alleged fact of international reserves coming in to sustain a continuing flow of disequilibrium trade has over and over again proved illusory. As Keynes pointed out long ago, gold or allied media held as reserves are either sterile and, therefore, meaningless in that form or they have to be used and, therefore, soon reach the limit of their capacity. The next stage, that is when there is no gold left, provides a more realistic limit, where the surplus country has to decide how much to import from the deficit country, and how much of its surplus exports it should itself finance. Where the deficit industrial country is in a strong position economically it would in fact seek to recover its lost gold by cutting down U.S. exports. And so this seesaw can go on, with no substantial strengthening of trading power by either country but only a generally restrictive, and as some have observed, inherently anti-growth bias. Where the industrial country is in a weak position, as was Europe during the Marshall Aid days, the U.S. will, if it wants to maintain its level of export trade, soon have to hold 'local currencies', and euphemistically rename the whole or part of it as capital credits. The interest paid by the deficit countries does not seem to be so much a charge for not paying in money for the imports made, as the price for being helplessly dependent on the imports. Among the Western countries today, it may be possible to assume with reason that countries are no longer helplessly dependent in this manner. One may assume that they could cut-back potential surplus countries' exports. It could thus be advantageous to all advanced countries to talk less in terms of transferring reserves or granting loans, and more in terms of settling disequilibria while extending exports and holding each other's local currencies. This in fact is really what has been happening in the North Atlantic Area from some years ago. The totem attached to the reserves idea has carried the fixation that the objective of national policies in trade has been to strengthen reserves positions. In fact, the sole objective of trade trends during the early seventies has been to achieve balance on an upward trend of commodity trade, with no one gaining substantial gold resources, but rather moving towards a system of governmental credit more in the nature of overdraft financing.

Thus, the position is that, except where local currency is being held, the international reserves accumulated by one country or another are constantly seesawing in a process of won, lost and won. Since this is more often achieved by contracting trade than by expanding it (that is by surplus countries increasing imports) the only consequences are stepping down of GDP in the export sector of the surplus country and of Gross National Expenditure in the import sector of the deficit country. Total world output goes down,[10] for the transitory gain (or recoupment) of international reserves. Under the alternative 'local currency' holding system, world income tends to remain high, with exports continuing at their own levels and imports by surplus countries very likely increasing. Among industrial countries the chances of equilibrating at a high level of total trade are much greater; while among developing countries the chances of others absorbing their exports are equally increased. Trade will thus be related not fortuitously to the holdings of world exchange media but to country's capacities in export and import.

In this situation deficit countries can find that imports are welcome so long as surplus countries care to hold outside currencies in exchange. Surplus countries need not face the same demands from deficit countries for importing goods such as primary produce, that they need not use, whether for reasons of cost or quality. The case of reducing unfair tariffs on primary produce would, of course, remain. As for the actual prices of this produce, they could afford to be determined, as they are, by market conditions which include the essential rational substitution of natural with synthetic raw materials by advanced countries. Such deficit countries' payment obligations over and above what their primary and other exports earn for them, would be met by payment in local currency. The surplus countries could now readily do away with their duties on primary goods and simple manufactures and enjoy a welfare increase by the import of these in the knowledge that overall economic activity will be more than compensated by increased exports. This expansionist process would also render much

234

Monetary and Investment Co-operation

easier the rationalisation of such internal sectors of an advanced country (of which the pre-War 'Lancashire' case was typical) as may be affected by the exports of developing countries.

The control function of international reserves was primarily to show that a country was importing more than it was exporting—and vice versa. The corrective action it prescribed worked against maximising world production and even world trade; it worked against efforts at development assistance to developing countries; and against maintaining high and steady GDP levels in advanced countries. The function of indicators will now be performed by the size of 'local holdings'. The corrective action called for will be action prescribed by national development policy and not by the unequal possession of gold, dollars, or sterling. In the same way as a developing country would not internally encourage luxury goods production, it would not, for fiscal and developmental reasons, encourage luxury imports. Yet the point is that curbs on import will be imposed not for 'balance of payments' reasons but for national income reasons. The test of this would be in the fact that the country could and would import capital and intermediate goods, as well as essential consumer goods, to the measure required by national development needs — something it could not have often done under the current system of trade financing. Developing countries may also, for reasons of building their national economies, grant protection to industries which in the long run will be economic. Subject to such saving clauses, however, the request to curb imports would really come from the exporting countries which have to carry the internal financing burden of effecting surplus exports. These surplus countries would also desire certain limits to their 'local currency holdings' and would, therefore, urge the countries concerned to develop exports, and would welcome such exports.

As also mentioned earlier, where countries run export surpluses, there is more money than goods within the economy with some price pressure involved, assuming unchanged fiscal policies. This is so, however, whatever the international financing system. The only point for gold or equivalent as a reserve holding is that the internal money — goods balance can be restored by financing imports from a third country. But this balance can be effected under the local holding system itself if the third countries too operate their foreign trade under the local currency reserve system. If, for instance, a deficit country (B) has settled its payment obligations in its own currency to the surplus country (A), but has 'local currency' holdings of a third country (C), this would be set off against A's holdings of its own currency, assuming that country (C) is in surplus with country (A). All this will be much in the manner of international transactions as now known. A residual global deficit, if it exists, will, however, be held not in gold or equivalent, but in a collection of local currency holdings. So long, however, as any country can import goods by paying in its own currency, the need for other media of exchange will not arise.

This process is, of course, international income transfer at its best and most realistic. Theoretically a developing country can meet huge portions of its consumer needs in this way. In practice, however, working arrangements are bound to emerge wherein local currency holdings by foreign countries will, if not limited by, be at least related to potential export capacities — a point which will now be more closely studied by exporting countries themselves than before, when export of almost anything would be sought so long as the receiving countries had gold or equivalent to pay in exchange. But, as suggested earlier, these export capacities will not be confronted by co-existing import curbs of one type or other by advanced countries. There is, on the contrary, likely to be a great endeavour among advanced countries to absorb various types of consumer goods, and especially to help in their future development. As for advanced countries, there is bound to be unrestricted flow of goods among themselves at an increasing pace, with trade either balancing at much higher levels or deficit/surpluses accruing again at much higher levels of trade than hitherto.

The discarding of the international reserve idea in its present form will afford unrivalled opportunity to developing countries to overcome today's critical obstacles to their development. The situation where masses of food, raw materials and other intermediate goods are available in the rich countries but

236

cannot be sent to the poor for want of international reserves, will cease to exist in these paradoxical forms. The historical special arrangement under PL 480 export, as well as the several soft loan arrangements mooted and tried, were indeed a recognition of the inevitable logic of the foregoing argument. These are indeed only marginal attempts towards this new approach, yet they are sufficient recognition of the rationale of a local currency holding system. Given the surpluses in Europe and elsewhere, and the great capacity increases in world GDP, a solution to international trade finance is obviously being awaited. As seen before, the lip service paid to the solidity of the international reserve idea has not prevented the governments and central banks of advanced countries from innovating a number of 'heretical' measures.

Mention was made of the approximation of the local currency system to a unified currency. It is, of course, clear that the approximation is not complete unless surplus countries' local currency holdings are themselves as freely utilisable within the deficit country as the currency of other income earners of that country. In practice, therefore, institutional arrangements would emerge which partly make this possible and partly render the deficit country liable to limits of sorts in the use of local currency systems. For instance, while payment in local currency would constitute settlement of obligations up to certain determined levels, beyond a point the deficit country may be required to pay a charge on the local currencies held by others (in other words the conventional foreign loan); for a further segment of local currency holdings the surplus country may be permitted to spend within the country on agreed investments and purchases; and so on.[11] The idea here is not so much to relate import capacity to international exchange media, but to relate total investment and consumption to current and potential GDP levels. It means also, therefore, that the relation is meant to avoid a country undertaking a level of Gross National Expenditure by means of uncontrolled inflation.

As also mentioned earlier, the local currency holding system would mean that a set of currencies of the world would now constitute the international reserves of world trade and play the

237

same role as gold, dollars and sterling jointly do now. Theoretically, the fact that under local currency holdings, international financing reserves would be composed of weak currencies as well as strong, could mean that an unacceptable basis exists in place of current exchange media. Theoretically also, however, this should not be so if every country concerned does partake in trade on the basis of local currency holdings. The fact that Germany for example may hold considerable Rupees would not hinder it from importing from the U.S. under a system where payments for the U.S. imports are to be made in Marks and where, in fact, the U.S. could take over Rupees to the extent that there is a residual balance. This is easy to see if one could only remember that the whole objective of reserves accumulation by modern countries is to be able to import — and this they are able to do under the alternative system with the added advantage that they are not forced when already in surplus to restrict their exports.

There is no doubt, however, that in history, the passage from one mental horizon to another has rarely rested on logical demonstration. In this sense the role that a World Central Bank can play in transforming the system could be both impressive and convincing. In the same way as governments have given respectability to paper money, the World Central Bank could 'transform' net local currency holdings into World Central Bank notes giving similar quality to international money as governments do to theirs. Perhaps something like a guarantee by strong surplus countries, in addition to pledges by all others, could be available to the World Central Bank, to provide the desired 'goods equivalent' (not 'gold') to claimant countries in the event of currency collapse in any of the country or countries whose currencies form part of the 'local currency holding' international reserves. These 'holdings', although of a deficit country currency, belong not to that country, but to the outside surplus country. What the latter is doing is essentially to put out this holding, instead of its gold, to finance international trade. If the currency of the holding in question gets debased, such local currency would revert as a charge on the country concerned. There would be no call for 'gold', but the country

238

will re-accept formal responsibility to repay 'in goods'; or in a later stable currency. Meanwhile, the claimant countries would receive 'goods equivalents' on the basis of the guarantees and pledges available to the W.C.B. with the 'local holdings' frozen out of international financing flow. Subsequent immediate trade by that country will be only on a 'barter' basis, relieved to the extent that foreign and international loans are bilaterally available. This is much in the way of what would occur under present financing systems as well. Once restored to financial stability and equilibrium, however, not only would the rehabilitated local currency take its place in international finance, but the earlier local currency holding held by the countries will be put back by the W.C.B. in settlement of used guarantee obligations and pledges.[12] In practice, institutional arrangements, to which reference was made earlier, would, as in present day trade financing, limit the unrestricted accumulation of local holdings even before a currency comes to a stage of collapse. If each local holding were denominated to a world standard of measure (and thus isolated in value terms from local inflationary collapses); and if the W.C.B maintained certain 'liquidity ratios' (between weak and strong currencies) the world of international finance would skip the history of 'bank-runs' that national monetary experience went through more than a hundred years ago, before it came to its present, fiduciary-based unassailable stage.

The trends and emerging practices as between industrial countries, as illustrated chiefly in the North Atlantic Area, make it clear that attachment to gold or equivalent is purposeless and unnecessary. No one country would suffer the other to carry on long with a process which brings gold or allied benefits to the other countries — and vice versa. Similarly, parallel trends and emerging practices for advanced countries vis-a-vis developing countries leave no doubt as to the fiction that is the international reserves idea. If one were to choose a limited adoption of the local currency financing system, it would appear safer to countries to begin in the industrial West; but to begin elsewhere in the backward areas of the World would be the more necessary step. The greatest need, however, is to overcome the mental subordination to past ideas. It would then be possible to cease interpreting the present world with a past theoretical instrument. As to the inevitability of change, there is no doubt. What is in doubt is whether the realities will be comprehended sooner, or later.[13]

NOTES

1   See e.g., Ragnar Nurkse 'International Investment Today in the Light of Nineteenth Century Experience', *Econ. Journal* 1954.

2   Weirn M.Brown, 'The External Liquidity of an Advanced Country', distinguishing between reserve and liquidity, contending that the former is an aberration and the latter is adequate for trade purposes.

   Conceptually, balance of payment deficits in one area of the world are surplus in another. Thus, there is no availability problem. The problem arises because earned foreign assets in surplus may be considered by that country as needed to build up reserves.

3   Kaldor and Trevithick, *Lloyds Bank Review, 1981.*

4   This is nothing new in a sense, perhaps; these were inherent in the Keynesian philosophy of approach and had to be implicit in the post-War structures that were created. See also my *Ceylon, Beveridge and Bretton Woods* (1948) for some early discussions.

5   While the responsibility for the frame is entirely mine, grateful acknowledgement is made to the opportunities of meeting Prof. Triffin during the late sixties, when the countries in the Asian region were attempting to grapple with these problems in the cause of formulating trade and payment cooperation arrangements.

6   Triffin, Bernstein, Kaldor, the 'Paris Club', to mention some active creative participants. Also, for example, Banco Nazionale Del Lavoro, Quarterly Review, March - June - Sept. 1966.

7   Economica, (May issue).

8   The preliminaries to the World Trade Conference had apparently some interesting postures taken up by countries. The advanced countries each suggested generous measures of income transfer of various types, in each case calculated to be more at the expense of its industrial neighbours than of the proposer. On the side of the developing countries a string of requests emerged adding up to an impressive demand for larger markets for raw materials and manufactures at prices specially advantageous to these countries, along with demands for more credits at lower interest and for longer periods. The fact is that under present systems of trade finance, such scales of income transfer become impossible. For example, the Common Market made timid concessions to trade liberalism one year in the late sixties and found its global commercial deficit double to the figure of $2,800 million. So long as international reserves are the

determinant of trading ability such policies will continue to be impracticable.

9 Note for example Haberler 'Integration and Growth of the World Economy in Historic Perspective', *American Economic Review*, March 1964.

10 The volume of world output, as Nurkse reminded once, is a truer criterion of world prosperity than the volume of world trade. Hans Singer recalls how under 'the original ideas developed by Keynes ... in Bretton Woods ... the IMF pressure ... was to be on the surplus countries ... rather than (the present) imposed IMF conditionally on the deficit countries...' (Adam Weiler Memorial Lecture, 1982)

11 All useful trade promotion measures familiar today would, of course, fit into the new scheme. For instance, the system of foreign investment on the basis of purchase of the outputs of those investments; or the 'division of labour' argument brought out in one of the resolutions of the World Trade Conference, where the simpler stages of an industrial process are desired to be undertaken by advanced countries in the backward countries— these are types of action which if desired, can be developed, and will probably find a more welcome atmosphere under 'local currency holdings.'

12 An alternative procedure would be for a special set of W.C.B. notes to replace this set of holdings, to be withdrawn from circulation later, when the currency in question has been rehabilitated.

13 Portions of the thinking and ideas in this Chapter are also reflected, as needed, at Chapter XV on South Asian Regional Co-operation (with some unavoidable, though probably essential repetitions). It was that the internal 'consistencies' of both may have suffered otherwise.

Chapter Fifteen

South Asian Regional Co-operation — with Particular Reference to Economic Issues

I. Reluctant Enthusiasm

Both the concept of South Asia and the concept of regional co-operation in South Asia, as it has evolved, and is today, are composed of two opposite realities.

The first is in fact that we have had in South Asia a geographical and, if we may use the phrase, a spiritual and *cultural* reality covering the region. We shall elaborate on this later on. This reality, which has ancient roots in a way, giving a commonality to the region, has lent this Zone or Sub-region a quality, therefore, of being 'ancient, abiding and real'.

The other reality is the *political*, economic and military background in the region. Quite obviously, it has left a legacy in recent times, of the region being 'amorphous, varied and conflicting'. In the experience of regions elsewhere, where conflict is at a minimum, and when also helped by a common external threat, there is a real chance for regional co-operation to emerge. Sometimes, conflict has an autonomous nature of reducing itself to a minimum in some of these regions. Some regions are not as conflicting within themselves as, perhaps, South Asia. Perhaps some are more, but when conflict is at a minimum and when it is helped by a common external threat, then regional co-operation emerges. This is what happened in ASEAN. It happened also in an area which many may not be as familiar with — the South Pacific. Of course, it happened in

242

East Europe and the European Economic Community. We are now on the threshold of a larger entity of the whole of Europe.

These conditions did not really prevail in South Asia. The situation till very recently was not of conflict being at a minimum, nor of international threat being profuse. Rather, threats to each other were profuse; and where the external factor was concerned, it was not so much an external threat, as of external 'partners' — each having somebody. Pakistan had China or U.S.A.; and India had the U.S.S.R.; Nepal had some links with China, which created problems, and made India feel uncomfortable. The exceptions were the Maldives and Bangladesh. Sri Lanka had sometimes looked over its shoulder, into China, though not in the same way as the countries of the sub-continent did; and sometimes looked at a 'Yankee' relationship as a possible factor. These are obviously reasons for the 'opposites' that we referred to earlier. All had some sort of favourite 'Uncle' in the Region, encouraged, of course, by things like the Indira doctrine, the Indian Ocean version of the Monroe doctrine, all of which became inimical to the formation of a South Asian entity.

Yet, there was an undercurrent which emerged finally in 1985 in Dacca, Bangladesh, for the formation of a South Asian regional co-operation association. Perhaps, it was a little more than a coincidence that it was Bangladesh which was in the forefront of the formation of this. As one of the least developed countries, she had enough problems herself, and need for co-operation. But, not having favourite 'Uncles', it may have been natural that she had originated and pursued the idea, more than the others. The only other country could have been the Maldives, but probably too small. In the meantime commentators, journalists and others were still full of suspicion, and hardly foresaw that this might become a reality. Thus we had phrases like this region being called 'a region of mistrust', a region which 'welcomed the absence of a co-operative regional machinery, rather than its presence'. So much so, that in 1985, that commentator was in a position to write that the concept of SAARC was 'fading away faster than the sunset'. The ink had not dried on the paper on which it had been written, when in Dacca, SAARC emerged that same year.

243

The Wealth of Poor Nations

How does one explain that there was this enormous contradiction between opinion and the reality as it come up later? One thinks it lay in two sources. One is what one referred to earlier as the feeling of abiding historical unity, or oneness of the whole region. There was a feeling that they had links with each other, whatever the quarrels, and that they could forge links. One had the experience well before SAARC was formulated, in the late seventies, to set in motion a process which resulted in the formation of a Community in South Asia, as recalled in another Chapter here. This happened when the Environmental movement gathered strength, after the Stockholm Conference of 1973. At that time there was a great environmental surge all over the world. Presidents and Prime Ministers were heads, in their own countries, of Environmental Ministries. There was the emotional, shared affection for One Earth and Planet Earth and kindred phases. The sense of ideological commonness of South Asia found expression it seems, when the UN found it necessary to gestate the idea.

In other parts of Asia, let alone the rest of the world, Communities had already formed. ASEAN and the South Pacific were there, and the Environmental movement found expression through the formulation of specific Sub-regional bodies, as ASEP for South East Asia and SPREP for the South Pacific and, briefly even for Indo-China.

In South Asia, it was a situation where there was no Regional Organisation, and no South Asian Community. Thus this writer, who had led the U.N. initiatives in all the foregoing, set about probing, suggesting, and coaxing into being, the idea of a South Asian Community. It seems right to say, that the response in South Asia was the product of the two 'binding' factors earlier recalled. One, the ideological pull of the Environmental call; and the other, that South Asia had links, and that they can link together if a 'thread' was found and was pursued diligently and properly.

Alongside if we come to 1985, although the area had no external military threat to put it together, in the sense that some other regions had, there was another external threat that was taking sharp form during the eighties. It started after the oil

244

crises of the seventies and countries became enormous debtors, to the point where the poor countries were paying back capital to the rich countries instead of receiving funds from them. So this aid, trade and debt trap, that the developing countries were falling into, came to be perceived in this region, as a common external threat. It was a substitute for the common classical, military threat, that forces people — as happened in ASEAN. At this point, sometime before '85, there was a stream of opinion which was prepared to subscribe to the thought that the countries were a 'single economic system'.

At the same time, it produced a peculiar type of conclusion, suited to local perceptions. So the countries, the major ones at least, declared a 'full commitment to a regional organisation, but also with full reservation!' This was about the time that SAARC was formed, in 1985. Hence, for example, the special emphasis that bilateral issues shall not figure in the discussions of SAARC. It extended to the components of economic co-operation itself, namely of full commitment on the one side, with full reservation on the other.

In the meantime, the World was marching on. The Cold War had ended. There was a 'new Europe' that was emerging, and the 'new Pacific Rim' or Pacific area was coming up. And there was a compulsiveness which led people in South Asia to think that they had to move immediately, perhaps faster than they have been. This, briefly, is the type of background which led apparently, to the position now in organisation. As to the content of South Asian co-operation, we should probably look at it under three categories.

First, the *political*. Politically the region was faced with giant external groupings. There was the North American grouping. There was the New Europe. There is USSR, for, whatever its present problems, in the destiny of the future the USSR is a giant grouping. And there is East Asia, that is Japan, a (later) united Korea and China. And others which are waiting on the sidelines. Further, as Lee Kuan Yew very rightly pointed out recently, Indo-China will one day link up with the rest of South East Asia, recording a type of rapid growth that will make the whole another giant grouping.

The Wealth of Poor Nations

That leaves South Asia. This then, is the type of political background in which it rests for now. The countries of this region have not sorted themselves out yet. We still have this big country/small country complex. One cannot ascribe blame, but looking from a wider background, it seems the countries should step back and try to 'think through' something strong and clear about it.

The next is the *structural* background. Compared to the giants, the South Asian co-operative unit that we have now, is what this writer once called a 'small South Asia'; it is not South Asia. Countries have to make up their minds, as to whether they are going to be South Asia in full or a narrower 'Indian Ocean Asia'. The latter is a lapse, because the historical perception of South Asia should not be, and is not simply, the Indian Ocean Area. Perhaps because of the Environment idea, the real South Asia came into being at that time, including not only the countries of the later SAARC, but Iran, Afghanistan and, provisionally Myanmar (Burma). If they do these, then they cease to be a 'small South Asia' and can stand up as an Economic Entity, with size and resource endowment, and variety and capability, that can fulfil the needs of a viable economic Unit or Area.

That is not only for economic purposes. It is also for fulfilment of the historical concept of South Asia. One recalls Iran emphasising over and over again in the UN, that people must remember that they do not belong to 'West Asia', but are Asians and belong to Asia. Thus Iran was not a member of the UN's West Asian Economic Commission, but of Asia and the Far East. So it was a natural structure, calling for response. Later, at the Islamabad SAARC Conference, SAARC took a hesitant first step without quite mentioning Afghanistan, and reiterated that if countries do apply, then they would be considered on the basis of unanimity.

The third aspect is the *substantive* component of SAARC - the economic side if one likes. This was the weakest. Here the countries established a basis for co-operation in SAARC but, to use a word that became common soon, still had only what were called 'sanitized' areas; that is, areas which do no harm, but do

246

South Asian Regional Co-operation — Economic Issues

no good either, with a little bit here and a little bit there. This is not to say anything derogatory. There were useful components in this schedule of sanitized projects or programmes. For instance, the food stock reserve that has been proposed, has its uses. But in terms of forging trade and regional economic co-operation, what were had were purely harmless sanitized areas. The areas were ephemeral, even deceptive, inducing the thinking they were co-operating, when actually not much was happening.

Essentially therefore, the crux of the substantive side of the future of South Asia depends on the ability to forge real co-operative mechanisms on *trade*, *payments* and development *financing*. Up to now, what we have had is a case of other countries doing a bit of India watching, and India doing a bit of only looking at herself! For the simple reason that India is large, she felt that she could develop economically and did not need the help of the others. She was a market by herself. Meanwhile, the other countries, who knew the advantage of a larger co-operative area, were watching every time for false steps, or surreptitious steps, that India would take, whether in fact those were false or true! To India, all her neighbours were security risks; to the others, their only security risk was India.*

They were also not entirely without foundation. Although Environment as we said, was a cementing factor, at the first High Level Meeting of officials at Bangalore, before the other steps developed and finally SACEP (the South Asia Co-operative Environment Programme) was established at the Ministerial Conference in 1981 held in Colombo, India carried a brief to oppose it, in fact to shoot it down. It was to the credit of the subject of Environment and, clearly of those who took part, the Participants and the Secretariat, that by the time the Conference ended, the Indian delegation, which was headed by a most charismatic representative who obviously played a key creative role, received a revised briefing from Delhi, and went all out to support the formation of the Organisation.

---

* A phrase well formulated by Alfred David, Sri Lanka's High Commissioner in Bangladesh at the time.

247

Thus it seems postures should not readily be read as realities. As we know, when Bangladesh prematurely suggested, at SAARC's creation in 1985, that they have an Investment Centre, India deflected it. Also, for two opposite reasons, India and Pakistan found themselves taking the same policy line, on many issues.

However, in 1988 some things began to move, starting in Islamabad. It was decided to hold, after the Summit, what was called the Fourth Meeting of Planners, to study and to pursue economic co-operation. In 1990, the Male Summit went much further. It decided to hold the Second Ministerial Meeting on International Economic Issues in 1991 in India, before the ensuing Colombo SAARC Summit was convened, in order to pursue hard, concrete possibilities of economic co-operation. There was also a decision to set up, or explore the setting up of, a SAARC Regional Fund.

Although not part of SAARC, the Indian High Commission in Sri Lanka offered to develop trade relationships on Rupee payment terms. Now, this was quite a notable statement although little came of it later. We have dealt with that subject itself in a separate Chapter, under Payments.

Thus, between 1989 shall we say and 1990, all the things that we have been saying so far, in terms of negative posture, were to a large extent overcome by a new feeling and resolve to forge regional co-operation. We are today in a situation where it is seriously possible to talk of concrete, regional economic co-operation. Not of course, that it will take place 'tomorrow'. Therefore, we should raise the question, if that is the situation, what are the chances then of co-operation taking place?

Before we come to the economic background, we must dispose of certain residuals in the political and structural areas that we discussed already.

Politically, the Region must continue the momentum and the process which the external world trends have made it realise. Structurally, as we said, it must convert this from an Indian Ocean area into a genuine South Asian Region. Then, economically or substantively, it could enter a phase, away from what we earlier called, of 'full commitment with full reservation', to one where we have 'economic co-operation without fear'. The need in order to do this, clearly, is to find *mechanisms* that will afford us this 'positive co-operation' without reservation, and without fear, in the three areas of *Trade*, *Payments* and *Development Financing*.

Even now, there is a danger of the area going into 'marginal' areas. We know, in the concept of marginalism, we do not accept failure but feign success! And then we go further into marginal areas. Here in one particular component, for example, the 'basic needs'; or 'poverty alleviation' programme, one needs to be quite clear that, as much as they are top National priorities, poverty alleviation and basic needs programmes, as instruments for forging regional co-operation, are marginal and misleading, and will only prevent them from looking at the real, essential ingredients of regional economic co-operation mechanisms.

As to the real steps, we do not suggest that we jump into a wholesale economic co-operation mechanism straight away. We cannot — because no other part of the World has done this! There is a case to be made for gradualism. That means going 'step by step'. But there is a gaping difference between going step by step, and ensuring that the 'content' of each step and the 'direction' of each step are correct. This is where the difference lies between adopting a basic needs, or a poverty alleviation programme, and going 'step by step' in programmes that relate to Trade Liberalisation, Payments Arrangements and Development Financing Institutions.

The region has to take these steps. If that is the case, what is the *package* that we have? Do we have anything before us? Has anybody put out any package which we can accept and work? This is the big question. In terms of 'philosophy', we do have plenty of philosophy. That started in Latin America, with Raul Prebisch, the very distinguished Economist — the first Executive Secretary of ECLA, and at UNCTAD — and the mentor of a whole generation of international economists. As philosophy, the Third World has plenty of philosophy on regional co-operation. But as for action, whether Latin America, the Caribbean, Africa or Asia, there has been very little to show. Even ASEAN was not really an exception, its path being created by other means. The result has been that the West, beginning in Europe, led in Co-operation; and the South led in the Arguments for co-operation.

The reality is that 'the instruments of co-operation' that we have talked about so far, are the products of what one would, for short, call 'intellectual colonialism'. We say so for the reason, in particular, that when we talk of regional economic co-operation we immediately talk of 'tariff dismantling'. This is the approach of the GATT type of tariff progress. The moment this is tried out — and it has been done in developing areas before, through the UN, or on their own — there is immediately an 'enthusiasm in principle' but 'doubt in practice'. Countries then end up with the proclamations and with marginalism, but little action. The reason is that under the tariff dismantling approach, there is no guarantee that a small country, or a less developed country, or disadvantaged one, will come out even vis-a-vis a bigger country, or a stronger country. In fact, the result, always, has been the opposite.

Thus, one simply cannot get to that 'regional co-operation without fear', that was vital. No only was fear there; but, it was a real fear! The solution then, as we said, has to be not 'assurances', but the adoption of the right 'mechanisms'. Here again we should separate them from 'instruments' of trade promotion. Entrepreneurs from across the border can get together, separately as Chambers of Commerce; or Governments can have agreements on trade. The *mechanisms* of trade co-operation, as one shall see, are quite different from just choosing the 'instruments'. What is essentially involved in this type of mechanism are three things in the three areas mentioned, of Trade, Payments and Development Financing.

In *Trade*, it is a change from 'import commitment' by countries, that is, a commitment to import through tariff dismantling, to 'export potential' to giving incentives to develop 'export potentials'. So, you do not hold down a country to an import commitment, but you encourage and invite export potential in trade. In other words, the country is to generate additional exports, not additional commitment to import. How this works, we have taken up elsewhere in the book, at Chapter XIII.

250

In *Payments*, we need a system (there is an Asian Clearing Union in whose setting up again this writer played a central policy role), where we may move from the level of reserves as a 'determinant of the capacity' to import, to the productive capacity of the economy itself as a determinant of the capacity to export and to import. This requires a new notion of what is a reserve, what is a common currency and if so how we move towards that.

Loans and debts are a characteristic feature of investment financing. We need a proper *Investment* Bank concept. SAARC mooted a regional fund. But we saw earlier the role that should have been of the Asian Development Bank. In SAARC, the ADB is the type of investment instrument that should be the main mechanism.

In all these three things of Trade, Payments and Investments Banking, the scenario that we have now is one of things being 'upside down'. We need to put them 'right side up'. This is a bold step forward.

II. Underpinning Commitment:
A 'South' Answer

Let us first take the area of *Trade*. The defect, also mentioned briefly above, in trade co-operation, was in what was called the GATT type tariff concessional approaches in bargaining between countries. There was a classic error of common sense, even professionalism or academic ability, which was strange, that countries did not see. This is why, as we said, there was full enthusiasm, but with full reservation. Countries were using phrases with counterpoints to illustrate this duality, of being 'publicly positive and privately negative'.

A simple factor which lies in commonsense rather than professionalism was that the tariff dismantling approach is something which is valid and operable between equals — that is, between countries that are rich. This is because, and this is a point that we should emphasise, it is feasible only amongst countries which already have 'advanced production structures'. That is a vital point that we have to remember. In other words,

251

countries must be so advanced that they have immense, varied, industrial and technological ability; and all they are looking for is the dismantling of barriers so that their products can go out to the other countries.

Now, if all countries are in this, or similar position, then it stands to reason that the more we dismantle the barriers in trade the greater the trade flow will be; because the capacity is there. But, what is the situation in the poor countries? Their situation was very simply that this productive capacity was not there. It is either an agrarian capacity, or an elementary industrial capacity; and it is precisely the creation of this advanced productive capacity that is at the heart of Development Economics. Something which has been totally forgotten, it is therefore also at the heart of any system of trade expansion and trade mechanism — for co-operation amongst countries generally, or in this case, of countries in a region. At present, it is not a question of bargaining between rich equals, but between rich and poor; or, in the case of South Asia, between big countries and small.

Now, therefore, if this is the situation, what we posit is really an entirely opposite concept, where trade co-operation is premised *not on 'import commitment'*, that is, not on a commitment to import — because you do not have the capacity to import more than you are importing now. You are badly off with what you are already importing but you have to import that, because otherwise you will not survive. So trade expansion or trade co-operation must be based in an alternative approach, that is not of import commitment, *but of 'export potential'*, in fact, of *creating presently non-existent export potential.* It is a concept where trade co-operation is conceptualised and effected not merely in terms of trade promotion, but much in terms of trade *creation.* It is in terms of an innovative, dynamic, trade creation programme, where there is a very strong linkage between national development and international export, and trade co-operation performance. In this then, in establishing a Trade System, say for South Asia, what we do is that we do *not request tariff reduction, but make offers of 'export promotion'.* What it implies is that the heart of the programme becomes creating maximum exportable capacity. In other words, the *export potential* that is created or to be created, becomes the *indicator of the import possibilities.* There is a strict co-relation between new export potentials and 'new' regional import possibilities.

There has been some thinking on this it is not that there has been no thinking. It is simply that countries have been hesitant to go into this because they are very hesitant to go into modes of operation which have not arisen in the Western world. There is still a very strange mental subjugation on the part of the poor countries, where they feel that if something has not arisen from the Western world then it is not something that should be followed. At the same time, in fact, the originators of this concept were Western, with some collaborators from this part of the world too. The two co-originators were, in fact a Frenchman and an American, particularly the former, a person called Pierre Uri, in the early seventies, who conceptualised this formulation about trade expansion. When it is done, like in most things, one is amazed how simple the concept is and why nobody thought about it before. As we said, tariff dismantling is simply possible only between rich equals and where production capacity is already there, not where it has to be created.

The type of trade co-operation which, therefore, we should have to take up in the setting of South Asia, will be based on what might be called a Commodity Flow exercise. In other words, an exercise where countries are simply requested to put out 'lists' of all current and *potential*, exportable commodities. The larger the number of countries the better. This recalls our insistence that countries should move from being an Indian Ocean region to a proper South Asian region. Basically it is that each country puts out, as fully as possible, recognising of course that this is not a 'once and for all' process, a list of exportable commodities of various types, whether agricultural or industrial, or intermediate, in a series of what one may call 'cross commodity' and 'cross country' Trade matrices, thus building up such matrices, in terms of commodities and in terms of countries. Basically this is the concept. What happens then is that, a whole Scheme of 'Lists' emerges. It would be a product of a series of techno-economic exercises within countries, between countries, involving the Secretariat of SAARC, and on the basis of a large array of existing and potential economic resource data. What comes out of them is, initially, a whole list of exportable commodities, which then becomes feasible for presentation as Trade matrices, leading to commodity and cross country commodity flows. The private sector could participate fully in this.

When this happens, it is also possible to visualize the operation of what has gone by the name of Say's Law, that supply determines demand, that a commodity you produce will have its market. The conventional economic Law is of course that demand creates supply. Now if the former happens, and we find a situation where Say's Law becomes operable in practice, then expanding supply can create expanding demand. With it follows another interesting phenomenon. Countries, and it is interesting for small countries like Sri Lanka, will then be able to move from small scale production to medium and larger scale production. This is because they are engaging themselves in a wider market. And the Machinery, Tools and Equipment (MTE) manufactures — see Chapter VIII on this — become economic even in the smaller countries.

It is also based on an interesting current position in regional trade. This is that the trade between the countries of South Asia at the moment is very small. Regional exports, that is the exports of these countries in South Asia to one another was about 4.1 per cent in 1982 and 3.4 per cent in 1989 — very small, indeed, compared to the total exports to the world as a whole. Similarly, the imports by these countries from one another in the region was 2 per cent and 3.6 per cent, respectively. Also, we may imagine, if this is the amount of trade — for it is so minuscule — the ridiculousness of relying on a tariff dismantling approach on such a trade basis. How may we expect a smaller country to remove its tariff barriers, in favour of another country within this region? In contrast a 'Commodity Flow' exercise, and trade negotiations or expansion on that basis, could easily foresee a Trade Expansion Programme. The reason is that the extent of additional trade possibility is *determined*, not by the extent of trade within the region by
254

countries among themselves, but the extent of trade outside the region. The extent of trade by countries outside the region is of the order of 96-97 per cent.

Thus, *the operational point* in this Commodity Flow Matrix System is that countries agree to divert a portion, or increasingly significant portion of their imports from outside the region, to imports from within the region. *This is what gives capability* to the Matrix. Now, if they divert imports to within the region, one could have a situation where, for example, Sri Lanka could export edible oils to India, to the tune of millions (India's need is about fifteen billion rupees and Sri Lanka may not even be able to handle that much at once). On the other side, Sri Lanka could import machinery and equipment, ideally on a joint venture basis, some of which could even be re-exported. All this could be gestated by a simple process in Sri Lanka, instead of importing this particular machinery from 'abroad', diverting it to import from India. It need not only be India. It could be Pakistan; it could be jute products from Bangladesh. Importantly, the scope for it comes out, only by a Commodity Flow review of the system; which also keeps expanding. This is done using the volume of extra regional trade as an indicator of the possibilities. It would be idle to look for *existing* complementarities because they do not exist. It is a rather ludicrous situation, for if there were complementarities already there will be exchange of goods and we do not need any mechanism. We need to create complementarities, and that is what the Commodity Flow Matrix seeks. If there is an existing complementarity, trade will take place. So the crux of an operative programme in the trade expansion is 'creating' complementarity not looking for existing complementarities. In this, the Secretariat of SAARC could play a very positive role indeed.

If it did so, there are a few features that come out under this trade mechanism. *First*, trade expansion becomes based on 'physical commodity relations' and not 'tariff relations'. *Second*, no country can lose — a basic point — but only gain. In other words, no country will gain at the expense of another country. And in that situation, there is no fear of India being 'big'; others do not have to pray that India gets broken up into a number of States! India can continue to remain big. *Third*, an interesting point, a potential 'surplus' country, in other words a country which has greater export potential, like India for instance, will seek imports, because under this system, the extent to which India could export to the region is determined by its local commitment to import from within the countries under the System. Surplus countries will seek imports and will not oppose them, or discard them. *Fourth*, tariffs will not determine the volume of trade. If there are tariffs, the country that will hike up the prices will be the importing country and this will not affect the exporting country. *Fifth*, there will be no call for 'short term' loss, like under tariff dismantling approaches, for countries to incur, for the sake of a 'long term' prosperity and long term gain. *Sixth*, there will be no burden on any one country for the sake of that phrase called 'the greater good' of the region. *Seventh*, there is no commitment, without time limit. One could always have a time limit for this type of arrangement. *Eighth*, again an important point, there would be no unwanted imports, because, as we may recall, the export expansion is based on diversion of imports from outside the region to start with. That was another problem in tariff dismantling. When they dismantle tariffs, countries are afraid — especially small countries. They have to import goods for the sake of regional co-operation which they would not otherwise have imported. *Ninth*, any country's total import level will not be more than what the country's planning system, or the governmental planning system, has already decided. So the import level will not increase, but the export level will increase. sounding a little impossible, this is really what would occur.

The only challenge to the countries is to set out their items for present and planned production and export. This is 'the basic offer'. This is what the countries are offered, and this is their only challenge. *The price to pay* is that countries offer to divert some of their imports from outside the region, to within the region. If one was committed to regional co-operation, that is a logical sequence; and a feasible and understandable sequence.

As we may see now, there will be *no* 'unknown' balance of

payments threats, as happens under tariff dismantling. There will be no 'pressure groups', as even in the European Common Market, the American Market, or Japan, standing against their tariff concessions. There will be *no* mistake of marginal gains leading to an illusion that we are progressing in regional co-operation, when we really are not. Finally, there will be *no* additional international debts, with trade dependence on the North, *to the extent* that we increase our own trade co-operation.

There is one aspect here that we have to note: that there is in Asia, under the UN Economic Commission, what is called the Bangkok Agreement for Trade Expansion, set up in 1976, following the final Meeting of a Council of Ministers, which set up a Trade Expansion Programme. The Agreement does not have too many countries. It has Bangladesh, India, Sri Lanka, Korea and Laos, with Papua New Guinea coming in, and Afghanistan. This again is a case which illustrates the need for SAARC to expand to include its South Asian countries properly. The question has sometimes been raised whether the countries should not, instead of developing a South Asian trade expansion programme or trade co-operation programme, just try to work their trade programmes through the Bangkok Agreement. The short answer is that one need not be considered competitive with the other. One could go with the Bangkok Agreement, which is a conventional system of tariff dismantling approach, but go on to establish a South Asian regional trade expansion programme which then on its own merits, may point the way to later linkage with the Bangkok Agreement, which cannot carry the same pace of development.

There is another component in trade, which is very important, that we mentioned earlier. This is the *Commodities* of World Trade, such as coconut, pepper, rubber and others. In these we have tended to rely, for trade co-operation, on something that we have to be very careful about. We have tended to rely on *what* are called *buffer stocks* and *price stabilization* schemes. The *direct gains* themselves are *very marginal* to poorer countries. One conclusion that has been made by a study by a Western economist is that, in fact the rich countries benefited more by the 'buffer stocks', than the poor countries;

257

whereas they were started ostensibly in order to benefit the poor countries. As we know, the basic objectives of buffer stocks and stabilization schemes are to get better terms of trade and to obtain more investment resources for the poor. These never occurred. On the other hand, as an FAO Study repeatedly pointed out, the prices of commodities in world trade generally went down, rather than up. This happened for instance between 1981-85, when a detailed FAO study was done. Also, the FAO reported that Commodity Agreements take long years, and were very burdensome operations. They reported further, that very few Agreements were signed, and that of those signed, very few lasted long; and in their economic provisions, were significantly disappointing. This was the general finding of an official organ of the UN on this type of support. But for want of anything else we still stay with these; and as we know, Third World governments still talk in terms of buffer stocks and price stabilization schemes.

What we need, is what we mentioned earlier, like OPEC for oil, a mechanism which was started in the late sixties in Asia, but had its problems with the multi-nationals and others. This is the formation of *Commodity Communities* which began with coconut; then it was pepper. In the case of pepper, they teamed up with Brazil, as the world's largest producer, although quality is of lower standard than that of Sri Lanka, Malaysia, Kerala or Indonesia. Subsequently, it was to be for rubber, tin and so on, in all of which, again, this writer had a lead policy role.

If this were done, then there was every chance of reasonable terms of trade emerging. Indeed, in practical terms, the world scenario is changing. It was one thing in the sixties or seventies and something else today. There are substitutes for raw materials. There are also reverse situations. In the sixties or seventies, people said natural rubber was going out. Some of us were among the few who said that the prognosis was highly suspect. Sri Lanka, then Ceylon, cut down on rubber plantations. That was a total error. Natural rubber came into its own, along with synthetic of course. It was a thing which had to be observed and studied. The International programmes for Commodities in World trade, have of course to be in association with other producers round the world, and not only in the South Asian region. Yet, there is no reason why a body like SAARC should not have taken the initiative in this.

In regard to *payments*, Chapter fourteen has discussed how that would operate. It does, not only in concept, but in effect, facilitate trade and act as an inducement to trade promotion. At the moment, apart from the SAARC countries, Iran and Myanmar (Burma) are also members of the *Asian Clearing Union* set up by the UN in 1974, which illustrates once more the wisdom of expanding SAARC to include the real South Asia, in this case Iran and possibly Myanmar. In the later, once its Army lets its hold, Myanmar's accession will bring to us a highly intelligent, forward-looking and liberal, civil leadership, who will benefit, and benefit others. The Asian Clearing Union worked on the basis of periodic clearing. There was no immediate payment in hard currency, with, at the end of each clearing period, the obligation to 'pay up'; that is to settle net obligations.

Again, it has not grown, because of the difficulty that rich countries had never thought of this, although they have come to this now. So, in our tragedy, we wait till they come to this, then find ourselves still where we are. The ECU, (European Currency Unit), is almost the foregoing.

A further 'alternative', is what is called *Local Currency Payment*. In order to explain, let us imagine the following in the South Asian region. There is ongoing import and export. Nobody pays in hard currency. Each country pays in its own currency. When Sri Lanka pays, it is a very poor, weak currency; but it pays in Sri Lanka Rupees. And similarly, all the other co-operating countries. This is the system of Local Currency Payment. Now, immediately what happens is it is the surplus countries, that is the countries that are surplus in trade, which hold the currencies that are paid by the deficit countries. For example, if Sri Lanka were in deficit to India, India, will be holding Sri Lankan Rupees; Sri Lanka will not be paying dollars, or whatever, as such.

So, therefore, for this region, there would emerge, what is called a pool, a reserve, of local currency holdings as a result of payments in local currencies. Now, we have to visualize this,

The Wealth of Poor Nations

not in isolation, but along with the Trade expansion scheme that we discussed. If we do so, then it is possible to justify, and to visualize in practice, a perfectly safe scenario. The system of Local Currency Payment will operate as an encouragement for the expansion of trade. In other words, the volume of trade for a particular country will not be determined by the extent of reserves that it holds, that is by the extent of 'dollars' that it holds, but by the extent of physical capacity as an economy to produce and to export. These are two different things. We may have the capacity to produce and export, but we do not have the reserves to import for our development investment. This is where a Local Currency Payment System works. Recently, as we noted before, India had offered a scheme to Sri Lanka, which may possibly figure in the next Economic Rounds between India and Sri Lanka. This is an arrangement for payment for imports to Sri Lanka in Sri Lankan Rupees. Coming nearer to the earlier idea, save that it is bi-lateral, it is not a visionary one. It should be fully worthwhile for SAARC to consider this seriously, as a necessary adjunct to a Trade, and Regional Co-operation Programme.

A final word on Payments. *The World Bank and IMF* were set up after the War, particularly with the leadership of John Maynard Keynes, and John White of the U.S. When it was set up, there were three components. The World Bank, the IMF, (this, to ease out trade balance fluctuations), and thirdly, what was called an ITO, (International Trade Organisation). Briefly what happened is that the rich countries 'overlooked' the establishment of the International Trade Organisation. That would have been the caretaker of the trade and trade promotion interests, of the Third World countries. These were to be the Bretton Woods arrangements. There was another feature, and this was very much in the concept of the economists who formulated them, that when countries ran surpluses in trade, the obligation to rectify the surplus was on the 'surplus country' and not on the deficit country. This was a very important component. These were not remote technicalities. They affect people's daily lives for years later, since the obligation to rectify the balance of payments and deficits rest today entirely on the deficit countries!

Thus, we have a very peculiar phenomenon now. Over the last several years, the phenomenon has been of deficit countries fighting to export because they are in deficit; and surplus countries fighting to prevent these imports. At the margins, there are a few exceptions, like the International Fibre Agreement. Thus one has very much of an 'upside down' situation, which has to be put 'right side up'. That is not obviously within the power of one country, or of SAARC for that matter. But if there was such an arrangement, or countries could simulate such a situation within the South Asian region, then all countries in South Asia, rich and poor, large and small, will be in an equal position. Because then this will be concerned not with upward reserves, but with upward trade — trade creation and not 'reserve creation'; and could provide far larger scope in export capacities.

The third area to emphasise was *Development Financing*, that is, investment capital. We did emphasise that the important thing in trade co-operation is to develop our exportable capacities, not just to dismantle tariffs. So investment financing is obviously crucial now, for this expected national development. Contrary to possible popular impressions, the rich countries have been quite parsimonious. The UN at one time, set a target, called 1 per cent of their GNP. That fell through, and finally, it came down to 0.7 per cent of the GNP. Even this has not been fulfilled, *sans* some of the Scandinavian countries, Netherlands and others. The U.S.A.'s commitments, for example, are far less.

The impression given is that all this is big money. Indeed it is. But let us look at some historical experiences of the rich countries themselves. From 1860 to 1914, UK's foreign investment was, not 1 per cent of GNP or 0.7 per cent of GNP, but 4 per cent; and during 1905-1913 was 7 per cent of GNP. This was, of course, entrepreneurial investment largely. But that was the situation. Let us look at it conversely, at Capital inflow to countries now developed, but which were developing at one time. All countries were developing at one time. The capital inflow as a percentage of national capital formation, that is, total capital investment that goes into the development process in a country, in Canada, between 1901 and 1920, was 40 per cent. For U.S.A. between 1869 and 1878, it was 11 per cent, Sweden, between 1861 and 1870 was 50 per cent, and between 1881 and 1908, was 79 per cent. So we see when developing countries ask in international co-operation for a larger flow of funds for investment, and talk in terms of 1 per cent, we may compare that with the actual flow of funds that took place. Mismanagement of investment is a different problem. We could be mismanaging some of our investment, and of course we should not.

In this context, in SAARC, the idea has come up that the countries have a Regional Investment Fund. As we said, Bangladesh at the time that SAARC was formed in 1985, raised this and it was shot down by India. The idea of a Regional Fund was raised in 1989 and it has been now accepted, in a new climate of endeavour. Yet, if we set it beside the scale of need for investment, then we have to ask questions. That is, how large, how effective, a flow of funds, will a SAARC *Regional Fund* be able to command by itself? By definition, the countries are developing; by definition they are short of funds, and if they were to organise a regional fund for capital investment themselves, then it is like chasing a very limited resource. On the other hand, the South Commission, which spent some three years on Third World problems, issued a Report in which, among others, it called for the setting up of a *South Bank*. This will be much larger and endowed with much more resources. But, we have to remember that this is going to serve all the developing countries of the world — again perhaps, with only too limited results.

Now we come to something of concern in this connection. A little before the Asian Clearing Union and Trade Expansion Programme were being set up as part of the scheme of things, there were gestated within the UN an Asian Regional Development Bank. This was the Asian Development Bank. That story has been told in Chapter XII. Yet, if the Bank had played this original role, as it is belatedly doing marginally in ASEAN, we might have seen the beginning of a more effective, meaningful Regional Co-operation programme and process in

262

Asia as a whole — and in South Asia — than we have had so far.

Perhaps, there is a role here, for SAARC and ASEAN jointly, to seek and to remind. Now the ADB is a rich organisation. The UN started it off with a little over one thousand million dollars. It may be a major point, and a good idea for SAARC to enter into a discussion or relationship with ASEAN, to try to review some component at least of this role of the ADB. If this was achieved, then it seems the essential Development Investment component of regional co-operation will at least be taken care of. Above all, the initial momentum, and psychological stimulus, of a Bank role would well prove invaluable.

The foregoing are the three Areas we mentioned. But before concluding, we must mention briefly, a fourth, the *Environment*. This is the area of SACEP, the South Asia Co-operative Environment Programme. There are two aspects about this. One is that, so far, countries have got enthusiastic about environment, but not used the Organisation effectively. The fact is that there are tremendous areas for co-operation which are available in environment and which must form part and parcel of a total package of South Asian co-operation. There is already an Indian Ocean Regional Seas Programme, which UNEP is supporting, and for which SACEP is the Executive Agency. It is a potentially massive programme, involving the whole Indian Ocean area, ranging from coastal areas and island eco-systems, to offshores and seas. Then there is the Himalayan eco-system, which is again a huge potential programme area. There is the Energy programme which eminently suits — it is also an economic programme — the co-operation of SAARC and SACEP, for they must co-operate. And there is the programme for Environmental Technologies, which is very important and vital for really Sustainable Development.

These are important roles, for both SACEP and SAARC to play, in bringing them to the forefront and placing them both on the World Agenda and in the Region. They need to work together; if they do so, not only will the Environment programme advance, but also the heart of the Economic programmes itself

The Wealth of Poor Nations

will benefit.

III. The Future

If one is to conclude to look at *the Future*, the countries need a *will*. There is something of this *will* now; but they need, secondly, 'subordination of past ideas to *new ideas*'. This they do not have as yet; and need to develop. Thirdly, the *will* too will not last long, if they lose themselves in marginal, or peripheral programmes. As we mentioned, poverty programmes having nothing to do with regional co-operation. We need to develop 'the central co-operative *mechanisms*'; and if we have the mechanism, then the confidence grows. And the goal that South Asian countries and SAARC set for themselves of 'building a strategy for individual and collective self-reliance' will occur. There is need to stop tinkering, or doing patch-work programmes, but to plunge directly into substantive, solid approaches for co-operation.

264

Chapter Sixteen

The International
Environment Compacts and
National Policy Making

I

Our main concern under this Chapter* is the international forums, and the international auspices under which the whole concept of environment development and management evolved. We saw in the earlier chapter on environment at the national level, how the idea of the environment dimension developed in the early sixties, from a sophisticated, esoteric concept with Western, rich country interest in wild life conservation, exotic species and matters of that nature. With usual alacrity, developing countries bought these ideas as if that were their problem. As it happened, that did not create much beneficial effect, nor serious ill effects for the developing countries at the time. Developing countries had also long lived with their own, often rich, environmental heritages.

At the outset it is useful to mention that, for the sake of cohesiveness, where so needed, some repetitions of issues and observations from the earlier chapter have been made.

---

* The reflections here derive, inter-alia, considerably from two Papers, "Brazil '92 : Whose Agenda? For Whose Benefit?" (August, '91), and the "Earth Summit : Bench Mark, or Non- Event?" (October, '92).

The Wealth of Poor Nations

II

When the Stockholm Conference, called the Conference on the Human Environment, was under preparation, we had, what was termed the Asian preparations for Stockholm. There was need to drum up ministerial level interest in these, and, of course, there were no environmental ministers. The poor countries were wondering what was in it for them, why they should get interested. It may be a surprise today to know that one recourse was an equivalent of the theory of labour intensive investment and development, familiar to economists. So the idea was developed, of pollution intensive industries, and indeed seriously touted in Asia, Africa and Latin America. That was until Indira Gandhi went to Stockholm and simply declared that poverty was the greatest environmental pollution in the poor countries, and development the only answer.

In that policy package was also an assault on the world's poor for its population growth. As we saw in the earlier chapter, there was a distinction between 'marginal' policies and 'mass' policies for population change. Yet, if the mechanics of this change was through these developments, then these were not recalled in the policies for the developing world population. In Stockholm, this was not directly argued, partly because, somewhat before that, the World Population Conference had taken place in Bucharest.

After Stockholm, the United Nations set up the United Nations Environment Programme. UNEP soon also set up certain slogans. Again, the pre-occupations following that are discussed in the previous chapter on environment. Meanwhile, as stated then, during the period between Stockholm and Brazil, UNEP had developed an excellent 'Environment Programme for Conservation', but had no 'Environment Programme for Development'.

The reason that the rich countries had for all this was of course quite clear. It became even more clear in Brazil at the Earth Summit. From the earlier run up to the Summit, through the Preparatory Committees (the 'Prep Coms' as they were called) that preceded the Conference, it became very clear that

266

the concept of the apocalypse, of ecological collapse, which had been held before the world, in the ozone threats, global warming and others, was based on a theory. Essentially, it was that the rich countries had the technology — we have dealt with that in the earlier chapter mentioned — to contain both the effects of pollution and those of resource exhaustion. But if the entire Third World tried to achieve the same level of living, then the world would surely collapse.

This was theory, and therefore, another phrase was developed out of it, that of 'ecological space', or environmental space, that is of a relatively fixed growth potential which somehow the world has to share. It even had some of our best Third World people accepting it, in total violation of any concept, as we said before, of the Brundtland 'Achilles heel', and the Keynesyian concept of perfectly feasible, varying levels of equilibrium. At the Earth Summit in Brazil, the Third World countries were thus talking to an agenda 'that was not there'. The Conference had a packed agenda on the 'qualitative' management of the environment, but none on the 'quantitative' management of the environment.

In the world of reality, it is wrong of course to hold that there would be ecological collapse if the Third World developed. It is a fact that if it developed on the present premises of international economic co-operation — and here we come closer to our field of interest — with only the Global Environmental Facility of the World Bank, the few UNEP projects, and some instruments and policies which we referred to earlier, which are not entirely relevant to us, without transfer of the means by which technology development can take place and the financial means that would aid this, then the world would indeed collapse. The fact of the situation is, as Lee Kwan Yew stated not long ago, no matter what other countries say, South East Asia, let alone China, will develop massively between 'now and the year 2000 and on'. Sub-continental India itself, although well behind, will go the same way.

Here, we have a situation where there has been marked asymmetry again between the policy packages that we have and the actual policies that we need. At the Earth Summit, the developing countries were so ignorant of their position that they simply argued on the percentage of aid to the Third World — the 0.7 per cent, or what it should be. They forgot that they already had the promise of 1 per cent in the sixties, when the 'first development decade' was launched.* As we know, the record was one of progressive breach of that promise. Below, we examine what came out of the Earth Summit at Brazil for the Third World, and what needs to be done now, at particularly international levels of action.

UNCED, 'Brazil 1992, the Earth Summit - these were the crescendo of wordings by which the United Nations Conference on Environment and Development, decided upon by the General Assembly, was described. Its stated purpose, from the beginning, was clear enough. It was to confront seriously the impending ecological disaster, possibly even collapse, that the Earth was facing — on the one side by the uncontrolled development of the North and on the other, by two phenomena or factors for the South, one present, the other impending. The present factor of the South was the on-going and threatened pollution of the environment from its over-whelming poverty, accompanied by unbridled population growth. The second Southern factor was that, if the South developed as the North has, there would result an unbearable addition to the toll on the Earth's resources and to its carrying capacity, as to spell disaster for all of us together. The Earth, after all, was the source of all resources, and the sink of all wastes.

The Conference was styled as being on Environment and Development. The means for attaining the needs in both these was encased in the catch word popularized by the Brundtland Report, called 'sustainable development'. As if also to distinguish itself from the Stockholm Conference of 1973 on Environment, the Earth Summit, 1992 was advertised as emphasising development for the developing countries, as much as environment for all.

---

* It was a case of 'arguing' the size of the zero, as a senior retired Head of a U.N. Organization, told an Ambassador of the 'Group 77' at Rio on the morning of the final negotiating Sessions.

The International Environment Compacts / National Policy

Earlier as we saw, UNEP — the United Nations Environment Programme — had invented words like 'Eco-Development', giving a lot of satisfaction, though nobody clearly knew what it meant; and 'Development without Destruction', though there is never any development, let alone existence, without destruction; until Brundtland came along and said 'sustainable development'.

Even this last phrase, around which the entire Earth Summit was in fact drummed up, as we saw, was without clear definition or methodology, too often, in practice, interpreted to mean the mere elimination of poverty for the poor countries, with no 'strategy' for real development alongside sustainable environment. The truth was, to re-emphasise, that there could be much higher levels of development than mere elimination of poverty, alongside sustainable environment. This indeed was the 'Achilles heel' of the Brundtland slogan of 'sustainable development', and held the seeds of the weakness of UNCED.

For this type of higher level of development, which was also in economic and environmental equilibrium, meant :
1. that rich countries had to re-define their life style and consumption targets, and
2. that in their own interest as much as of the South, they had to make freely available, their new environmental management technologies to the South in order to,

(a). contain the pollution accompanying rapid development;
This never figured at UNCED. Indeed, the South kept on asking at Rio for the traditional Aid and Trade concessions, which in any case, they have been voicing at dozens of economic forums elsewhere.

As for the Conventions, UNEP itself, under the persistent leadership of its earlier Executive Director, had carried all these ideas and more, and even succeeded brilliantly in getting countries together — the last of those being the Montreal Convention. So in this way too, the Earth Summit simply did not score any great success. The point is, there was no need for an Earth Summit to do all this.

269

The Wealth of Poor Nations

What then was left of it? Verbiage — Yes. Zeal and sentiment to group and student generations? Yes. Chances of any real redress to ecological deterioration? Hardly any prospects yet.

Who is to blame? Apart from the Secretariat,* the North, primarily, had not given that lead in survival and growth together. The phrase 'Environmental Space' itself, by which the South sought to persuade the North, was not a happy one. Both history and experience of Environmental management had shown, if we cared to look at it, that it was not 'sharing' a 'fixed space', but vast increases of resources and enlargement of opportunities to all that served the peoples. This also created new 'technology', that then made *continued management* of the environment feasible.

As strongly pointed out earlier, the South's thinking on its strategy was itself totally wanting, by failure to declare its position as one of rapid development, inviting the North to give or not to give its response in such situation. In that event, 'lapse' meant accepting ecological collapse. Funding should have flowed implicitly from these positions and the acceptance of them as given. The *principles* flowing from them — and not setting of target figures of percentages as Aid — would have yielded far better co-operation and collaboration with the South by the North; and the *great link* should have been between Aid and *Technology supply*, with strong *indigenous capacity creations* for the latter.

People returned home from that Summit, clutching conventions which for the most part only the North can implement; and 'Action 21' (the agenda for the 21st Century) carrying hopes without assurance of any fulfilment of them. Perhaps now the pieces need to be picked up. Quiet follow-up

---

* All these are no reflection on the outstanding commitment and efforts of the Secretary-General of UNCED, Maurice Strong, who strove right through to carry the message and the specificity of situations of the developing countries. For instance, during the preparations he had emphasised that 'the traditional foreign aid syndrome was not a sound or equitable basis for North-South relations and we have to move to a new basis'.

270

by the South and getting on with their development, with the North progressively facing up to the Earth's sustainability should perhaps be the next scenario. It is more than noteworthy that, amidst the outcries of the South, there were none heard from South Korea (or, by proxy, from Taiwan). It was also another developing country within memory. These remain good lessons for the South to pick up and good basis ultimately for a World that would be more co-operative in working together, and safer economically and environmentally.

(b). maximise the use of Alternative Resources through invention, technology application, and various other means which only development could create.

Obviously, the North had not arrived at that point, of being willing to talk on these positions, whether at the Earth Summit or in the two years of the preparatory processes, that went before it. This was best seen at Rio where, as we saw, of the two Agendas essential to the Conference, namely, an 'Environmental Programme for Conservation' and an 'Environmental Programme for Development', only one was there and the other was missing. The result was that UNCED became simply a matter of discussions and attempted conclusions on climate, on bio-diversity, on forestry and so on, which, while in many parts highly commendable, were all in the group of what is best termed, the 'qualitative' management of the environment. Totally absent, therefore, was the agenda for the 'quantitative' management of the environment, namely the question of how to manage the enormously increased resources that the South would necessarily be using into the year 2000 and beyond, whether the North liked it or not.

Surprisingly, the North was not the only party responsible. UNEP had, since Stockholm, built up a very responsible agenda, with delivery of results, on the qualitative side of environment, and had allowed the quantitative, development related, side, despite motions of studies on 'environment and development' to go completely by default. UNCED simply copied this, not able to show more creativity, even under the urgings of its proclaimed Conference Title and its masthead of Sustainable Development.

The Wealth of Poor Nations

The poor countries of the South themselves compounded this, by not formulating their position — contrary to the urgings of a very few — as one of 'giving notice' to the North that they would become developed countries, even if over a time, across large areas of the world, certainly protecting their own environments as best as possible, but not in its global dimensions, *given their resources and their technology*. The import of such notice would have been that, either the North saw its 'own self interest' in global ecological security and lent its Technological support to the South, or the World went under.

Thus the position was that the Earth Summit, billed as the World's largest Conference then, concluded with its outcomes inconclusive, but its message clear — that the poor countries must find their environmental solutions in the context of development, and not outside it.

III

It is now no more a question of how good 'Brazil' was, but of facing *the future*, into the year 2000 and the 21st Century. In that sense, the problems of the poor countries were not simply of Global Pollution and the Global Commons, though they were of serious concern to them, their solutions lying dominantly with the rich countries. The major problem of the poor countries was how to manage their resources of the environment, while pursuing growth that required massive increases in the use of these resources.

It was not just elimination of poverty, which 'bred not only pollution, but also bred people.' Yet, *the Policy Packages* being used by the poor countries for environmental management were, unfortunately, the policy packages devised by the rich countries for themselves, and handed over by them. A new approach was necessary. At least, the thinking for that was available; and the future lay in that.

As for policy positions and strategies, the developing countries themselves, and not only the North, are standing environment 'on its head.' We all claim to be experts on

272

environmental pollution and degradation. Nobody has answered the question how environmental resources management has to be handled in the *factual situation*, to which we pretend ignorance, of at least five to ten times the resources that we are using, being needed, taking that convenient time post, by the year 2000, for minimum economic and welfare satisfactions of peoples (not reaching out to anything like the twenty or forty-fold standard of living of the North.) Even that former, more modest, target requires,

(a) resources management *techniques*, of which the environmentalists are simply unaware now; and

(b) from the World Bank and the countries symbolized in it, a commitment to supply, not 'dirty' industries, or some financing but *technology* in range, scale and terms, to meet these needs, of which we have no signs yet.

Development should not be 'destruction'; and 'environment' should not be stagnation. In that felicitous phrase, quoted earlier, of the King of Thailand 'Development is the Creation of Livable Environment.' If the latter does not exist, then there has been either under-development, or over development — the former as much seen in the poverty of the poor countries, as in their international debts, inflations, and social deterioration; and the latter, in the environmental profligacy and planetary threat by the rich countries, typically in their urban enclaves.

UNCED, despite its verbiage, proceeded in ignorance of these needs in environment action or development co-operation. It provided a forum for loud Third World argumentation on their needs. What had been left, at Brazil, was a swallowing of the West's prescriptions for environmental management, with all the attendant effects on poor country prospects and welfare — as, of course, longer-term ability to manage their own environmental resources.

The implication is that these peoples will be permanently ensconced in a future stagnation and dependency on the rich, beside which past historical parallels of unequal relations, of colonization, or of the 'gap', would be each a lesser phenomenon. These lead us to the issues that must then be directly accepted and acted upon. We group these below:

273

The Wealth of Poor Nations

1. The North

1. The issues before us were, and are, being presented, among
others, as of one earth, of global warming, the ozone layer,
tropical forests, wild life, and the Third World's Population
growth. It is that there is one environment, and one
question, namely the threat of planetary collapse, or possible
redemption by immediate action by all countries.

2. Yet, the reality has been otherwise, of One Environment,
but Two Perspectives. It has been a leadership by the
'North' that was largely irrelevant to the 'South'; and of
needs by the 'South' that have largely not been served by the
policies or inclinations of the 'North', a South trapped in
poverty, and having to pay heavily for needed technology
for both development and environment.

3. In important ways, the North has by now developed an
excellent Environmental Agenda for itself – on the one side,
by internalization of environmental costs, by increasingly
impressive pollution control and treatment methods; and on
the other, by visible re-cycling programmes and even if
slowly, acceptance of limits to air and water pollution. All
this has been made possible only through a pervasive
development of technology across all the areas of
environmental management and economic production. For
'Development is not merely the cause of resource use, but
also the means to resource sustenance.'

4. To recall, what all this adds up to is that, of the two types of
Management essential to a true Environmental Programme,
only one, the 'Qualitative' management of the Environment
was addressed by the North. The aspect of 'Quantitative'
management of its Environment has received little
recognition and even less implementation — that is, both of
excessive resource use by the 'North', and heavy resource
need by the 'South'.

5. This means, that the level of use of the World's resources by
the 'North', by far the greatest user, has remained the same,
and threatens to increase.

274

2. The South

1. Where do countries of the 'South' stand in this? By one, extremely valid reckoning, which we quoted in the earlier Chapter that, for the 'North' on an average, an individual uses/disposes as residues of wastes about twenty to forty times that in the 'South'. The population of Europe for example, if 400 million is, 'environmentally' in fact, 8,000 million.

2. Secondly, even to stem the growths of population of some countries of the 'South', poverty, as we said, is not only a polluter, but a 'breeding ground' of people; and it is the 'mass' change (as opposed to 'marginal' change) of development that will, in fact, finally arrest population growth.

3. Thirdly, simply by way of comparison, too many countries of the 'North' have a higher density of population per square mile than the South, without at all attracting any policy strictures. For when, during their industrial revolutions, their populations spurted — picturesquely called 'the vertical invasion of the masses' — in Europe last century and around, their levels of resources use increased in parallel tremendously, by domestic exploitation and external expansion.

4. The almost explicit request to the 'South' now to use resources more modestly for development, emerges in this light as an 'asymmetrical' prescription from the 'North' to the 'South'. The International Community completely overlooked the enormous question of the levels of resources use at both ends of the 'quantitative' side of environmental management.

5. Finally, examples abound on the failure of this quantitative management in the North, too many to list here. One estimate had it that the U.S.A. used 40 per cent of the world's resources, with 6 per cent of its population — that it would have been more profound it had attained its successes using only 6 per cent of the world's resources. Another found that if India used the same energy levels as the U.S. in its agriculture, all known oil reserves would be over in twelve years. And so on.

275

6. What remains the moral for us in this, both 'North' and 'South'? Again, we draw from our previous observations. Firstly, the massive technological capability that the 'North' has developed for itself and continues to — in pollution at source — has placed it within sight of warding off Global Environmental Cataclysm.

7. However, this has a premise, namely that — given little Nothern intentions to share technology or money — the South does not use the same, or anything like, the resources in 'replicable development', as the North is continuing to do. For, then, the world would certainly collapse environmentally on both accounts, namely (a) the vast new mass of Resource Use Levels; and (b) on a base of Environmental Management Technology that is primitive and totally insufficient. The apocalypse then, would be for sure. The Agenda of the 'North' is based on this unspoken premise, and the appurtenant theory of the Apocalypse.

8. This is the crux, containing the two 'Problematiques' of Environment and Development, whose 'intersections' - to use the phrase of Ph.de Seynes, former U.S.G. of the United Nations - has still to be found. And this, was not in the Agenda of 'Brazil 92.'

9. The 'South' needs, as we said, on a modest estimate, at least five to ten times the resources it is using now for Development, and for Environment. Thus, the 'South's Environmental Priority at Brazil was not less resources, but far more resources than now.

3. Measures

How may this be achieved, and the Earth too kept in ecological balance?

1. Firstly, an ideal is for the North to come forward to participate in a Resource use Containment Programme for itself, apart from all other current agenda.

2. The context for this is that very significant areas of the 'South', by the year 2000 or threat, will surge forward as developed countries, with enormous additions to the world's

276

resource use levels, whoever likes it or not. When that happens, the Global Environment at the given levels of technologies will become unmanageable.

3. Left in that situation, *pollution* on large scale will occur, until these countries too become fully developed; and can use those technologies that will manage, contain and solve the problems of the environment alongside growth — unless, well before that stage, the world environment itself collapses; or unless the North brings down its technology and resources to South.

4. It is, thus, more than a question of what we are prepared to 'give' as donors, or 'do' as receivers; or *'bargaining'* on either. In the compulsive future that will evolve, there must occur a massive use of resources and massive development all over, if we go in one way, with safeguard to the Earth and to World Order; if in another, with cataclysm and conflict.

5. The 'contribution' to co-operation needs, therefore, to be seen *not as Aid, but as 'own Self Interest'* and as global contribution to the Eco-System, outside the economic aid and assistance framework that we see entrenched now.

6. Such an agenda, given good sense, had *to be found* place in Brazil, with vision into the year 2000 and beyond; but was not.

7. If these may become so, then a set of *Principles, Programmes*, and *Special Activities* can be seen, as below, which must, in one way or another be adopted.

4. Principles

(i) Recognize the historical *asymmetry* in resource use levels as countries struggle to become developed.

(ii) Agree that *development* is the *means ultimately to* commanding the resources and the *technology* for the same environmental threats that development and, before, poverty created.

(iii) Agree that the North will increasingly set Resource Use Limitation target for itself.

277

(iv)   Agree to set out appropriate Resource Use Expansion targets for the South.

(v)   Accept that Development, in the striking phrase of the King of Thailand, is 'the Creation of a Livable Environment.'

(vi)   Reject the 'Consumerist, Mercantilist and Commercial' type of development as manifest in many cities/enclaves in the South, *passing off for development*.

(vii) Agree to set *technology* supply *transfer targets* from the North — and linked financial resources - for successful environmental management in the South.

(viii) Agree to set Global Pollution Control targets, for North and South as appropriate.

(ix)   Accept the setting of Consumption targets for Select Resources, such as tropical forests, genetic resources and other select renewable and non-renewable resources.

(x)   In that connection accept the relevance of the 'Polluter Pays Principle', also *at international level*.

(xi)   Commit to the support of Resource 'Expansion' targets as set out, by combination of technology with Restoration, and Maintenance methods, the use of Renewable and Reusable Resources and Wastes, and search for *alternative*, 'friendly' *resources*, in all areas.

5. Programmes

(i)   Establish 'Resources *Balance Sheets*' — global, regional, sub-regional, national — for all major Resources (macro-level; ex-Ante)

(ii)   Account all key Natural Resources as Capital Stock, with provision for depreciation, re-equipment, etc., and with 'Reverse Discounting' in strategic cases.

(iii) Conduct *EIAs* (the micro-level; ex-Ante) only on the basis *of prior Resource Balance Sheets* as above.

(iv)   On the basis of the above, move towards converting all EISs into Integrated Environment/Economic Cost-Benefits systems, fully integrating all cost and all benefits.

(v)   The North to take Technological/Financial

Responsibility (with South co-operating) *for Global Warming* (CO_2 sea level rise, ozone, CFC and other issues of the Global Commons).

(vi) All projects in the South *using Renewable or Re-usable* Resources and Wastes to be eligible for Grants/Low *Interest Loans* from international lending countries and sources.

(vii) Implement an International Polluter Pays Principle (cost-sharing) for the World's Tropical Forests (as its 'carbon sinks') *Genetic Resources* conservation and *related areas*.

(viii) Accept and foster the UN initiatives for establishing Expanded Environment-Economic SNAs (macro ex-post)

(ix) Accept and foster the development and use by enterprises, agencies and others concerned, of Environmental (Green) Audits, which are also development 'sensitive' (micro ex-post).

(x) Subject to the foregoing, the South to be fully *responsible* for all degradation/pollution during *its development*, as its commitment to the Global Eco-System, and to itself.

6. Special Activities (Academic, Research, etc.)

(i) Vast fields of study await attention of the world's universities, institutes and other centres, in all sectors - *in ideas* (e.g., the future of city planning, transport and the motor car); in *science* research (e.g., as energy alternatives, pollution prevention, bio-technology); and in across-the-board *technology* development, promoting both the economy and environment.

(ii) Socio-political fields need fundamental thinking on *policies, administration and systems*, with need for distinction between 'protectionist' and 'productionist' approaches.

(iii) *Legislation* must distinguish between enforcing the law on poor polluters of wastes, and enforcing systems for their 'conversion', by governments and agencies, into

279

economic product (from being a residue to be disposed of, to a resource to be converted).

(iv) The entire *education content* of environment management needs fundamental re-arrangement, from pure pollution orientation to resource restoration, management and use.

(v) The world's *N.G.Os* have a particular function and capacity in all these areas, - (a) to help environmentalists and governments to do their 'home work', and (b) to 'speak for the grass roots and intercede with authority on the grass-roots on the other.

(vi) A *'New Economics'*, absorbing environmental resources management, awaits formulation out of the foregoing thinking, with no room by either discipline to conceive of themselves as 'opposites'.

Over the decades, economics has, in fact, absorbed non-economic categories in the past and will do so again, given effort by the environmentalists, to go beyond the 'slogan' of sustainable development to the methodology of 'sustained maintenance of future resources levels' called for above.

(vii) A draft convention, embodying commitments on the foregoing, would have been a truly appropriate contribution form Brazil '92, for the future peace and welfare of the Planet. The difference between *prosperity* for all, or *disaster*, must lie in the ideas here presented.

7. Regional Co-operation

(i) At least three major areas of key importance must be noted:

(a) The first is the need for positive and innovative *designs*, at macro and micro levels, for *integrating* environment and development;

(b) Obviously research at *University levels*, sadly deficient, or superficial, or segmental if in-depth, has to be pursued intensively, as well as priorities in education and training;

(c) Thirdly, the development of *indigenous* environmental *technologies* must be given topmost priority. Energy remains a key element, but the technology priority should obtain for all areas and all related disciplines.

(ii) All these require, without doubt, the ingredients of sensible, professional and co-ordinated regional co-operation *mechanisms*.

(iii) Across the board co-operation by Government, *United Nations bodies* covering Asia and (in Asia), the Asian Development Bank, must be forged, and be forthcoming.

(iv) - At the level of inter-governmental organizations, in Asia, ASEAN and the South Pacific Forum have successful environmental co-operation organizations (ASEP and SPREP).

- For South Asia, the most obvious thing to do is to give political support to the full use of what is known as the South Asia Co-operative Environment Programme (SACEP), established in February, 1981, as the inter-governmental organization for this region.*

- Yet, the South Asian countries themselves have been forgetting their first lessons in co-operation by initiating somewhat confused parallel programmes in SAARC, which obviously has its own separate rationale and high purpose over-all.

8. The United Nations and World Bank System

(i) The chosen instrument out of the Earth Summit for United Nations responsibility was the Commission for Sustainable Development (CSD). Apart from its capacity to exercise leverage, let alone power, the manner of its approach to assistance, as already shown do not seem to give promise of help to the developing countries.

---

* All these incidentally were initiated by this writer during the Seventies and turn of the Eighties from the United Nations.

The Wealth of Poor Nations

Firstly, environment is a dimension, and cannot and must not be split up in management and policy-making. Secondly, and flowing from this, a CSD decision to pick out block areas from Agenda 21 for attention each successive year flies in the face of both conceptual meaning and ultimate value to the countries.

It is not the picking up of so-called environmental areas here and there, but the promotion of the comprehensive environment development management methodology, consisting of macro and micro resources management *systems and tools*, leading to both the best identification of key *resources*, their management *points*, *policies* emerging from them, the *technologies* involved for the future, and the *integration* of all these economic management, that would really serve the causes of the developing countries, and *should have been the concern of the CSD*. Countries would then be able, to be *comprehensive in scope, managerial in approach, and integral in the environment development imperative* rather than, having to pick random, even haphazard, 'priority' resource areas.

All these, inter alia, the UN Statistical Office's advanced programme on the system of integrated environment economic accounts (SEEA), the replacement of the narrow environment impact assessment in countries with integrated environment development cost-benefit framework, the preparation of national resources balance sheets for all major resources and the promotion of environmental (green) audit as supplement to financial audits, are all crying out to be serviced, with the CSD, perhaps, not even sure of its priorities in its deliberations.

(ii) The World Bank system, very briefly, needs to reflect all these in its appraisal and aid policies and programmes.

(iii) *The global conventions*. As mentioned already, the conventions on *climate change*, and the consequent policies concerning the ozone layer*, can only be understood for developing countries on the basis of,

(a) primary responsibility being assumed by the developing countries; and (b) a full and frank *global*, indeed self-interest based, *technology transfer* and *technology creation* programmes for developing countries as they develop.

The *bio-diversity* convention, needless to say, is of deep concern to, and valid, for the developing countries without reservation. This is entirely different, however, from the right of the developing countries to their bio-diversity heritage, and the total absence at present of any safeguard to this resource wealth of the developing countries, assisted by the patents and royalties provisions of the GATT and Accords.

It clearly is a matter for the CSD, if not for anybody else, and, of course, for others in the global system - countries as well as organisations.

While the bio-diversity is with the developing countries, the bio-technology is with the developed countries.

---

* The foregoing, of course, overlooked the fact that of the twin-house gases,

    (a)   water vapour was the most important source; and

    (b)   under CO_2 the natural source emissions are at least ten times rather than anthropogenic. Doubtless, under the later fossil-fuels account for 85 per cent, and thus the North have most of it at present.

D. The Future Context

Chapter Seventeen

Culture, Religion and Politics

Culture

While it may not be customary to afford a place to cultural or spiritual attributes in describing the conditions and bases for development, in truth no group motivation and group action, which is the bedrock of means to success, has been possible without such a basis.

This may go by several names. It may be seen as social ethos, ethnic trait, national cult — based on tradition or leadership, religion, or plain materialism. Some of the articles of faith which may have served well at one time may have also lost their relevance subsequently and become a hindrance, instead of being a help, to further progress. But a new article of faith has to be discovered, else the society stagnates. It has been said, cynically, that the God of religion does not exist, but that civilisation needs religion as a matter of life and death.[1] If we may use the word God for successful rallying points as well, history is full of examples of these essential rallying points during the surge of humanity at various times. The ritualistic and social organisation at least 2500 years before Christ, in India, the cults of some of the fascinatingly well organised community arrangements in Africa and in pre-Columbian America, the creative force of the Islamic genius in the era of its powerful economic expansion, the great puritanical ethic of European modernisation, the materialist ethic of the Socialist revolutions, and the materialist secularism of the recent upsurge of the four 'little dragons', for all their apparent polarisation, bear closest affinity, in terms of this essential ingredient of a transforming cultural ethos, to put together and to carry forward the inert forces of growth towards creative wealth and welfare.

Culture may be considered the result of attributes developed over a time by a society in a multiple set of fundamentals, essential to its organisation. Such attributes, being specific, can vary from society to society. They are not aesthetic or spiritual alone. The political organisation of a particular society, its social pattern, religious inheritance, and literary or artistic development, all combine in a result which we may call its culture. Such a culture, then, is also the culmination, or fulfilment, of a society's purpose, since it could represent the expression of its 'welfare' enjoyment, on the basis of its socio-politico-economic — spiritual foundation.

But the formation of a national culture is at the same time a continuous process and it is thus also a means to stabilising the particular character of the society. In order to do this, it would establish a system of totems and taboos in which, respectively, there are major hallowed symbols which may not be desecrated; and major dictates which may not be violated or trespassed. These may not, in fact need not, be expressed in political or legal terms. Historically, their expression has been rather in mystical, social, religious and other symbolical terms, which perhaps have bound societies to them even more strongly than laws and regulations. So much so that some of the most enlightened societies are still themselves victims of such inheritance, even if perhaps out-of-date now. Peoples are replete with flags, symbols, labels, slogans, patron saints, and, in the less advanced societies, a much larger crop of superstitions and customs that are considered invaluable.

Past development theories and efforts, in particular international cooperation prescriptions, have been notable for mis-interpretation and misjudgement of components of national cultures as inviolable in pursuing and advancing economic and social development. Typical have been the postures of those social anthropologists, who were very active during the colonial period and indeed made redoubtable contributions, but who studied the totems and taboos of tribes, societies and nations and called for their sanctity or inviolability, with consequent prescriptions for policy that deepened rather than overcame their economic and cultural 'traps'.

As we saw earlier, in looking at social change in development, it is development itself that overcomes most of the mass problems of social change; and similarly it is development itself in the widest sense, which automatically overcomes the social fossilations that have sometimes falsely been held to be sacred values of a society. Where this has happened, cultural deadwood may be said to have been weeded out and stronger cultural foundations established with newer sets of totems and taboos. We have the examples of the free market ethnic, the call by Nehru to look on the country's huge dams as the new temples of India, concept of economic crimes under the new priorities of the socialist revolutions, the idea of the work ethic as supreme, instead of race and religion, in Singapore, and many others. In some instances, perhaps best illustrated by Japan, deep cultural inheritances have been turned to advantage as powerful support of the new development and new ethic; such as, in the life-long employment concept and relation to the factory.[2]

In too many developing societies today, the rigidities of past inheritance seem still to be with them, to the detriment of a more certain attainment of wealth, welfare and social harmony. It manifests within countries, as also between countries, perhaps its most acute expression arising in the form of religious differntiation or confrontation. There is hardly any part of the world where, either as a minority problem or an inter-state problem, this does not manifest as a drag.

It remains among the great unsolved needs of humanity, since an 'ethos', which is what social religion is, is needed as a matter of life and death; but this same ethos can be a drag to enlightened social action for social welfare. Historically, religion has been the source of some of the greatest works of creative genius - in thought, in painting, in sculpture, in architecture, and in music - capable of being loved all at the same time, by all races and at all times. Tragically, it has also been the cause of some of the greatest abuses, murders and genocides [3] In one sense the reason at least, if not the solution, is not far to seek. A credo, once developed into an organised religion, becomes indeed the basis for a society's most powerful totems and taboos. Since nationalism is the central character of homogeneous group, all organised religion becomes a form of nationalism and a support to it.

As much as the 'territorial imperative' or proclaimed national boundaries gave a sense of national security, the imposition of a human organised religion did the same. With political expansion and conquest, organised religion too expanded, to extend its sway and to strengthen the newly imposed homogeneity, under a new set of boundaries. This is not to deny that alongside were devoted groups with earnest mission to spread the 'word' whether it be Islam or Christianity or any other, but also if needed, by force of arms or worldly benefit.

The confusion as to the supreme dominance of a single revealed truth — apart from the dire consequences of competition between two claimants of supreme truth — has also resulted, perhaps, in a new type of social dependence with implications for growth and welfare. If successful development is the result of a total favourable set of pre-conditions, both material and non-material, that are a complex indigenous evolution, the transplant or imposition, of an extraneous cultural, spiritual pattern must in fact detract from the capacity of a given social base to grow on its own strength or genius.

The periods of Protestant economic expansion in Europe, of indigenous Japanese growth later, and under a different ethic of Soviet and Chinese economic development, are fair examples of success, compared to countries that had cultures and prescriptions 'imposed' on them. A vital question is whether peoples cannot live together in peace, hold different views, without looking down on one another or imposing one on another. It is a deep and fundamental question in which the issue of sustained development may also lie. It is particularly one that should hold the attention of youth of tomorrow as a long awaited challenge that can only be overcome by them. [4]

Culture, Religion and Politics

Religion

Below, in what may essentially be relatively new ground and in which one may only be suggestive, some thoughts and ideas are set out on what may be a universal or perennial philosophy of truths and 'knowns' in the realm of spirit and spirituality. It has no bearing on particular religions; and all religions may continue, each appropriate to its own place. For example, not a long time ago, a group of intellectuals in an East African country considered that the basic beliefs in the African civilisation formed a deep, more socially and economically appropriate and perhaps essential basis for the evolution of an African religion and African salvation.[5]

In a study of African heritage is the following ancient philosophy: 'According to ancient African belief there exists in every person, every animal, indeed in everything, a power that influences and conditions life. The supreme god is necessarily remote. He has contact with humans through the spirit world, expressed through all things and in the souls of forebears.'[6]

From another area of the world, of a remote group whose practices would have been superficially branded as 'paganism', it was said[7] 'the word animism has commonly been used to describe this sort of belief in this part of the world. I suggest this is inadequate and in effect, derogatory. We are dealing with something deeper, wider and more imaginative than that. Instead, I propose the term Universalism. For this system involves conceptions of the whole universe of man, animals and plants, stars and cloud patterns, sights and sounds and smells, observations, visions, provisions, fantasies and dreams with a total effect that is truly philosophical - and at times almost beyond the reach of the formally trained Western mind.'

It seems most essential to distinguish between pure religion and organised religion. There can be complete harmony in the realm of the former. There has not been harmony in the latter, though it can be forged to society's advantage if organised religion were seen as social religion and, therefore, as varied as societies are varied and relevant to them in their different places, without the least provocation or cause for conflict with others.

291

Spiritual truth cannot really be expressed in logic, much less in words, because the human possession is of the finite senses and the only instruments of expression. Eternal reality, the 'non-contingent', may not be seen through the 'contingent' senses,[8] thus not as sensory perception but only as 'intuitive apprehension'. In this humility, some ideas of this ultimate reality of a perennial philosophy are set out below, as they seem simply common to all 'pure religion'. On such a basis and, someday, on true understanding of organised religion as social (relative) religion, people may get a universal inspirational basis for their common advance.

There can in fact be many ways of even expressing such a perennial philosophy. Words are but limited instruments of conveyance, and the moment a reality is translated into words (this is the core of doctrine, dogma, and 'organised' teaching) obviously distortion begins. Thus presentation here is not unique; we have just chosen one.

One such has been the Indian metaphysical tradition. All traditions of humanity evolved from very simplistic beginnings; from animism through subject worship, to questioning and to essential realities. The old *Rigveda*, some millenia before Christ, too, began this way, as perhaps also the Indus religion that existed prior to this at Mohanjadaro and Harappa. It was a stage of fire worship and sacrifice, followed later by brave and noble questionings as to origins and why and wherefore, till they culminated, some centuries before Christ, in the *Upanishads*, the magnificent renderings of the concept of ultimate reality and of perennial philosophy.

Alongside, as in all societies, was a social religion called Hinduism, originally beginning in the Indus basin and with the name derived from it, and later referring to all those in and beyond and east into South East Asia. This was an established, organised religion, simply part of the particular society and with codes, customs, totems and taboos that, for that time, devised masterly mechanisms for social and cultural conduct, stability, and even development. When they became irrelevant, even inimical to the needs of later economic and social needs, they turned into obstacles and hindrances, as they still are in many ways. Thus it was as myopic in the name of social anthropology to stand up for them later, as it was urgent to understand the need to create new sets of organised customs and totems that would carry the new development, but based in the national genius.

In the meantime, the metaphysics of the perennial philosophy stood unsullied by 'this other religion' and it is this that seems most essential to understand. This 'pure religion', or philosophy which was not Hindu if by that is meant a 'label', could not refer to any exclusive doctrine or institutionalised religion, whose hallmarks could have been dogma, rule and ritual. It is of the essence of unity, diversity and universality, beyond religion and therefore accepting 'all truth being simply one, while the paths may be many'.

While this may be a weakness for organised religion to concede, in a perennial metaphysics it is a strength not a weakness, of understanding or of conviction. So one may say, for the Buddhist metaphysic, which shares intimately with the *Upanishads*; and so too for the Tao metaphysic; as also of the pure mystics of other great faiths. Such original essence of truths transcend, as they must always, the 'labels' which are attached to peoples as soon as they are born, and the schisms and feuds that result by 'organising' truths into exclusive and conflicting moulds. Beside the eternal reality and its comprehension, the 'possessiveness' of social and organised religion seem so divisive and small.

What religion to hold is immaterial; the metaphysic is universal and that is material, to future personal salvation as to social peace. Thus in a perennial philosophy the supreme or universal is all that is proclaimed by all religions. In the finiteness of human capacity in which the contingent may not see the non-contingent, it is impossible to describe the reality by means of words that are only finite. The first words which describe also carry the first distortions; and it goes on therefore to the end! This then gets embodied in doctrine and dogma and book and institution and becomes the basis for conflict and controversy. In an annotation of ultimate reality, it has been well said that 'the reality of the supreme is not a question to be

293

solved by a dialectic which the vast majority of the human race will be unable to understand. Dialectic in itself and without reference to personal experience cannot give us conviction. Only spiritual experience can provide us with proofs of the existence of the spirit'.[9]

A universal religion is such as must, without limit of time or space, embrace within its synthesis the whole gamut of the human spirit from the crude fetishism of the savage to the creative affirmations of the saints. 'The reality is formless and the true Tao; and it is the unreality which has form. Those who are on the road to attainment care not for these things (words), but the people at large discuss them. Attainment implies non-discussion; discussion (controversy) implies non-attainment. Manifested Tao has no objective value, hence silence is better than argument. It cannot be translated into speech; better then, say nothing at all. That is called the great attainment'.[10]

As we said, most indoctrinations have led to mistaking and confusing dogma, symbolism, and parable for the reality. There would be many ways in which this reality can be described, no one inferior to the other. Any particular way chosen would be simply because of a location and origin. On this premise, what is set out below bases itself, as we said earlier, on the terminology of the Indian tradition, but in fact bringing together without limitation the varied mainsprings of eternal truth from the recesses of all religions; and so is one description of the perennial philosophy, from source of creation (brahman) to union (moksham), as follows:[11]

- the ending of *samsaram,*
- the merging of primordial consciousness,
- the attainment of universality, clarity, intensity and purity,
- the union of creation, preservation and destruction,
- in timelessness of fulfilment,
- the universality of Hindu/Taoist Gnana,
- the clarity of Buddhist dharma,
- the intensity of Judeo-Christian Maitrya,
- the purity of Islamic Anantha,
- beyond religion, beyond code, beyond doctrine, of life and beyond life.

294

As we said, there would be other ways of presenting a description of this reality. Within the Indian tradition itself one could perhaps do so in terms of the triple aspects — known as the Trimurti, of Creation, Preservation, and Destruction. This accords with the ancient metaphysical concept — which may have parallel in modern scientific theories of the universe as 'expansion' from a cosmic energy/mass concentrate — of the cosmic cycle of 'emanation to contraction' (from the infinite, through the finite, back to the infinite). Or, it may be possible to present the reality in terms of a much wider known triple concept, of the Trinity of Christendom, which may perhaps be an embodiment of the highest essence of creation — of the Creator, the Created and the Life Spirit (the Shakti of the Indian metaphysic); and so on.

In societies which eschew organised religion, these may not be burning questions at all. But there will be others in other forms — the new 'secular religion' and 'rival' secular religions - for societies will continue to need 'religion', although nothing to do with the old ones.[15]

Politics

As we mentioned, culture is also the product of the political organisation of a society. From the point of view of development, the break in continuity of an organisational evolution, with the introduction from outside of a so-called enlightened political system, may not have assisted growth after all. We saw, earlier in this Book, the socio-political premises, involving democratic welfare statism and the like, on which international co-operative support for development was posited.

We also mentioned that no country in history, at the time of its transition to development was a political democracy. Whatever the arguments for or against, it is clear that the co-existence of an imported political system with an inherited culture, was a 'conflict situation', at least in the purely technical and scientific sense. We referred before to the manner in which development leadership organised itself in the West at the time

295

of the Industrial Revolution; or was forged in the Socialist countries this century; and shaped in those countries, such as Japan, which did not have such a conflict. Within the parliamentary democracy idea itself, developing countries have switched from say, the British system, to the French system or the American system, or a combination of them in the search not only of development leadership capacities, but for harmonies of political organisation and culture. As in economic prescriptions which we talked of in an earlier chapter, the political prescriptions, brought in good faith from the West, were those developed by the countries for themselves.

It was well-known and freely admitted that the administrative structures, excellent as they were within limits, were good only for 'law and order administration' and not for developmental administration. These were the subject of much attention and strenuous effort to overcome in the developing countries during recent decades. A similar limitation, while fully existing at the political level, did not, however, find similar priority attention addressed to it. Its consequences for the pace of development may well have been quite serious, even though unnoticed. The reason for this neglect may have been the fear of being considered reactionary.

Of course, there were only two systems of political organisation, the Western democratic and the socialist democratic, if one might leave out any autocratic systems. But as we also saw before, where poor democracies succeeded even somewhat in development attainment, it was because they had the 'umbrella' of a 'single person' personal leadership. This must have been the approximation in the Nehru era in India and certainly has been with Singapore.[16]

It is clear, therefore, that the political system must be capable of providing for the primacy of development achievement, seeking the democratic linkages through identities with inherited cultural patterns. Apart from the well-documented Japanese case, bold initiatives on resource-based village level democratic planning, and similar 'guild' concepts derived from cultural patterns, may well have to be sought vigorously.

Culture, Religion and Politics

Perhaps not very often an openly expressed view, but nonetheless reflecting more than a few who may be silent, was a recent analysis from Singapore on political organisation and people's development.[17] 'The claim that an opposition would make the government perform better is a pathetic and dangerous belief which must eventually end, as it has in many countries, in parliament being reduced to a madhouse and the military or a dictatorship taking over to restore law and order. It is a fallacy to think that an opposition enters parliament to help the government perform better. The purpose of an opposition is to make good government as difficult as possible so that the ruling party would be thrown out in a future election and the opposition voted in. (One) must get away from the idea that the essence of parliamentary democracy was an oratorical boxing match between the governing party and the opposition. We learnt pretty fast in the arena of practical politics that things do not work out the way they do in political textbooks.

'For example, the government made no bones about detaining without trial supporters of the Malaya Communist Party and secret societies. These actions of ours were denounced by people in Singapore and outside as transgressions of democratic principles which, theoretically, may have been so. (Yet), life on the whole was made better for the people. All you have to do is go back to 1959, when people lived in squalid huts and cubicles, unemployment was rampant, secret society gangsters preyed (around) and communalists, and communists periodically staged big and small riots.' One does not have to agree with everything in this, to see the dilemma faced.

The London Economist once described the Singapore administration in the seventies as one of '24-carats honesty and frightening ability'. We have had it repeated too often, in studies of development, that corruption was an inherent malaise in the developing societies and was a major block to development. If there is a technical truth in this, it must be as much marked by a fallacy in interpretation.

As for the truth itself, as Arthur Lewis observed long ago, more ruin has been caused to development in poor countries by poor decisions than by bribery. Again, as observed once, it is not that corruption is a monopoly of the poor societies, it is also an art in the rich societies, perhaps even more. The difference was simply that, while the latter could afford it, the former simply could not. But given that there is corruption and that is bad for development, the case of Singapore is an outstanding contrary example of a special political system, a newly forged cultural ethos and a non-elitist leadership. Most curruption in the developing societies are either the result of the class and vested interests and the derived, elitist structure of the leadership, whose priority concepts for development are themselves influenced by their class; or, have been the result of foreign governments bolstering non-representative coteries to national leaderships and then, perforce, condoning abuses.

Solutions, to be found now by developing countries, involve a hard road, perhaps even travelling back to find the roots before travelling forward; or socialist revolution.[18] The West has never had a matching country model for Third World development, not having quite learnt even how to use its aid and trade assets to advantage. But the search must be made, in which various leading segments of society must needs be involved, including the youth.

The Issue of Nationality

It is a serious contention amongst scholars and observers today that the nation state, which after all was never that old, has entered upon a stage of erosion of its validity and continuity. It has been argued that the reality today is between globalism on the one hand, as manifested already in innumerable political, judicial, economic, environmental, and other international regimen, not to mention the technological networkings of communications and information systems; and on the other hand what has been perhaps honestly termed 'tribalism', is a phenomenon which emerged with a force in recent years that surprised many sophisticates and radicals round the world, but perhaps did not ruffle other social philosophers or thinkers who distinguished between creations, however noble or well intentioned, and realities or truths based, as we termed, on 'organic' realities.

Between these two, namely globalism and tribalism, the nation state, it is alleged, is fast disintegrating, and even destined to disappear. At least so goes the inference of argument. In the global-tribal dualism, the former seems to be growing in strength, while the latter is making its eternal character better understood.

Future global scale conflicts have thus even been predicated by some as to be, not between nation states, but between civilizations, 'Western, Confucian, Japanese, Islamic, Hindu, Slavic, Orthodox, Latin American, African'. It is not necessary, of course, to describe this as a new scale of 'star conflicts', identified by civilizations, since that may not stand scrutiny or acceptance amongst peoples. If the key identification of a group (family, community, race, nation, or civilization) is as of a people with a strong sense of identity, then there are enough groups around the world, perhaps fortunately, sporting the same language or religion, or even same 'ancestry', who still work disparately, even belligerently, against each other. If tribalism, as seems to be the case is an unbending unit of identity, then the possibility for any larger identity out of that would be only, if we may identify 'an enlarged tribe', if one may say so, which in varying cases may be a nation, a so-called civilization, or even a federation of nations. It seems a key to success in creating a confluence between such 'intertribal identity' and a national identity is what has been happily described as the 'federative' idea.

It has been suggested, for example, one thinks correctly, that the Soviet Union's disintegration was because of its betrayal of the federative idea with which it began. By the same token, the American spirit of open society was particularly conducive to the generation of the federative idea across its States and Groups. The eventual history of British and French national identities today, built as we know on application of sheer physical force, is again, as pointed out, the outcome of confederative or federative principles and concepts leading to equalities, equal opportunities, equal rights, and generally a removal of what may be termed 'identification marks of differentiation', in favour of "identification marks of identity".

In any tussles between tribalism and unsatisfactory nationalism, the former must prevail. It is not that nationalism is set to disappear, but that a given tribal identity (here, community) will set up 'its own' corresponding 'national' identity. It is clear that it will not also surrender to globalism, however much, like all others, it conforms to, even uses to advantage, the new and ever widening international regimes, charters and conventions. The apparent association of a nation state with some different, larger entity than the tribe, is a confusion with the efforts of a tribal identity to seek its own self-expression. Not only, as in Europe for example, are homogenous national identities doggedly remaining so despite Union, but innumerable micro communities, which never had to fight for separation from a larger entity, exist profusely as tiny nation states. It is the imperfections or failures in arranging for satisfaction of tribal identities that have, historically, threatened the particular states.

The historic, future norm would, therefore, have to be one of either satisfactory 'confederative' nation states, giving true satisfaction to the constituent communities; or of individual micro-states, composed of quite homogeneous communities. In a given situation, the choice and challenge, is for the given State, more than the tribe or community, to make. It is this, more than any other, that marks out what we may call the 'perceptions and realities' of National identity. So long as the Nation State represents the 'enlarged' tribe, there seems no reason why it will fail. The diminution of a Nation State is not of 'nationality'; but of the particular State not fulfilling the needs of nationality.

The Essential Identity

It seems then that what we have to know first is what 'identity' itself is. As we said and we all know, the Nation State itself is a relatively new creation in history. In that situation, the primary building block of identity must surely be something else. I had occasion to state in many contexts elsewhere, that across the world and down the ages, the only 'organic' unit in a 'body politic' was the village. All other units, through region, nation, and the globe, were conscious creations out of needs, opportunities, missions, hopes, even oppressions.

Yet, the 'core' identity in our consciousness does not start even at this point, of the primary organic village or unit. The essential unvarying identity for all, and at all times, is that of the individual. Rooted in birth and in instinct, apart from in philosophy and metaphysics, this individual consciousness and all that goes with it, is the fundamental, or inherent, 'mental' identity. From that proceeds, if one may see them as concentric circles, the 'family' identity — equally inborn and fundamental — thereupon the 'enlarged families' or the 'primary' tribe, (the geographical village identity coming somewhere at this point), with the tribe and community following as equally unalterable constituents of a Group identity. Also, historically at least, they would be characterised by common genetic, linguistic, religious and cultural codes.

In the course of human pursuits, such communities may and do frequently see advantages in working or coalescing with 'associate' communities, generally contiguous to one another, and if so, they become a Nation. At this point, as noted earlier, the new national entity bears heavily, the responsibility for maintaining its cohesiveness. It is indeed strange that political thinking whether as history or analysis, has bypassed this essential reality, and therefore often failed to recognize the roots of successful nationhood.

There is, therefore, an important consideration, based in reality, that we must keep in mind. Given that a Society recognizes explicitly the essential identities — from the individual through family, to tribe and community — all such community groups develop and perceive sentiments and values in the larger entities or units as well, of a wider area, which has its own strong common denominators notwithstanding community differentiations. That is the crux of nationality and national identity. How that is consolidated, sustained and strengthened is the essence of State formation and Statesmanship. Where these exist with success, each component community unit, in a wider nationality, is not only committed to the latter, but as repeatedly, proved, even prepared to die for it against foreign disruptors.

Nor was this an idle consideration for Sri Lanka at certain times in the past. It was in the fullness of such a background that I, and I am sure others too, had occasion to tell our leaders more than once in past times, that their confusion of the interests of what is called 'Ceylon Tamils', as being identical with, and having affinities to those across the Palk Straits, was totally misplaced, was a creation of their own unfortunate thinking, and only fuelled differentiations, ultimately even invocation of a wider Tamil identity for support against those differentiations.

These considerations are, of course, quite different from that where a group or settlement — as has happened repeatedly in history, and in this country too — finds itself, by voluntary migration or as left-overs from a receding foreign occupation, living peacefully in the midst of a larger indigenous community. Time and again, in such cases, the former groups have, over a period, shed their original racial or linguistic identity, and become part of the endogenous whole. Examples abound right across time and in the world. In this country, whole masses of populations in the so-called 'South', are now Sinhalese fully and entirely, who were purely Tamil, centuries or even years ago; and the same phenomenon may be observed in the 'North' with large numbers who are now Tamil, who were completely Sinhalese earlier in our history.

This could yet happen, imperceptibly or marginally, both ways, even now, given, however, the unfailing condition that neither State, nor any dominant group, imposes anything whatsoever towards this coalescence 'from above'. The history of this country precisely, of course, is that it is just the opposite that has happened, in ways and on occasions that are too numerous to document here, and in any case should be too well known to the honest and the discerning.

302

The Anatomy of National Identity

Given the foregoing truths, we could now seek to set out for ourselves, what may be considered as factors or conditions, which need to exist, or must be brought to bear on ourselves, if we may successfully repair, re-establish, or stabilise a national identity. In the course of doing so, while illustrating from elsewhere as well, we shall obviously be focusing on the Sri Lankan experience and position.

When security is high in a society and when expectations of employment and economic opportunity are also high, its people even if mixed, tend to think of themselves easily as an entity within their country. In such circumstances, they readily feel and accept that any issues or problems between segments in their society can also be solved within the concept of themselves as one larger entity belonging to one country.

In a 'homogeneous' society, these issues can be economic, caste or class, religious and others. In a 'heterogeneous' society, they can be also these, plus their differing language or communal characteristics and specialities. Each will pursue with acceptance, often with participation by others, its own fulfilments of cultural and other creativities. They would not only accept the larger belonging to the country, but even develop very much cross-cultural characteristics, idiosyncrasies, aims and satisfactions over wide areas, including dress, speech, common beliefs, arts, foods and many others.

Extremism or chauvinism is managed to be kept in its place; and predominance of one racial or religious group in particular areas such as employment, landownership, business or government are seen in a vortex of overall movement and change, rather than of one at the expense of the other. True for many countries round the world, this certainly was very much the perception amidst Ceylonese/Sri Lankan society up to about five, possibly four, decades ago.

But when security ebbs — by collapse of institutions, political as much as of law and order — and insecurity stalks, that wider identity becomes the first casualty, taking the form

303

The Wealth of Poor Nations

of and seeking refuge in a group (community) identity, which from being a means to creativeness and fulfilment, changes, and becomes its means to protection and self assertion. Most often, it is powerfully aided by economic stress of one type or another. Once such a process begins, it also becomes progressive. Discrimination and repression take turns with resentment and self-assertion, with none gaining.

Self-assertion itself can take innumerable forms depending on the country and its own situation. For example, it can take the form of the dream of dignity in the society, as with Martin Luther King; or desperate struggle, as in South Africa or the Palestine; of solutions through federalism, as in India; of separate states as in Bangladesh and, elsewhere, Cyprus. If secure physical and political conditions could be created, it could even take the other forms of envisaging reunion, as for Vietnam, China-Taiwan, the Koreas, and the two German Republics.

History of course has many examples of union, in Switzerland, Belgium, U.K., France, Italy and others. On occasion, this has occurred also by colonization of one community or the other in a country, or of both. In the old days, decimation or forced absorption may have been tried, but none would be foolish, in his own interest, to think of these today. Voluntary absorption so profuse in ancient times as we saw, and till recently here, may still obtain up to a small extent today; but it would be a very tender plant to grow and, certainly, not one that can be manured with the use of force. The more likely modern emergence, given healthy conditions, would be highly visible and positive common cross-cultural national traits, habits and particular identities, making for mutual acceptance of each other.

One country and a national identity obviously mean free and easy existence of the various component communities over the country generally. But, apparently, there is a limit to this. For, when a non-traditional population increases beyond a certain number in an area, it seems the traditional population begins to get uncomfortable, lets slip those so called natural values of non-racism, non-discrimination and the like and takes a turn which from then on becomes unpredictable. Often, the

304

latter role-playing is not by a majority, but a traditional community, now almost a minority overwhelmed by a migrant mass, or a 'major' force, as in Assam, Fiji, Malaysia, South Africa. In many cases in the past, the latter have taken over completely — which explains, of course, the countries of Australia, New Zealand, Mauritius, West Indies, U.S.A., Canada or the Latin America Republics as we know them now.

A minority facing encroachment would more easily associate such threat with demolition of its territorial base, so essential to identity and with a basic fear of extinction. There is a beautiful letter written last century by Red Indian Chief Seattle to the Big White Chief in Washington, when the latter offered to buy his people's land. Considered by many to be one of the most moving documents on a people and their heritage it is preserved in Washington and was on view at American Expo '74.

Thus there could be four streams which a crisis of unity could swell.

1. In a majority, such a 'critical mass' or limit, could occur when an immigrant minority has reached a size that the former feels is socially, culturally, economically or in all these ways, a threat; or

2. Even when an indigenous minority which has flowed into majority areas, reaches such proportions;

3. In a *minority*, or a numerically larger number treated like a minority as in East Pakistan, such a limit would arise when it feels its self expression seriously impinged or thwarted, physically or economically; or

4. When an almost effaced group, like the Red Indians or the Australian Aborigines, has grown enough to reach for the minimum rights and dignities taken away by the intruders.

When, precisely, a community sees another's presence as such a critical or pressure phenomenon, to be resented, is not something that can be precisely stated. At least it is not a given mathematical figure or ratio. All one can state is that there is a perception of something like a critical mass, or population ratio, in the minds of the resenting group, beyond which values and value systems begin to get attacked, sometimes savagely.

However, the beginning of such a crisis is determined by a number of specific factors which, as in earth-quakes, even if not enough to predict when a system will break down, will certainly show that one is coming. Sometimes it is a few of these factors, sometimes almost all, invariably it is not just one of them.

The timing when a dominant community will resent and the subservient community rebel, would also differ from country to country, according to those specific factors; it would not be the same for the U.K. or U.S.A. and so on. It is also noteworthy that these same factors perhaps provide the mainsprings from which to find the solutions. So they are important. Some idea of these factors may be obtained by listing them, even though they are not isolate.

1. Somehow, a large country, of continental *size*, tends not to see a minority presence in the same way as smaller countries. Its perception of this as an ethnic threat is not one of its initial or early reactions, though it may sometimes be misguided by contempt.

   Small countries would tend to see a problem of the same proportion in a different way and therefore, much earlier than necessary or wise, even to itself, as a threat. Again, this may not necessarily be so, as shown by Singapore which employed some of the other factors, as we shall see below, in highly positive ways.

2. The *ratios* of the various populations within a country, large or small, obviously determine how soon or late they begin to be seen as pressures, by one side or the other or by both. We have the U.S. (Negroes), India (Pakistan, Bangladesh, the States of the Union), the U.K. (Blacks, Browns), Cyprus, Palestine and now, Sri Lanka. When the minorities are very small, majority intolerance gets postponed, even indefinitely, seemingly in the name of high and liberal values, and minority fear or assertiveness is either not yet, or not necessary.

3. Even given sparse population, or thin ratios, *concentration* of a minority in areas within a country can spark off an otherwise dormant sense of intolerance. Strong polarization of cultural or economic background, or rooted self-opinions based on history, race, colour or creed, would usually be involved in this type of crises creation. There are the US 'South', Ulster, UK's Southall or Birmingham, Spain's Basques and Sri

Lankan plantations. Conversely, encroachment, or its threat, by the majority in a minority area under State Power — for example, Palestine, Sri Lanka's North and East — can be an equal phenomenon.

4. The level of economic *development* of a country, reflected in the sheer availability of goods, services, jobs and job expectations, overwhelmingly influences the stalling and eventual avoidance of an otherwise certain onslaught on the system, the latter often becoming a more broad based revolt by all the poor against the State. In inter-communal terms, values get dropped, and balanced, sane and healthy arrangements to take care of minority preconceptions in a larger unity go by the board. Virtually all developed countries, east and west, north and south, capitalist and socialist, big and tiny, bear witness to this.

   Some that had not yet been developed, held it as a dedicated goal before the people, spurning both self-assertion and oppression, and succeeded. We have Singapore, USSR at that time, in some way now India, perhaps one day Sri Lanka.

5. Obviously cementing or obstructing national unity is perception of the country's *history* by each group, of its origin, links and characteristics, whether as shared perceptions or as opposing concepts. Clearly, there have been variations in these histories, simply because, otherwise, there would not be different groups today in such countries. But bias in place of realities, suppression or neglect of long standing commonalities, clearly throw a wall that should never have been there. Where the sense of shared history is strong and encouraged, countries ride the pressure of separateness and 'episodic' histories much easier than those that do not. Quite obviously, Sri Lanka has been in the latter position, despite the valiance of a very few.

6. The richness of a country's *culture* and traditions, of music, dance, literature, drama, and epics, and of mellowness and maturity in understanding of other cultures, will again determine whether perceptions of intolerance seep in earlier or later, giving less or more room thereby to overcome any recipient crises in time.

The Wealth of Poor Nations

Very often it is not a people's culture but its violent interpretation by leaders that determines everything; true, there must be underlying situations that make possible such leadership. Nazi Germany is the example all hold out, but we might well admit that all countries have a little of it. 'Dhamma, Vedanta, Bible, Quran, we want to preach it to others, as if they are the heathens; we need to preach it to ourselves, for it is we who are'.

7. The principle of *equal rights* and opportunities is a fundamental one, the absence of which must bring on early clashes of interests, and erosion of unity.

   Obviously related to the level of development, apart from perceptions of history and culture, in terms of capacity to provide the services and facilities for all, in under-developed countries such as Sri Lanka this is where the sense of national unity perhaps first breaks down.

   In the UK, England wanting Home Rule from Scotland is only a good joke; and the US have the means to make that dream come for the Blacks. In a poor country, it remains a conflict situation, worst for the weakest, such as the Indian estate population, or simply both the Sinhalese and the Tamil poor all over the country.

8. *Human rights* is a part of rights overall, but so special that any breakdown in vital aspects of it will deeply embitter the minority, render the majority marked and noted, and open up other effects such as separation and armed struggle of one type or another.

   They finally entrench minority positions deeper and let the majority divert from its primary obligations of restoring all rights as its foremost function.

   Profuse dossiers of human violations are there round the world. Sri Lanka itself (Ceylon before) had an enviable record of standards and conduct and it must have been a remarkable exercise in unintended deviation, for this country to have come to international attention in this regard.

   Yet a thing does not come suddenly. Perhaps when the first lapses occured it was never realized — as in most lapses — where it would lead.

308

But one gave silent sanction, as it were, to the other, until they came to be openly acknowledged, even by the country's leaders, as having built up from 1956 or 1958 up to now.

9. Finally, underpinning all these is the nature of each country's *constitutional system*, structures and provisions affecting minorities and the use of the *permanent ethnic majority vote in democracy's name*. These concern the legislature and the executive, and the centre and the regions. If these were lacking, especially combined with a negative score on some of the other factors earlier mentioned, discord and disunity could be fast indeed. Almost without exception, all countries with minorities have provided for their involvement in nationhood, in varied and several ways. These have included chambers of nationalities, federalism, regionalism, provisions within the legislature, participation in the executive and, generally, non-imposition by fiat of language, religion, or settlements of population.

Such countries include rich and poor, big and small and capitalist and socialist. In this, Sri Lanka seems a notable absentee. In all cases as above, national unity has clearly emerged. Left to itself — certainly not by force — strong elements of homogeneity have also appeared subsequently, such as the use of one language by all without at all losing one's own. These are great advantages to be desired and worth striving for.

   *   *   *

Thus indeed, Culture, Religion and Politics, would need to be an integral part of organisation for successful development. Aspects of politics, social structures, religion and arts are all involved. An area which awaits much more attention than has been given to it, it requires a great new endeavour in thinking, research and application.

NOTES

1   Bernard Shaw.
    Voltaire remarked that if God does not exist, civilisation would need to
    invent him.

2   The result is Western observers are scurrying to study this socio-cultural
    pillar of economic success, which was absent, or long wiped away, in their
    own culture.

3   Within a religion itself, such as for holding that the earth went round the
    sun, or being a low-caste and entering a temple, a milder form being
    separate pews in church for the elite; or between religions, simply for
    belonging to another religion!
        Within organised religion, perhaps Islam is the highest example of
    egalitarianism among its adherents.

4   One of the strongest strands in today's youth 'unrest' amidst other
    confusion, disillusionment or rejection, is still a yearning for true peace,
    manifest in their 'sit ins', their 'mod' songs (the 'ballads' of today)
    wondering 'when will they ever learn', saying the 'answer is in the wind'
    and very much dreaming they shall overcome, 'truth will make us free',
    'we shall live in peace one day'.

5   The same may be said of the South Pacific. Going back to Africa, while
    varied figures have appeared, it seems that in Nigeria for example, of a
    population of 90 million nearly 43 million are said to be 'observing
    traditional religious customs'. To what extent this may not be a superior
    basis for integrating culture with social, economic and political attainment,
    is a question worthy of the highest thinking, particularly by leaders in
    their own areas.

6   Africa: Tribal Art of Forest and Savannah. The issue here is not whether
    there is animism or religion in it. It shares essentially with a perennial
    philosophy. All religions have props — the 'tendrils' of Indian thought —
    to overcome human limitations of trying to relate to the Infinite; the
    reference above to spirits may thus be no worse than, say, saints having
    seen the 'sinful Popes of the Middle Ages actually burning in Hell'.

7   Tom Harrison, Preface to Volume 13 of the Sarawak Museum Journal, on
    the Iban religion.

8   Radhakrishnan, the Oxford Hibbert Lectures, later published as *An
    Idealist View of Life*.

9   Radhakrishnan, *The Bhagavadgita* (second edition, 1970, p.20).

10 Lao Tze (Soothill: *The Three Religions of China*, second edition, 1923,
    pp.56-57).

11 It is also in these renderings — and neither as idolatory or dogma — that
    Hinduism was taught to the young in Bali, Indonesia.

12 Since everything is part of the Ultimate, wholly and entirely; to be not,
    being contradiction of itself.

13 A universal truth. Even our own bodies cannot live without 'destruction',
    every moment along with creation and preservation. So with ideas; so
    everything in the universe. A 'destroyer' is not necessarily 'bad'. Action

Culture, Religion and Politics

itself is neutral; the 'motive' gives it character; action is 'matter' and motive is its 'soul'.

14 Both being parts of reality, only, the human 'perceptions' of matter being purely 'relative'.

   The ultimate reality of all things is as 'non-matter' (as consciousness) and, therefore, One; not one matter 'over', or superior to, another matter.

15 At a minor level, on an issue concerning nudes in newspapers, the Peoples' Daily in early 1982, had to stress 'true beauty lies in the unity of ideological content and artistic form'. For 'ideological' in another society, read 'religious' or 'spiritual' or some other equivalent of the particular society, and one comes down to the question of a shared social need.

16 Hongkong was not an independent democracy in any case; Taiwan, under Chiang-Kai-Shek after the experiences on the Mainland, may be considered to have been under a unitary creative leadership (actively assisted by the world's strongest country, the U.S.A., as its partner).

17 Excerpts from speech by Second Deputy Prime Minister (Foreign Affairs), January 1982. (Text released by Ministry of Culture).

18 As one worker put it, a revolt against lack of 'feeling' for the poor; and to ensure minimum needs for the working people; not to reach the next higher level of wealth which at a time of backwardness and privation is not an issue.

Chapter Eighteen

The Information Order

Getting the message across has been one of the greatest achievements of successful societies from ages down. True, the message needs a content. There had to be a basis, of a society having satisfaction of its wants and needs, and a social, political and cultural fabric which is its own creation. Upon this, the leaderships would want to spread the widest possible understanding among the people, in order to ensure stability of that foundation, as also its further advancement.

While communication today is on the basis of a frightening array of sophisticated technologies, which are not only audio-visual but are instant and can reach millions simultaneously, it may be sobering to think how, much more simple, but different systems left indelible marks worldwide in the form of the great literary and cultural heritages. There were writings, the great epic creations of ancient periods, on heroism, on values, customs, religion and the arts, on almost everything that had meaning for the lives and systems of those days. Some of their inheritances have been so strong and deep that they still remain, to most nations, the basis of their philosophies, cultures and much of their values.

It was so whether in Hellenistic Europe, or in China, or the Greater Indian culture of South and Southeast Asia. Perhaps the most powerful means of communication of these at large was word of mouth, in prose or in song, as story-telling, as mime, or as drama. They occurred spread from village to village over whole countries and centuries. Compared to that epoch, one is not sure whether the powerful modern media systems have been capable of a similar infusion; and whether there is one single example that may be taken as a creation in modern times.

True, the configurations of understanding have advanced, with literacy, high education and profusion of materials and equivalent adjustments in ways of communication. Thus, there are innumerable numbers of intellectual journals; yet one is not sure that we at all have the means by which the 'Conventional Wisdom' may from time to time, be advanced, ennobled or further consolidated, as must be for a Living Society. Much less, when we come to the much larger raw material of the daily communication systems today, both of print and radio or television. We need adjustments for survival at all ages - ecological, nuclear, religious, economic, morall - none of which need be threatened, save out of social folly.

In fairness to the power, or otherwise, of communication systems, it must be said that this is not a problem that could be solved by the media alone. Forging of national visions and resolve are the result of the combined force of leadership and peoples participation, for which media is a supportive arm. The media cannot substitute for the former.

However, there is a serious question in many countries today which are struggling to attain economic, social and cultural goals, grappling with transplanted social systems and values, and carrying almost certainly other human defects such as corruption, of entitlement to unqualified enlightened assistance by sympathizers. That includes, in particular, the media.

There has been an open question whether the media, by and large, has fulfilled this role, or whether, as constituted, it can at all fulfil the role. The question may be seen at two levels, national and international. At the national level, it is predominant problem of national media sources, perhaps without conscious intent, not being able to formulate a creative posture or line for themselves that may be really sensitive to the deeper needs of the people, and not merely to 'sensational' issues.

313

The Wealth of Poor Nations

At the international level, for developing countries, there has been a problem of a dominant First World media structure which has its own pre-occupations; and only marginal, or patronising and, therefore, basically irrelevant interest in Third World needs. This is not a conspiracy by the world media, but simply character of an organic system. The first World media could as well be unhelpful to the First World governments, except that, as we said in connection with corruption, those governments can economically better withstand neglect by it media. These are the sum and substance of what is behind the posited new international information order. The proposed new order may itself be overcharged with emotion and its prescriptions for solutions may even be in parts worse than the problem, but the reasons for its origins are more firmly valid and plausible.

There is no ready answer for these things. One can, in truth, only perhaps consider the existing systems for their weaknesses and strengths, and look at some of the illustrations of the weak and strong points. For instance, the so-called lopsidedness between the First and Third World media, has produced certain responses. Statistically, developing regions are perhaps not as neglected as they were in the past. Regional press initiatives, such as the Press Foundation of Asia, have helped to create not only a brand new source of information flow, but perhaps have been a stimulus to First World press agencies working in the Third World, to reflect a little more, the problems and priorities of the Third World countries.

But perhaps it cannot still be said that there is an understanding in terms of peoples' needs and their media priorities. There has been nothing to substitute for the country-wide folk communication systems we talked of earlier as having been the basis for the lasting embedded values that served societies so well. In the past, it may have been culture and religion that were promoted. The 'religion' now is development; and neither leaderships nor media have really forged the mechanisms for this mass communication. The newspapers even in the local languages have not proved to be a substitute. The most positive contributions often have been on spreading the latest sensations, rather than the latest rural technologies or

314

even the achievements within areas of the country. One interesting equivalent of the ancient system may be rural mobile units,[2] which combine today's audiovisual technology with the means of communication that simulate the ancient genius. There is no easy answer to finding the best mechanism; what we do know is that what we have now is far from what is needed.

Let us leave this particular question for the present and go on to a central question which has vexed all segments of society and, hopefully, the media. 'The great art of journalism' said Dr. Han Suyin[3] 'which is a marvellous one, is to combat myths for reality.' This may be interpreted in two senses. One is what we have tried to grapple with earlier, namely, the question of what priorities to reflect in communication. For instance, is it hot news or economic news, and so on. The second is a question of truth versus truth. In other words, the objective of good communication is to spread the truth. Sometimes, this may suffer not even by an open distortion, but by ellipsis so that the real things that must be known do not get known. A cynical version of this was the Shavian view that 'Journalism consists in saying Lord Jones dead to people who never knew that Lord Jones was alive'. The more direct by-passing of truth has of course been the subject of the greater attention for obvious reasons. Political leaders do not as much like to be exposed with truths, as perhaps many sources of media themselves love to convey, regardless of the real truth, under temptation of being sensational.[4]

Distortion, of course, is a world wide disease and occurs in government, in international negotiations, and the like, as much as it could in reporting. It could well nigh be a situation of to each his views'. In theory, the media is a special institution in a body politic. It is the Fourth Estate in the hallowed company of the other three Estates of the Legislature, Judiciary and the Executive. If it is not, like Ceasar's wife, above suspicion, it must in any case take the posture of being so. An Asian weekly in a lighter moment, once observed 'The only persons entitled to refer to themselves as "we" were kings, editors, and people with tapeworms'. Yet, as we know, all things in any Establishment do not remain sacrosanct for their

315

own sake for too long, but have continuously to prove themselves.

Whether inside the Third World or outside, there seem to be two issues round which the quality and validity of a media structure may be seen. These may be expressed as two relationships of (a) the media versus the countries' leaderships and (b) the media versus the private individuals. It is clear that in these things some very basic considerations become a determining factor. These are such as the ownership and control of the media; the distribution network; the technology required to maintain itself; in some countries, even the language or languages involved; and so on.

At the bottom of this are questions such as: Who is the media actually? Whom does it represent? Has it developed a system of 'referral' to reflect at all the peoples' views? Does it stand for freedom of the press, or freedom for the press, as once remarked, with licence to represent nobody but itself? It is a uniform principle derived of experience that who owns the media determines its content. In a state-owned mechanism, the contents would be state determined priorities. This may be good and adequate or not adequate. They may represent the most important components of economic production and culture, while not reflecting others. The question is not one of value judgements, but of an indisputable fact of this relationship between ownership and content. Similarly where the media is based on plutocratic funding, content must be heavily loaded in favour of vested interest concerns and commercialism, including daily nudes on 'page three' if that is what the commercial interest has decided.

Apart from these considerations, a uniform requirement under any situation is of course quality. Quality has never been and perhaps cannot be, provided for by means of professional degrees or similar benchmarks. On the other hand, mediocrity can go under the mark of high professionalism, to the detriment of both public causes and the cause of journalism and good communication. Under the protective power of ownership, there was once a case, perhaps a nadir as such cases go, in which an individual who was distinguished solely by his abilities in the playing field, found it possible to take a high professional look at a complex international problem, simply because the subject had become a good hobby horse for a headline. These are rather, and can be deemed, eccentricities, in a world where the pinnacles of journalism must draw nothing but admiration by critics as much as by supporters.

A much more common problem is a more subtle one, which may involve journalists of honesty and repute, seeking either to expand their influence or to publicise a problem. In the life of the Third World, cases have been too often where the media has just found itself incapable of comprehending the total problem and therefore, all the real causes and the crucial remedies. Very genuine national and international initiatives have sometimes greviously suffered at such hands.

In the late sixties, for example, there was a concerted campaign in some of the columns on the inadequacy of international organisation in development co-operation. Without going into the intrinsic limitations or achievements of the organisations, it is possible to say that in certain crucial programmes that would have made a difference to the developing countries and in which the saboteurs, in conferences and outside, were the developed countries participants, the media failed to see, either for not wanting to do so or inability to do so. Similarly, there have been cases of programmes, national or international, condemned outright in one part of the world because it had become 'trendy' to do so, while colleagues of the media in another part of the world were praising quite the same type of programme to no end.

Two such illustrations of inadequacies, by a contradiction between the reality and the communicated word, and one illustration of sound prescience, may perhaps usefully be given here. Of course there must be many round the world; these are simply among those better known to us. In the late 1960s the United Nations Economic Commission for Asia and the Far East (ECAFE), which had a study and conference type[5] programme on shipping services, tried to take up the logic of assisting shipping development in a direct form. Apart from the record of the already developed countries, including Japan,

317

there were also encouraging instances such as those of India. Besides, there were examples of inter-country assistance, such as China's effort to help build a dockyard in an African country in order to build ships, rather than to advise on chartering and services alone. The particular component in the proposed Asian programme included similar dimensions. For example, it was known, on the basis of studies, that the Indonesian Archipelago had a given large number of vessels for whom also the obsolescence rate was known to have become considerable. The posited programme was to help in ship building, rather than a services and a loan finance programme to purchase ships. Needless to say, at least one or two developed countries had on their drawing boards, plans to provide such a supply of boats. It was perhaps natural that such a programme met with stout opposition from such developed country sources. The media at that time found it beyond its interest or range of knowledge to reflect this and serve as leverage in assisting the international effort for development. In addition, much praise[6] was showered on the services and conference components of the programme, in good faith, lulling most people into feeling comfortable and eventually making it possible to ensure that nothing more developed.

The second case was the more straightforward and typical one, of the type of queries sometimes raised as to what a particular international body is doing or not doing. Some years after the Asian Development Bank (ADB) was established by ECAFE,[7] queries and comments freely appeared in the media purporting to evaluate international contributions in the region, which declared that while the ADB was making a solid contribution through investment finance to the countries, it was not clear what ECAFE was contributing to development. This not only overlooked the chronological fact that it was the regional commission that created the bank, which had to be looked at together; but also that the contribution of the former, as a regional spring-board of the U.S. system to stimulate and to create the requirements of development in various forms, was a different and, by itself, fully substantive role and contribution.[8]

The Information Order

An example of perception and positive media support to international development was when, for the first time ever, a programme emerged for the ten countries of South Asia to set up an organisation for co-operation. It happened to have originated under a new dimension of a worldwide environment programme concept, as the management of resources for development. It was particularly important for the poor countries, which needed many times the amount of resources that were available to them and who at the same time were experiencing degradation and exhaustion of their resources through poverty or national mismanagement or international market mechanisms.

Following on a declaration by a Ministers' Meeting in 1981, a constitution under the name of 'Articles of Association' was adopted, for the important process of 'ratification by the Parliaments' of each of the countries. It was also an arrangement in which, apart from a headquarters, each country through a focal office was accepting responsibility for a particular area of the programme, on which it would formulate the action plans for adoption and implementation by all of the partner countries. It was thus what may be called also a 'participatory' type of co-operation. Needless to say, funding contributions by each member to the secretariat was part of the agreement. A situation in South Asia in which forging such an agreement would have been unique under any circumstances, this was indeed an achievement and a tribute also to the countries.

In all the stages through which this slowly evolved, including early official meetings and the later ministerial agreement, as well as the subsequent parliamentary actions, the media proved to be not only a true reflector of the import and potential of the steps, but in fact, by its almost uniform high level handling, gave confidence to the leaderships of the countries and, in that way, certainly played a role in assuring success.[9]

So there are clear potentials and an even clearer role for the information system. That there may have been inadequacies should by no means be confused for the absolute need for media systems and the media. There are genuine problems of capacity and empathy, objectively speaking, with no malice to any side. Even if there may be no ready answer in sight, it is worthy of the

319

most intense involvement, at the highest possible levels of openness, by all concerned. This must be not only national leaderships and international organisations, but the media itself and the silent majority, 'who look up and are not fed'.

When it comes to information and the individual, the gulf is even wider than with the governments, by reason of the wider technical and financial disparities between the two sides and, above all, in the final resort, the press being the arbiter of its columns. No matter that a Prime Minister of one country may condemn journalists as those who could not get any other job; or that the Deputy Prime Minister of another country may stress the ability of the press to print white as black and black as white; and so on. These are not relevant to the analysis, except that behind them is a real and genuine unsolved problem of how to balance the prerogatives of the purveyors and the readers of news and views. Perhaps one solution may be to approximate to a system in which the readership is accorded a position with the press, as if it were a 'co-owner'. This may involve the reversal of a hallowed principle, that the editor does not have the last word on a matter that has been an issue. Alternatively, or additionally, it may just be that one day there would develop a system of a Press 'on the Press'; in other words, a newspaper that writes about newspapers.

It was not our hope, or intention, to be extensive, much less exhaustive, in this review of an 'information order'. There is not only a mass of material on it; even more importantly, the whole subject belongs to a highly evolving and highly unresolved area. It is also partly because one cannot conclude in terms of 'black and white' in this matter, even of 'checks and balances'. Some things can, and perhaps, must be done, like the rural/ people's dimension. In the meantime, the attempts for a new international information order remain still imperfect. It seems this is one area of support to development where we have to live, for the time being at least, with what we have.

The Information Order

NOTES

1 Not the morality or immorality associated with hell and purgatory, but that which leads to 'organic' disintegration and disequilibrium — as much of persons, as of a society.

2 Recently, in connection with environment, resource management and rural development, an experiment was initiated in Thailand and supported by the United Nations, with promising indications.

3 A noted Chinese journalist, married in India.

4 One problem may be, as Imelda Marcos, First Lady of the Philippines, observed on a visit to the U.S., that power is distributed among many strongholds in society, while responsibility is fixed on one called 'government'.

In another variation, it was said that congress had the power without the responsibility, while the President had the responsibility without the power.

5 A favourite way of programming and goal achievement among U.N. and similar systems, often rightly, a target of cynicism by the press.

6 Ably assisted by speeches of developed country representatives at conferences. The occasional attacks sometimes helped media personnel to find themselves in U.N. postings, a process heartily welcomed, perhaps even initiated by top U.N. management; some of them undoubtedly of high quality .

7 The question of fulfilment of ADB's role itself has been discussed at Chapter VIII.

8 The same thing sometimes has happened elsewhere, such as, for example, in the catalysing and creative role of UNEP, not only with UN's regional commissions but with various agencies and bodies, and then the question as to what UNEP is 'doing'.

These are all different from genuine questions of over-laden bureaucracies and the like, which we openly discussed at Chapter Eight.

9 Something which the First World media failed to pick up, reflecting one major aspect of the pressures for the new information order.

A recent example of positive reporting from the First World position, whether one agrees or not with the views, was a piece in early 1982 entitled 'Cuba's Achievement and the Price it has to Pay', showing the differences between Cuba and the other poverty-stricken populations of Latin America in straight, objective terms; so much so that the title could have an additional phrase 'and the price in the other poverty-stricken countries'. (Boston Globe, Field News Service).

Chapter Nineteen

A Manifesto

I. PREAMBLE

In the unfolding of history, the development of peoples has indeed never been even. It has been so in the advancement of wealth, in early agricultural as in present day industrial civilizations; and so in creation of the sciences, arts and cultures. The capacity to develop has not been the preserve of one people alone, as has been sometimes imagined in a few quarters in this century, based on innate development capacities of, say, the temperate climate countries, or the limitations of the tropical. Both history and emerging present experience hardly validate such a view. Particular historical developments within a strict time-frame, such as economic expansion by one group supported by military strength, and resultant de-stabilization of the affected countries socially, structurally and cumulatively, may naturally make the road back to stability and development a long haul indeed, which may, therefore, even sound impossible. It is these that have lent form to ideas such as of 'soft societies', incapable of leadership or character to emerge out of poverty into wealth.

But the movement of peoples goes on. In one place, it is by a total simulation of the model which it was thought a poor society could not replicate. In another, it may be by overthrowing old shackles in an upsurge, leading to the creation of a new system. It is in the nature of peoples that this surge and the probe must go on to the realisation of an end, a symphony which may at once be delicate as torrential, until wealth and welfare are attained. Sometimes there may be failures and the symphony must repeat itself as if unendingly and when it cannot, as in the frequently fruitless world discussions during recent times between the rich and the poor, the memory keeps the music and it is never dead. During such times, the discussions may not even be all too clear. The yearnings may as well remain incohate, instinctive and elemental, ranging from the simple thoughts of ordinary people, to the sophistications of political or economic idealists. But the results will emerge. If the rich and the poor could reverse some entrenched doctrines as to their self-interest in mutual co-operation, they could emerge much more quickly and with more uniform benefit. In a very modest manner, this is the substance of this Book.

We talked earlier of several 'system' determined traps which developing nations had inherited, some before they started developing and others in trying to develop. The heavy weight of giant economic strength on one side, the difference between the 'spade and the hydraulic forklift' that we talked of, is a trap by itself. one in which further cumulative growth of the former, the so-called ever widening gap is simply assured by that very fact. From this followed the gaps that we noted, of incomes, of trade, of technology and others. They not only made it very difficult to climb out of the pit, but worse, led to persistent erosion in development and governmental processes. The implications of modern state government — necessary and natural — for surplus generation, re-investment, consumer demand management and organisation for development, are nonetheless also a trap, unless vehemently confronted, as in some countries such as we have observed earlier.

In the course of their trying to develop, we saw well-intentioned theories and ideas, which also contained within them the seeds of possible contradictions to growth. These were such as the basic needs trap, the growth engine trap, the infrastructural or social pre-conditions trap, the employment intensive trap, the 'oscillation' trap, for industry solely or for agriculture solely, the 'loans' instead of trade trap, the soft society corruption trap, the cultural trap, and others.

The Wealth of Poor Nations

Associated with these, therefore, even if not always resulting from them, were prescriptions for growth that were often partial and inadequate and, in some important cases, what we termed 'upside down', which had to be turned right side up. Some of them were as national policies, and some international. Inside a country, were policies such as bureaucratic planning from top in place of resource based planning from the ground, planning for financial ratios of Rostovian minimum savings instead of for wage goods industries, employment-intensive planning without capacity for surplus creation, capital investment programming without development of indigenous fabricating capacity, financial resources planning without national resource balance sheets or technology policy for application to resources, political and cultural bases without sufficient local foundation, information systems without developmental dimension or people's participation, and so on. Between nations, the international co-operation institutions have well nigh neared the point of cancelling each other in their usefulness by their proliferation and their styles. The framework for trade co-operation remains perverse and upside down. So too, the monetary and investment co-operation systems, with their capacity to be problem-creating rather than problem-solving.

We have not, in the above, said anything more than the substance of our discussions in previous chapters. What we have with us is a challenge as to the future context and future calls of action for poor nations. We may perhaps say the following to start with.

Firstly, much as all genuine people would like to see to the contrary, we must presume, particularly in the perspective of a decade or so to come, the intransigence of the existing aid, trade and overall development co-operation patterns that the world community has with it as of now. It is an unfortunate commentary that it should be so simple to see the feasibility of complete co-operation, not merely for the growth of the poor nations, but also for the self-interest of the rich. While conferences of GATT, of UNCTAD, of the rich in OECD, and its likes, of the Group of 77, of the Non-Aligned States, of the U.N. in World Summits, and many others, will continue, we

324

have to conclude that none of these will yield the mass-scale change required for the upsurge to the needed growth among poor nations. Changes brought by these, while welcome, would be marginal. One can only hope not lulling the poorer countries into seeing them as singular solvents for their problems.

Secondly, therefore, the pattern or structure of a strategy for growth has to emerge among the developing countries, in which all such support as may come from the developed, while welcome, will be only as part of that strategy. While one could have hoped that the 'South-South' Conference may have initiated an entirely new phase, it did not succeed much beyond the fact that it put certain needs together. The hope expressed years earlier by the then Austrian Chancellor, quite correctly, that there should be a Third World Marshal Plan is, if anything, too sanguine, at a time when perhaps the world system is in 'neutral', if not reverse gear. Any expectations of such a prospect cannot certainly be interpreted from the present configurations in international postures for co-operation.

As we have seen before, sometimes among the developing countries, the philosophies of minimum needs, employment-intensive approach and small technology, as well as narrow refuge in cultural pasts, have on occasion taken pride of place. Leaderships have been found sometimes to state that what the poor people of their country want is simply some clothing, and housing and food and they are so simple and so pious that they would be satisfied. This is somewhat near to the remote pictures of an idyllic countryside, drawn from the comfortable distance of an urban centre and almost always totally wrong, unknown until the ferment becomes a social revolution. On the side of the developed countries, the ideas of less than optimal growth for the poor countries has been based, apart from so-called technical arguments of trade propelled growth that we saw earlier, also very much on a premise that all these will take so long and in any case will be so uncertain, that what is needed is some significant upping of *per capita* incomes. Thus, there is no catching up and, of course, no internal sinews of self-reliance such as of a wage goods pattern or fabricating industries, and the like.

The Wealth of Poor Nations

One may be almost certain, that if Japan had not become a developed country — which it did without clearing a strategy from the advanced world of the time — the developed community today would truly be saying that they need not try to catch up, but could simply move to eradicate their poverty, provide employment and, with assistance from the developed world, provide for steadily improving incomes. One could see the parallel with many other developing countries today, certainly with different time horizons for attainment, but as much justifying their aspirations as discounting the international co-operation mechanisms, that have up to now given little more than marginal growth.

Given a dynamic co-operation pattern from the developed world as we have discussed earlier, the record should certainly have been different and the future, for the developed countries themselves, much more assured, not only in terms of overcoming their own economic strains, but also of social unrest overall. Assuming such a policy in the past, say from and after the forties, one could perhaps say in Asia, that countries such as Malaysia, (even Cambodia, Kampuchea, and Laos), Thailand, Sri Lanka, India, would have been in a self-reliant and sustained growth league already; and Indonesia and Philippines, given certain social, cultural pre-conditions. Vietnam remains the product of a complex political see-saw, which otherwise could have been one of the earliest success stories; such as, already, the four 'little dragons'. So it need not only be Japan or the Western countries. Yet the realities are otherwise. In the possibilities just cited, we posited enlightened international co-operation from the advanced countries.

II. FOUNDATIONS

What we now have to see is the prospect of a difficult road, which would require firm resolve by the poorer countries and perhaps a slightly longer time, but which will certainly lead to a stable basis for wealth. This is the road of self-reliant, co-operative development, using, but not depending on, developed

country aid and trade 'mantras'. Basing ourselves on our past
chapters, we shall try to draw out those options that must
comprise a manifesto of future actions. These activities lie at
two levels, as national actions and as co-operative actions
among developing countries. The set of actions could be
grouped in three broad categories:

1. The political organisational basis of development;
2. The international co-operation system; and
3. The constituents of a true mechanics of growth.
We may look at needs, therefore, in these terms.

1. The Political Organisational Basis

The political structure, as the organisational basis for
development, is the first area of need, a fundamental pre-
requisite, for all other policies to succeed — economic, social or
cultural. As we saw, such a basis for development has been
established in some countries, appropriate to each country.
While being one mould, they are also each varying and different
from one another. We have to look at Japan, Taiwan, Korea,
Israel, India, or Singapore, to see this diversity. Even the
Socialist bases of political organisation carried a refreshing
range of variations, from the original mould in the USSR,
through China, to Yugoslavia, Cuba, or Vietnam as examples.
Whatever the variations, therefore, and whatever one's personal
value judgements on each of them, the incontrovertible perceived
need has been a firm, development supportive, organisational
basis for a country.

A country may even go back in search of some of its own
strengths, legacies which may have lain buried under the
impositions of modern constitutional patterns. This need not
mean the creation of a fourth political mould, assuming the
nineteenth century Western political system is the first. Already,
as we see, there are mixtures, with a little of the French, British
and American imprints, reflecting also the wide spread of mixed
economies, sometimes proclaimed as democratic socialist and
sometimes as socialist democratic. Presumably in the democratic

327

The Wealth of Poor Nations

socialist structure, utilities and services are 'socialized' upon a basically private enterprise philosophy; while in the socialist democratic structure, public ownership of the means of production is perhaps more 'socialized', while attempting to preserve the Western democratic modes.

Except where societies have found an answer for themselves, one salutary approach may be to probe for stability and potential in *a guild concept*, inspired from past ideas of village and rural-based self-determining organisations, which then temper the basically unproductive and often contra-developmental nature of the standard two-party democratic governmental systems that had been imposed.

Then we have, at least immediately following revolution, a magnificent phase of fulfilment of *the 'Marxian dynamic'*, in which the means of production are organised to rid the society of stark privation and to fulfilment, at basic level, of that highly moral socialist declaration, of obligation of the State to provide employment. *The next phase*, of 'take off' to higher growth, begins to present the inescapable problems of rising expectations and of political organisation to meet them; and related economic organisation. Where socialist societies have ensured adequate organisational basis for continued growth, we may obviously accept them as solutions. But where socialist societies have not done so and are obviously probing, a basis has to be stimulated, not necessarily the same mould of the free market democratic countries, but nonetheless an additional evolution. It seems, even as two-party systems in the political democratic countries were of no help to organisation for development; so the one-party system in the socialist economies has, in quite many cases, been no help at all to this second growth place.

The concerns under both political structures, while being understood, must yield to realities.[1] One does not cease to be 'socialist'; and the other does not cease to be 'capitalist', as political systems. Although the latter, in concession to its tenet of 'freedom', concedes the existence of communist parties, the system expects that socialism will always be introduced only by democratic process; implying, that it may also be voted out. Anything less would be anti-State. It should be possible to apply a similar principle in socialist countries, in which two-party elections could prevail, but on the unconditional premise of fully socialist platforms. One should think that such a recourse would positively enhance the capacities of socialist economies also to provide for healthy successions to leadership, as much as to carry an economy through to the next, higher, phase of rising expectations and ramified growth. Remarkably, the foregoing passages, on limits and change, have been entirely from the First Edition of this book.

Much later, in 1993, with the eclipse of Gorbachev, I was to write, indeed vindicating the foregoing, as follows:

> Any attempt to enable a shift from an under-developed Society, to one reaching towards the high mass consumption levels of advanced development, is both a political and economic exercise (involving a 'Perestroika' in both, as distinct from only 'Glassnost' in the first), in which essential change had also to be modulated, for success with the political as with the economic process.

By the same token, going back to our observation on a 'guild concept' in free enterprise democracy, it seems necessary to look seriously to establish a pattern of economic democracy, in which the mode must be 'participatory development'. We could see this in concentric circles, from village area upwards. We may even thus have a happier international situation since, on the one side, we would have free enterprise two-party democracy with intensive participatory development; and on the other, intensive socialist planning from down up and up down, but with two-party elections as well.[2]

2. The International Co-operation System

a. *At the international level*, we have one set of decisions that developing countries must now take. It belongs to de-emphasising their total *reliance on the developed countries* for their own growth. More than the physical, it appears to be a major psychological step for most of the Third World, away

329

from a posture originally created by the First World, but in which the Third World has allowed itself to be trapped. Its hallmark is the system of international conferences, plans, programmes, declarations, resolutions, calls to developed countries and development institutions, and so on.

The proclamations of *self-reliance* by the Third World have often been merely slogans, with total continuing structural, financial and resources dependence on the First World and its international systems. Thus, also, when it came to co-operative mechanisms among developing countries, global or regional, the proclamations have not proceeded beyond verbiage; and countries have continued to go back, almost exclusively, to the offers and mechanisms of the international aid institutions and systems. So too in the latest South-South conclusions and recommendations of which much was expected. This has to break, if the developing countries are to break through to genuine co-operation among themselves, as one major support to their developmental aspirations.

Thus it is necessary, even if it may come as a shock to some countries, to re-think the emphasis given to, and energy spent on, drawing up charters of new international orders with hopes of activating global leverages. As we have reiterated, what flows from global capacity should be welcomed, within nationally determined policy frameworks; the catastrophe has been to rely on the former. So much for the GATT/WTO accords; the Earth Charter; Services and Intellectual Property Rights and Patents; even the Bio-diversity Conventions; and others.

b. As a counterpart to self-reliance, a serious examination of the major international system — namely, *the United Nations* and the allied Specialised Agencies — must at least begin to be made, for a complete overhaul, both of the *type* of development support it could give and of its overgrown and duplicating *structures.* Hopefully, such an examination should be made and an overhaul completed as a high priority on the international agenda.

Obviously, a rearrangement of a structure such as the United Nations system and its ramifications requires an intensive, separate look at its origins, the reasons for its various ramifications, its realities and essentials and its future credit worthiness. The *problems* and *solutions* have been and will be *both political and management*.

There seems to be a co-existence of *two political stances*. Contrary to a general concern, and even conviction, that the growth of the United Nations system should be arrested and if possible reversed, a whole array of 'sectoral' clientele inside governments make decisions at international governing bodies which have been always expansionist. Often they have also been divisive and conflicting in terms of new bodies or offices created.

There is also another peculiarity that has been allowed to emerge inside the United Nations bureaucracies, which is again a co-existence of *two contrasting characteristics*. On the one side, it is overloaded with people whose work cycles seem to be getting together pieces of paper and organising conferences, many of which may as well not take place. On the other side, for substantive research and hard ideas for development breakthroughs, with very few exceptions, there is serious inadequacy. Too often a serious problem of this sort is handled by farming out to outside personnel, with the finances needed to develop internal capacity for work on this type of work already taken up by the regular bureaucracies.

With the *end of the Cold War*, a third, somewhat amazing turn took place. The political security agenda took over from the economic. When it was next to impossible for Secretaries General to process Peace-Keeping operations in the past, these now became commonplace. The Economic and Social Secretariats became constricted, even de-emphasised, and the Security Council took more control than ever before, vis-a-vis, the General Assembly. The manner of choice of the Secretary-General, needless to say, also had an unfortunate role in this. The issues of Peace-Keeping and Security cannot be studied here and need urgently to be done elsewhere. Here we look at the economic and social prospects in the United Nations system.

c. Amidst all these limitations, one may be vain to visualize a radical transformation, such as one must hold is, in any case, necessary. Yet, even if it may not materialize immediately, it may be worth seeing the lines of such a real transformation.

At the base, has to be one interdisciplinary United Nations system and no more, for each developing *country*, whose main function shall be to prepare a pre-investment and investment assistance programme, as counterpart to the country's development plan. Its purpose should be not merely to serve as the framework for the small, United Nations assistance, but as a 'frame of reference' for all assistance sources, whatever be the source of the assistance to the country.[3] This is the strongest contribution that the United Nations character and capacity can ever make to a country at the country level. No matter that a new trend, such as recently from the United States for the private sector and the market-place, emerge or is canvassed. Neither this nor other assistance stances make sense outside of a single aid plan or frame - insofar as the country benefitting itself is concerned. It is a function in which the United Nations, more than any other source, can be the most valued contributor. In order to fulfil this, the United Nations system in the country must have two supports. One is that its country office must have, at the top, not only known general capacity but technical capacity and understanding of economic needs and priorities.

The other, and even more important, is that there must be a single United Nations organisation at the *regional* level for each of the regions presently designated or such other regions as may be marked out. At least from the viewpoint of the countries, there cannot be room for a system of bodies and agencies and others all purporting to help. This does not mean elimination of some and continuing one; but elimination of all first. Pursuing their own furrows when not 'developing conferences', there is need to reconstitute a much streamlined and inherently capable single regional United Nations for development. Its main thrust will be (i) to forge the much needed international trade, monetary, commodity and other co-operation systems and sub-systems within its area, as well as transregional arrangements on them, and (ii) to provide, by virtue of its wider specialized human resource base, concrete inputs to the country United Nations system, for the preparation of the pre-investment and investment assistance programmes that we talked of earlier.

At the *global* level, there is probably greater proliferation, duplication and non-productive use of human and financial resources than elsewhere in the system. Agencies have, ostensibly, their own separate specializations. However, components of the system have distinguished themselves as often by specializing in bits and pieces of the others' specializations, with justifications that were entrenched in sophistry as well as, mandates from their governing bodies. Meanwhile, committees on co-ordination do not co-ordinate and contributors to programme funds remain increasingly unimpressed. A solution may indisputably require that the entire global level structure should be located in one place, perhaps in Europe, such as the European Office of the United Nations; incidentally, with considerable release of funds to productive activities, now tied up on often in unproductive, in any case duplicative, personnel. Any concept of dispersal of UN presence must not be by distributing global head offices, but through an 'outlying field' offices concept. These may not only be the re-arranged regional headquarters offices, but sub-regional units of both regional and global headquarters, as needed.

The *unified character* of a United Nations structure is indispensable if we may look forward to a future value out of the system. It may be sobering to reflect, not only that countries developed in the last century before a United Nations system existed, but that all those that became developed this century did so, very much irrespective of United Nations inputs, even if in certain cases these were indeed visible. The United Nations economic and social system has still to find its capacity to create a developed country out of a poor one.

d. *The developing countries* must stop paying only lip service to organisation for regional trade co-operation, pursuing global 'will-o-the-wisps' in hope of largesse or miracle. The Third World has to take itself seriously, recognising that success involves serious re-orientation, honest hard labour, and an assured outcome. It is in this background that we considered a pattern of regional trade co-operation in an earlier chapter.

The Wealth of Poor Nations

In *trade* the developing countries have been trying to seek refuge in commodity and stabilisation arrangements and other concessional devices, all marginal palliatives (save in OPEC type initiatives). They all ended up in the same place. Developing countries simply continued with a market disadvantage, being weak and non-resilient economically, and not being able to modulate their production in trade terms, since their policies were determined by the sore needs of sheer subsistence, well before development. Even otherwise, the vast mass of social, infra-structural capital that is demanded in all development, became a fixed import commitment, over whose price or quantum variations there was little capacity for control.

We saw earlier how the International Trade Systems, dominantly represented in the GATT process and Accords, were consistently developed-country oriented, and with much the major benefits flowing to them. In the same vein, upon the final break-through in December, '93 on the Uruguay Accord - and the World Trade Organisation (WTO) to boot in the wings - an effort was again made, perhaps even unconsciously, to give all these a mantle of a World Trade 'break through'.

Possibly, in the euphoria of 'the day after', the lead Editorial of the London Times, titled 'Beautiful Victory', called it 'a political achievement comparable to that of (Keynes and others) who created the Bretton Wood system'.

The further acceptance of a WTO, it said, was 'a completion' of the Bretton Woods task where the latter contemplated, but failed to establish, the intended International Trade Organisation (ITO).

Yet, not only was its ebullient estimation of GATT partial, but the comparison of the new WTO to the lost ITO, totally misplaced. The dominant fear of the new WTO by the developing countries is not its possible toughness or speed, which the Editorial commends, but fear that the power within was heavily in favour of the developed countries; and not only in Trade, but on the new, threatening areas of Services, Environment, Patents and Royalties, Bio-technology, and others.

A letter sent at that time to the *Times* when this writer was visiting at the London School of Economics, proved ostensibly too difficult for that doyen of public thinking to carry. The main text of that letter, stated:

'The World Trade Organisation — ITO — which you mentioned, was to be an integral part of that System, and its absence did not merely mean one omission, but the effectiveness of the Bretton Woods mechanism as an entity.

The reason is that, unlike GATT (which came to negotiate and institute tariff based approaches, primarily for the rich countries) ITO meant what its title said, and was to function as integral part of the policies for redress of short term imbalances (at IMF) and for reconstruction and development demands (at the World Bank).

The central concept in such an ITO role, at least in the run up to the Bretton Woods Acts, was to invest a lead, if not primary, responsibility on the Surplus countries to redress their surpluses by more imports worldwide, with the secondary responsibility on the shoulders of the Deficit countries to create exports. This, of course, was the opposite of the real world situation before or after, in which the burden of adjustment was with the Deficit countries.

Contrary to your view, American doubts about ITO were not on the 'bureaucratic sclerosis which affects the UN' — something in any case no one could have asserted at that time, when the UN had yet to get itself established. The prospect of wide membership of ITO, among other things, would of course, have been a real fear for the Americans at that time — something they had to contend with all along later at the General Assembly.

As for any comprehensive benefit — to the whole World — your hopes conceal too much: on unequal benefits, constraints on 'catching up', hidden walls, and the long time-frames.

The Final Act is indeed a significant milestone on the rough road that, alone, humanity has known to take. Perhaps left to a Keynes, the content of a 'beautiful victory' may have been had."

In the Third World situation, there was a mutual conflict, of clear enthusiasm in principle along with intellectual doubt in practice, as to the scope available for *trade co-operation*, in which a western type tariff dismantling approach was dominant. It

335

represented an obvious 'upside down' situation, which has to be turned 'right side up'. The formation of a positive programme of trade expansion and co-operation must be based on an opposite principle, of the basic condition to co-operating countries of 'additional export' rather than of an additional commitment to import. This idea of a commodity flow matrix, based on quantitative rather than tariff bases, introduces a system that depends not on request for tariff reduction but on offer for export additions. The structure provides assurance because of its promise that no participating country can lose, but only gain.

Similarly, although this has global implications, the Third World should take up for consideration, as well as lead, the institution of a sensible *monetary co-operation system*, in which the financing limits to international trade are set by the capacities for growth of all, rather than the ability of one to block the imports of the other.

The *financing of international trade* based on deficit countries fighting to export and surplus countries resisting imports, was a clearly 'upside down' phenomenon which had some day to be set 'right side up', if a world order were seriously contemplated. This indeed applies as much to the developed as to the developing world. Such a lasting solution, in fact the only possible durable solution, is tied with establishment of the idea of 'local currency' settlements, wherein globally deficit countries' currencies made out to the surplus countries in trade balance settlements constitute the resources for the monetary 'International Fund'. In this idea, implying automatic creation and adjustment of the required foreign exchange media for settling the net dues of international trade, we have a different situation from what prevails. What prevails is an essentially unnatural limitation on the scope of such trade imposed by the volume of monetary reserves available in the case of strong countries and by the volume of international income transfer decided upon in the case of weak countries. In either case, import or export possibilities are not determined by internal economic capacity, as evident in the case of trade between areas within one country. Clearly the important missing factor at the international level has been the absence of a single currency. The task is to achieve this or, more correctly, to re-outline financing methods in a way that would approximate to this in the ultimate. Under a local currency holding system world income tends to remain high with exports continuing at unhindered levels and imports by surplus countries tending always to increase. Among industrial countries, equilibrating at a high level of total trade is much more likely, while among developing countries, the chances of others absorbing exports are equally increased. Widely ramifying investment and technology developments will emerge almost naturally out of this, with global benefit overall and developing countries' genuine self-reliance in particular.

While being essentially a series of national initiatives, still the evolution one day of a sensible understanding of world *cultures*, by each understanding its own in a wider arena, is a needed basis for development, as for global peace. It is a priority for all, not simply for the Third World. Perhaps here, more than anywhere else, it gives an opportunity for the highest minds to provide leadership and example.

So one may state, also for an *information* order of the future, which must be both national and international. At the national level, getting the message across to the people is perhaps as foundational as any of the other foundations we have listed; at the international level, it bears close affinity to the aims and aspirations of cultural advancement.

3. The mechanics of Growth

Preferably on the above bases, but in any case, we need the essential constituents for a *national mechanics of growth*, that can be called self-reliant, or self-managed, and sustaining. Let us check-list them here briefly.

The first need is to adopt a complete, changed, resource-based planning system at *ground level*, involving the people as producers at all stages, of planning, programming and implementation; yielding the first resource creation needed for sustained investment and development. We have discussed this. Given the political structure for development and resource-

337

based 'participatory' planning, land reform will find a solution, as examples of Japan, Taiwan, Korea, China and others have clearly shown. To cry out loud for land reform as basis for development, which indeed it is, without the former, is to be sterile from the start; and the reason for the poor records seen in many politically disoriented societies.

The second national foundation - with exceptions such as small cities, states and very large countries where additional requirements are involved — must be the early establishment of a pattern of *wage goods* industries as we have discussed earlier.

A third national decision which, as we pointed earlier, is a vital one for growth, is the institution of an early pattern of development of *'fabricating capacity'* for machines, equipment, and machine tools. As we have mentioned before, it does not mean making all, or most, of these things, even in the categories that are related to national production. But the only road to economic self-reliance and to a basis for growth is the creation of this capacity in major categories, such as each country must decide for itself. It is not only a 'one-step' economic benefit. It creates an expanding pool of human skills and, importantly, a permanent 'fabricating culture' in the country. It is, as past experience of all countries that have travelled this road has shown over and over again, the only road to national self-assurance, leading to a multiplier capacity in later years in science, technology and capital goods production.

The fourth foundation has to be a concerted *sharing* decision among partners in the economy — on the apportionment of *national product* between consumption and surplus re-investment. The partners in the economy are the owners of the means of production — entrepreneurs or the State according to the political system — the workers, and them together as consumers. A political system such as providing for 'participatory development' as we discussed under free enterprise democracy, or for the two-party elections in a socialist democracy, should obviously lead to better decisions on this very important constituent of continuous development. The chances of the various partners accepting realities, as well as working together for targets, should be much greater.

A Manifesto

We said early in this book that there were three growth models in history. The pattern of self-reliance for developing countries and their co-operation do not mean that we require a 'fourth model'. The open market model is in vogue. Yet, as we said, countries can continue to belong to socialist or free market systems. What we require is confirmed action in the directions involved. The resources and the potentials in both of them are there; a vast stock of potential human skills; and vast resources, with capacity to make up for imbalances in endowments through development and application of technology to natural resources.

As a case in point, the export of some of these resources in their natural form yields large incomes at present. Examples abound, especially in the tropical zone countries. For instance, in the early eighties, Indonesia earned about $ 1.5 billion per annum by export of timber, but obviously at the risk of incalculable destruction of forests, soil and other reproductive ecosystems, all these none else than economic bases for continued development. In this sense, the country was converting some of its assets into a non-renewable resource: as was remarked in another instance, it was 'living on capital'. The immediate economic gain can be dubious. This could be so not only by the exports being used for import of consumer goods. Even if used for capital goods, if these continue to be imported, while nothing is done to set up machine manufacturing capacities with these proceeds, these products share a characteristic with non-renewable resources that work for classic dependent economies. For example, in South-East Asian countries, tin is exported in primary form, without further processing to finished stage and, therefore, with loss of the major portion of benefit to the countries. Unless the proceeds were used to build up capital goods and other value added capacities, in this or other domestic sectors, this type of 'dependent development' is obviously self-defeating.[4] As we said, therefore, it is not a question of inventing a fourth growth model for international co-operation, but of resolutely following the implications of the present, and the potentials of the future. In the long run, we shall have in any case, not several, but one integrated planning concept for development.

339

The Wealth of Poor Nations

The whole question of *dependent development*, full value added, and fabricating capacity[5] is so central to creation of wealth and welfare, that they must be considered fundamental and foundational, making for the lasting differences between the rich and poor countries — tying down terms of trade, income, sustainability and capacity. Our Chapter Eight was simply devotion to this.

In my '*Economics of Full Employment in Agricultural Countries*', published in the fifties and frequently referred to in earlier pages of this book, we stressed the opportunities that were about to be lost then for a proper and positive aid role for West Europe in a global context. A distinction made between the Reconstruction Aid from the United States to Europe, which I called 'Viability Aid', and the needed Development Aid to what we now call the Third World. For failure of Europe to play its role, the United States had assumed both roles in large part, whereas what should have occurred was Viability Aid to Europe from the U.S. and Development Aid dominantly from Europe to the Third World. It was to have been over wide ranges of wage goods production and machinery and tooling capacity in developing countries. This unfortunately failed to take place, in fully that form for conceptual as well as political weaknesses, in thinking, in a loss of opportunity to both 'Europe and the developing world'.

The same portents seem to be before us now, and we do not learn. UNCTAD VI, and its successors, have rolled to a close, unfortunately as we feared, and the post-War Aid Trade Model may no longer be valid, unless an Aid role is found as we have emphasised and pinpointed here. Essentially and singly, this is for the transition from 'dependent to non-dependent' development. What should additionally be clear is that such a role is enormous even in quantitative terms, if the developed countries could see beyond their present mental frame. *Europe*, now as OECD, may miss a proper and positive *Aid opportunity* again; eventually to the loss of Europe, in particular with its lag behind the United States and Japan in the new technological revolution.

It is of course possible, if one must, to outline something like *a fourth development model*. The basis itself is the invariable

340

means and conditions for growth as we have seen at Chapter Two, and applicable to any model. Surpluses have to be garnered while an income and consumption policy has also to be managed. But we are at a point of time in which dependent economies have been created. One of the most fundamental starting points for an effective fourth model must, therefore, be the ability with which a country may depart from its pattern of import dependence on a number of semi-luxuries, which have even come to be considered necessities.

Thus, motor cars, household equipment, a number of tertiary, tourist and other services, and a host of other categories, become ultimately tied to established policy thinking. Secondly, the eradication of these in vacuo would immediately depress incomes, employment and other benefits so drastically that a policy change, particularly as a governmental decision, may be inconceivable. Yet the success with which and the degree to which an economy could change to a different track would determine the speed with which it could implement such a fourth growth model.

The examples are there in a historical sense. Japan after the War, Taiwan, India and so on, in which such imports were held back for the purpose of capital construction — as the socialist economies term it — or creation. We noted in an earlier chapter the psychological condescension with which aid patterns have looked on such restrictions. Immediately after the War, Japan for example, in building up its investment surge, not only contained consumption, but developed a priority mix in investment, holding down on many road systems and cars, houses and even some light consumer goods, until the fabrication basis had been established. After all, even in the U.K. right up to the early fifties, it was easier to have delivery of a new car for those who had foreign exchange than for the locals; and so on. Such a direction also gave a better bargaining power in the traditional sense for a developing country's exports.

- Given such a basis, and recalling some of the points we had already raised, we could list the *foundations* for the fourth growth model. They are,

The Wealth of Poor Nations

(a)   A strategy for wage goods industries;

(b)   A selective, but firm and determined capital goods fabrication capacity;

(c)   An effective regional co-operative trade and monetary
system, the latter hopefully widening into global;

(d)   Selective commodity co-operation arrangements;

(e)   Such available aid and trade of the 'third growth model'
type as the developed countries agree upon; and

(f)   Within this framework, the other national and international components of a model — namely, resource based
ground-level planning, wage policies, governmental and
cultural foundations, and an information order.

To sum up, therefore, self-reliant, self-managing or *self-
sustaining growth* has yet not won the fight for the Third World
because of the gap between what went under those names and
the reality. There was a transition from the 'shovel to the
hydraulic fork lift'. For too many cases, this transition was
simply the end of the indigenous shovel industry and the
beginning of an expanding hydraulic import industry. There
was no transition in which a machine or component became a
prototype to 'fabricate and to multiply'. The distinction runs
like a golden, or not so golden, thread dividing all prosperous
countries and the so called developing. The immutable basic
approach, apart from a clear package that includes 'wage goods'
industries and a new decentralized agrarian 'participatory
development', has to be the establishment of an early fabricating
industrial capacity. Given these, all other so called panaceas of
recent decades fall into place; without them, economies would
not even move. More important than even 'catching up'
therefore is the establishment of this type of self-sustained
growth; catching up will then take care of itself.

What comes as aid to the Third World is a small part of what
would have been 'value added' resources within these countries.
All countries that are developed had gone through this change
first — incidentally putting them in a position of superior
trading, payments, and '*aid giving*' power. Not having done so,
the developing countries had no autonomous growth capacity
and no own created surpluses. Their *concepts of growth* were

then beset with concessions, grants, loans and aid and continuing ways of seeking short-term relief. *The real growth path* for them was elsewhere.

III. TRENDS

In talking of the wealth of poor countries in these chapters, we have ranged over varying types of needs, economic and non-economic, contemporary and prognostic. We have talked of shortcomings on various sides, nationally and internationally, and not only of one side or the other. We have called for a departure from sterile postures or verbiage, at both national and international levels, and for the test of courageous action, again at national and co-operative levels, as the only means towards a serious new turn for the countries looking to a different future.

These have to happen with the responsibility spread wide. The leadership have to become responsible; so the intelligentsia; and the people. While a change may be spearheaded by an elite, it can be sustained only by the peoples. That change must occur is an inevitable inference from the course of events as they have occurred and the world has so far witnessed. We do not mean that any of these may materialize, or be achieved, overnight. What is serious seems to be the lack of signs of a beginning in these directions, and in the areas in which we saw that changes were needed, as minimum necessary bases for wealth. These are nothing more than the changes that countries which broke through to development did undertake. The first steps, if taken, may be the most important.

At regional level, in limited ways although too general so far, countries had shown this capacity to take a first step to realise an objective as well as to expand from it. As Asian countries, in the history of ECAFE (now ESCAP) when it was first established in 1947, provided a modest example. At its inception, ECAFE had to be an effective point of 'communication' between nations, many of which were newly independent, helping in the establishment of a new pattern of inter-country relationships that never existed before. Next, it provided a 'forum' for professionals and policy makers, to begin to exchange information, ideas and possibilities. It led to results such as regional statistical systems, improved national planning and programming, preparation of region-wide economic surveys and analyses of the countries as a whole, and so on. From these, the interchange led to co-operative programmes on 'institutions', such as a common institute for economic development planning and others of this type.

A further sophistication came with possibilities of co-operation 'round natural resources', particularly larger ones; from this emerged the Mekong Project at that time, and perhaps still, the largest United Nations led initiative of this nature. Then came co-operative initiatives around 'infrastructures' which led to the well-known Asian Highway, and proposed plans for a Trans-Asian Railway Network. A more difficult stage was reached with the establishment in the sphere of 'financing', amidst considerable opposition from outside, of the Asian Development Bank. With more confidence the countries moved to the adoption of a comprehensive declaration subsequently on 'trade and monetary co-operation, leading to the first initiatives on co-operative trade systems, clearing union, reserve bank, and so on. About the same time, a series of 'commodity communities' arrangements became possible, such as on coconut and pepper. In support of these, 'subregional groupings' that began to identify themselves at the time, launched serious initiatives on specific potentials for their co-operation, such as on large industry, marine resources and so on. While sophisticated economic union was obviously not a practicality, the vision and the process were clearly practical and creative.

Much later, in the formulation of a South Asia Co-operative Environment Programme for development-related environmental management of major resources, there emerged in effect a South Asian community arrangement, with perhaps unique significance in international law, for co-operation among developing countries. The grouping emerged under an agreed constitution adopted at ministerial level through Articles of Association, and was ratified in the parliaments of the participating countries; a step, at the time, of true significance indeed. It contained the other constituents, such as a headquarters, administrative arrangements, and community contributions, the last feature again a significant one. When we consider, for instance, that one of the programmes accepted was a Himalayan ecosystem management plan covering a huge span of six countries with an estimated 1,000 million people living by the year 2000 in the shadow of the Himalayas, and that the assumption of focal point responsibility for the programme by Pakistan was consented to by all the other countries involved, it does speak for the possiblilities of large and real co-operation if countries will it. In the case of this particular grouping, as was said at the time of its establishment, the programme was related all the time to development and to overcoming the poverty situation. It developed gradually, from small beginnings, without ruffling sensitivities or creating fears, moving to *ad hoc* activities, to programmes, to tentative arrangements for co-operation, to strategy for organisation and, finally, to setting up of structure.

In this as in all such others, within countries and between countries, *the necessary philosophy* must be 'to look for areas of agreement'. The easiest thing in the world is to find areas of disagreement; but an area of agreement, however small, provides a starting point, round which one builds. With the experience of working on such areas, which more often than otherwise soon dispels fears and suspicions, the real potentials begin to get discovered; and then these, surely and certainly, expand and blossom out into creations that give satisfaction. Barriers give way to bridges, no matter that there are many more barriers still left. These acts of peace building, the 'other side' of peace keeping, spread over areas and over types of human association, from economic to cultural to political.

Looking now as a whole on the future context and prospects for the 'wealth of poor nations', one is inclined to look at trends in three categories, namely:
1. As a continuum from past foundations;
2. As completion of initiatives that have already begun and have developed a momentum and;

3. As compulsive needs, such as of survival, or from threat of upheaval, so imperative that we have to act;
whether we like it or not.

Looking at the future context in these terms and spanning the various issues which we have tried to bring out and to discuss, let us look at them in this context. Before doing so, we must admit that some trends may need to be seen rather as 'non-trends'; namely, not as things that may happen but unfortunately as things that may continue to stagnate. Also, some issues may, as is natural, figure under more than one of the three categories we have here.

1. The 'Continuums'

As a continuum from past foundations, *most* of the trends seem to be indeed as *standstills*. We see them as follows:

❏ The political organisational *structures* which could effectively create structural capacity and development leadership are not likely to emerge and will continue in the short-term as *largely non-developmental* for the least developed countries, with the others growing on the backs of the open market developed country investments flows.

❏ Notwithstanding, a very *few more countries* may add themselves as *developed* in the coming decade to the 'four little dragons' (or not so little) with luck. It may be countries such as Malaysia, Thailand, India, Brazil. They will still have a long road to go after that, yet the take-off may have occurred.

❏ Social *cultural conflicts* and cultural inadequacy seem likely to *continue* and will be a drag on strong thrusts for development.

❏ *'Dependent development'* — namely, the absence of a solid wage goods industry base and of machine fabrication capacity — seems likely *to prevail*, except in the few countries that may 'take-off'.

❏ One of the main reasons would be the *still unfortunate drag in* setting up bold, positive, *regional* trade *co-operation*.

346

A Manifesto

- *International trade* systems will almost undoubtedly continue with the *same gap* between professions and practice.
- The machinery for *international financing* co-operation is also likely to *continue 'up-side-down'*.
- It may be *just possible*, though almost certainly for reasons connected with political interplay rather than intellectual enlightenment, a much *streamlined United Nations* global machinery for social and economic development would begin to emerge.
- There would possibly be a *better* concept and practice of *resources management* for sustained development.
- Following from this, but also from frustrations with the multiplicity of sectoral planning priorities, there is *possible* chance of much more *integrated planning* and programming emerging.
- Very *likely*, wide areas of *renewable resources* would be *tapped* in large volume, not only for energy but also as other resource inputs of development; at the same time, it seems certain that nuclear energy utilization will expand.
- The world's conventional resources would continue to erode, but most *likely* with marked *slowing* down in their *rates of depletion* or deterioration, particularly soils, forests, aquatic resources.
- The *transport* system, particularly of *Cities*, would continue to *remain confused* with just some chance of radical reorientation in one or two in the world, which may then hopefully give a lead. In the meantime, the main break-throughs to make life possible in Megalopolis would be rapid transit sophistication of one type or another, helping here and there, but not necessarily overcoming its space-time dimension, or solving the problem of neuro-psychosis of a so-called modern life style.
- *Megalopolis* will continue to expand; so too would marginal settlements in absolute terms though not relative; and rural emigration would continue to take place.
- Rate of *population growth* may for once be brought to *manageable level*, though with little import for wealth and welfare unless cities acquire quality, and the rural country side acquires economic efficiency.

❑ Absolute unemployment and relative *poverty* are unfortunately likely *to continue*. Overall national income would undoubtedly grow, with the opportunities contained therein depending on the type of economic structures and development leadership created.

❑ Large *'enclave' dependency*, under guise of development, could take over in quite a few countries through so-called free trade zones, tourism and similar so-called lead sectors, and so on, diverting from or *choking out*, the scope for laying the *structural foundations*.

❑ The concept of the *'global commons'* would be *advanced*, but the *First World exploitation* of the resources of ocean depths, outer space intellectual property, and bio-diversity seems *certain*.

2. Initiatives Begun

On particular *initiatives* begun, which have acquired momentum, it seems that most of them would be *led by the First World*, even some of those that are of concern primarily to the Third World. An indication of them may be as follows:

❑ A more rationalized global, international and national *information system* may be set up, considering the momentum that has been created and the *inability to hold back now*.

❑ The moves for a *new global energy mix*, given the series of worldwide initiatives already begun, have gained a momentum now which will not stop.

❑ At the level of international relations and politics, the *law of the sea* should expect to be a *reality*.

❑ Specific *sub-regional co-operation* movements which have developed a strong thrust in recent years *would* definitely *last* and grow.

❑ *Some work, not much recognised yet*, but of significance for developing countries under integrated planning - *such as* the preparation of *'national resources balance sheets'*, and *integrated cost-benefit* presentations - could with luck carry

348

the momentum of solid work started and profitable applications *should begin*.

❑ The *family planning* momentum would see something like a *fulfilment*, though not a final attainment. This is not to say that population will cease to grow (a statistical phenomenon, among others); nor that economic welfare will thereby increase (quite a different thing from simply limiting families).

❑ Environmental *sanitation*, under leadership of WHO and a record of achievement already in certain areas, will *probably carry the current momentum* generated under the slogan of 'Water for all by the Year 2000'.

❑ The *microchip* and 'robots for workers' *technologies* will progress to their *logical conclusions*, whose final configuration it is not possible to define fully immediately. In this, as under oceanic and space resources, the gap between the advanced and backward countries could widen dramatically.

❑ The momentum on the *space programme* will obviously be carried, with a *few more countries* joining in.

3. The Compulsive Needs

On the compulsive *needs which must be met*, one may see it *mainly* as the cumulative force of *various 'up-side-down' positions* we have in the world of co-operation and development today. They may be something as follows:

❑ There is no question that the *Third World has to provide itself*, and be provided, with a *large multiple* of the *resources* that is *now used*, say, anything between five to twenty times. While the First World should be using less resources, although unfortunately it will not be, for the Third World, the issue is not less resources but many times the present available resources. So *this will be found*, whatever the way.

❑ The *political organisational base* for development *must be found*. If it is not under present patterns, it will still be.

❑ *Unless* a likely *streamlining* of the United Nations system, which we said may occur for other reasons, fairly solves

349

serious deficiencies, there will be irresistible *pressure for a United Nations* system that is quite *different from the existing*.

❑ Either there will be a *reformed aid, trade and monetary system, or an alternative* pattern which could, sadly, bypass this, the outlines or leaderships for which remain still unclear.

❑ *Compulsion will dictate* strong *regional co-operation* organisation, on trade as well as commodities and related matters.

❑ Sooner or later, including reasons of resource needs by the Third World, a *global resources management system* for development and management of outer limits to growth, *will have to be confronted*.

❑ *Similar* confrontations have to be made *for* the delineation of new *Energy Maps*; new *Urban Systems*; and the establishment of genuine Lead sectors within economies.

❑ Countries that have not taken steps, would be faced with *inexorable compulsion to establish* strong *technology bases and machinery fabrication capacity* as absolute needs for their development.

❑ The world's still *inadequate understanding* and appreciation *of genetic resources* and the *habitats* for them, *could be catastrophic*. It would lead perhaps to one of the nicest areas of peaceful world co-operation, in which a widespread network of genetic resources pools for man's existence would be set up and maintained. That, in this whole world, only the plant manufactures its own food may become, once more, a golden thread of human culture. Yet, *present international concordats* weighted in favour of the North, *may place all these on hold*.

4. EPILOGUE

Whatever we may say, or feel, on needs or trends, seeing them as likely or compulsive, we have to fall back on a *hope*. It is the hope that, through people, we shall have understanding and determination. Understanding is both 'awareness' and

A Manifesto

'mutuality'; determination is both vision and honesty. What we tried to set up in *these chapters* is *only the basis for action*; *action itself* is truly *a human force, conditioned* heavily by all the economic, political and cultural environments, *but beyond* them and coming from the power of peoples — its leaders, its elites, its masses.

Perhaps one may well conclude taking refuge in a reflection made some years ago, on a distinguished occasion, on *the four gifts* necessary for true achievement.[6] They were set down as the gifts of: *seeing* the problems and the tasks of their generation with a clarity and detachment given to few men; *perceiving* how to break through the constraints imposed by politics and public opinion; *(carrying)* their contemporaries and changing public opinion sufficiently to make things happen; and *being animated* not by lust for personal power or aggrandizement but by desire to benefit the nation and humanity.

In such a manifesto of action, one may not perhaps seek to predict the future course. But one must hope. In this hope, this Book started by addressing itself to the youth. The needs and the goals mentioned here are, of course, more important to them. Their attainment may also depend as much on them, for the future is, so often, in the present. Yet, the youth of today in a decade enter middle age; and in a decade more may as much become answerable for failure just as, if they will it, for outstanding success. It is a measure of the need to caution ourselves against complacency; and of the strength of the exertions we must make. Together, they are, indeed, not difficult of realisation.

We said at one point earlier that this Book was not about revolution. It does not seek to establish yet another development model for the world. But what it is about, and calls for positively, is a revolution in the use of the three extant models; a revolution in which the leaderships — under parties, caucuses, cells or en masse — force the changes within their own models, irrespective of which model, or whether a country tomorrow moves from the 'first' to the 'second'. *Models by themselves*, Open Market or Dirigiste, *will never achieve*.

The call is for the great internal revolutions — such as, for example, in the 'first' for participatory development, or in the

351

The Wealth of Poor Nations

'second' for two-party organisation, or in the 'third' for all the things that this book has urged; and among all three, for an essential new 'religion' and a new 'culture'. The elites need to awake, so the people may not wait in need, or surely find a different elite and new leaderships. Our judgements may be human, but the thoughts we have traced are inevitable. In the new revolution within their own societies, the dimensions of these thoughts must need to pierce; and be discussed, enhanced and carried into their own set systems, of economics, of culture and of organisation. People await this leadership in all the 'three worlds'. Of one thing it may be certain, that it is time. At the end of these long pages, perhaps unavoidably pedantic in places, one must hope that their purport and urgency may be fully seen. Perhaps new leaders and new forces from within peoples will emerge to see common cause, to take these up, to improve them immeasurably, and to go forward.

We have, of course, not talked of War. Turbulences have been continuous, out of the fissures, of varying size, that have appeared in all areas of the world. Major upheaval, leading to holocaust, will throw out all hopes expectations, for the matters that we have talked about. When, or whether, we may renew a discussion of the creation of Wealth is another matter.

NOTES

1 One of the oft noted commentaries on the two systems is in fact their unnoticed approximation in many important aspects of economic organisation and management. The different, recent, Chinese initiatives for the four modernizations have certain similarities to our discussion here of the second phase of rising expectations.
2 May well be the political counterpart of the 'conditions and invariables' that we referred to under the mechanics of growth at Chapter II.
3 In a spurt of early contributions between 1965 and 1969, ECAFE produced a presentation of 'Technical assistance programming and economic development planning', under an activity called national co-ordination of technical assistance; undertook a sample Economic Survey of Thailand as a basis for such programming; and outlined the above technical assistance role for the United Nations system in its comments and proposals on what was called the United Nations Capacity Study on the subject, prior to the institution of the United Nations Development Programme system in its present form.

4   A point which was very well expounded in connection with the integrated cost/benefit work referred to in an earlier Chapter. It is a forceful illustration of the place of machine and machine tool making capacity — the fabricating capacity — in a true development strategy, as the first essential for ability to obtain the highest feasible value-added benefit from natural resources; built-in bargaining power in trade; and, of course, framework for sustainable development.

5   Francois Mitterand, President of France, at the Summit Session of the seven industrialized countries held June 1982 at Versailles, provided a long felt lead when he 'called on other Western leaders to approve a programme of using technology to pull the world out of economic recession and spark growth in richer and poorer countries'. *(Reuter)*

6   Austin Robinson, Cambridge, First Keynes Memorial Lecture of the British Academy, 1971.

Index

355

Index

357

Index

Index

Index

Index

Index

367

Index

Index

Index

Index

Index

The Wealth of Poor Nations

Understanding 312
Understanding and determination 350
Undeveloped resources 53
UNDP 168, 169, 170, 172, 173, 179, 187, 188
Undue growth 81
Unemployed 5
Unemployment 21, 45, 46, 61, 66, 110, 117, 297,
Unemployment problem 43
Unemployment situation 44
UNEP 169, 170, 263, 266, 269
Unequal pay 81
Unequal relations 273
Unequivocal 17
UNESCO 170
UNESCO description 132
Unfailing condition 302
Unfortunate drag in 346
Unhindered levels 337
UNICEF 114, 169
UNIDO 169
UNIDO Lima Conference 24
Union 300
Union of Soviet Socialist Republics 175
Unit 144
Unitary 69
United Kingdom 34, 39, 117, 175, 178,
United Nations 25, 26, 41, 164, 165, 166, 167, 171-175, 178-180, 183, 185, 191, 266, 276, 281, 330, 331, 333, 344,
United nations character 332
United Nations conference 159, 268
United Nations conference on Environment 129
United Nations development programme 165
United nations economic and social system 333
United Nations Economic Commission 184
United Nations Educational Scientific organisation
United Nations Environment Programme 266
United Nations Headquarters 169, 177, 183
United Nations inputs 333
United Nations organisation 164, 171
United nations structures 170
United Nations system 167, 170, 172-174, 178, 179, 330-333, 349, 350

United Nations World Conference 129
United States 5, 77, 120, 156, 175, 188, 198, 340
United States economy 120
United States Government 188
United States Participation 189
United States to Europe 340
Unity 141, 293
Universal 291
Universal Postal Union 164
Universe 131
Universe or eco-system 132
University levels 280
Upanishads 292, 293
UPU 179
Urban enclaves 273
Urban system 350
Urban/rural human settlements 145
UREA 201
UREA project 201
Uri Mission 221
Uruguay Accord 3160, 161, 34
US (Negroes) 306
US 41, 47, 230, 233, 238, 275
US Budget 232
US Congress 197
US Dollars 104
US economy 232
US Exports 231
US imports 238
US Secretary 118
US Source 196
US Statement 202
US system 3186
US treasury Department Special Report 197
US 'south' 306
USA 98, 176, 194, 208, 224, 243, 261, 262, 275, 305, 306
USG 276
USSR 168, 191, 243, 245, 307, 327
Utility of theory 66
Utilization of by-products 53

V

Vaccine Project 201
Vacuo 341
Valid project level 147
Validity and continuity 298
Value added 87, 96
Value added capacities 339

380

Index

Value added component 74
Value added export promotion 98
Value added item 88
Value added production at home 98
Value added terms 88
Value of imports 101
Value of Imports by principal commodity 102
Values 312
Various population 306
Vast resources 339
Vedanta 308
Velocity Joints 201
Verbiage 270, 273
Vietnam War 188
Vietnam 187, 304, 326, 327
Vigorous import industry 93
Village area 34
Violent interpretation 308
Vishnu 141
Vortex 303
Voting strength 191

W

Wage and general welfare 79
Wage and related issues 76
Wage constancies 79
Wage decision 75
Wage differential 81
Wage earner 79, 92
Wage earning sector 74
Wage fall 67
Wage good industries 342
Wage goods 78, 92, 96
Wage goods industries 34, 324, 338, 342
Wage goods output 94
Wage goods pattern 325
Wage goods production 340
Wage goods structure 38
Wage increases 79, 81
Wage is investment 77
Wage levels 158
Wage policies 74, 342
Wage problem 74
Wage regulations 82
Wage responsibilities 74
Wage settlements 82
Wage share 68
Wage structure 78, 82
Wages 64, 71, 74
Wages and employment 163

Wages and productivity 77, 79
Wages forward 78
Wages fund 73
Wages or employment 64
War 85, 341, 352
Warranted growth 73
Washington 305
Waste-assimilative 150
Wastes 144, 278, 279
Wastes conservation 145
Watanabe 190
Water 144, 145, 163, 349
Water pollution 274
Watersheds 144
WCB 239
Wealth 9, 91, 343, 352
Wealth and welfare 323
Wealth creation 90, 91
Wealth of poor nations 345
West 115, 239, 250, 295
West Asia 169, 246
West Asian Economic Commission 246
West Europe 11, 93, 169, 340
West Germany 120, 138
West Indies 305
Western 299
Western commentators 116
Western Countries 77, 233
Western democratic 296
Western democratic modes 328
Western economist 257
Western Europe 77
Western European Economic Group
    Member 187
Western formulation 73
Western mind 291
Western policy 115
Western political system 327
Western type 210
Western world 253
Wheat 115
White smoke 65
WHO 172, 179, 349
WHO Campaign 179
Whole truth 132
Wide-ranging 67
Wide-spread opinion 158
Wil-o-the-wisps 333
Wild life 265, 274
WMO 179
Women and development 83
Women's wages 83

381